THE WIND AT MY BACK

May God sleep on your pillow
May He hold you in the hollow of his hand.
May the roads rise with you
Fair weather to your heels.
May the wind be ever at your back . . .
And may you be a long time in Heaven,
Before the Devil knows you're gone . . .

Old Irish benediction . . .

THE WIND
AT MY BACK

The Life and Times of Pat O'Brien

by Himself

DOUBLEDAY & COMPANY, INC., GARDEN CITY, NEW YORK

To my beloved parents and my wife,
Eloise, whose love and understanding
have sustained me through the years

Contents

Before the Curtain Rises

Before the Curtain Rises:

In this book I have written down the story of my life in my own way, in my own language, hoping to review one man's life on earth, not as a record, or a warning, but as a summing up, a look back and a look ahead. It would not have been done but for the editorial help, advice, knee action and professional knowledge of Stephen Longstreet, who labored long to impress on me a sentence must have a point, a chapter a climax, and that commas do exist. In his unwavering loyalty to our mutual typewriter, and the probing of my memory, I want to thank him for his help and kindness.

My wife Eloise, too, has read the first rough versions and her suggestions have presented a more polished, detailed retelling of our long life together. To all others—named mostly in the text— I also offer thanks.

CURTAIN
GOING
UP

1

Thank You, Alexander Graham Bell

There's an old saying—by an Irishman I'm sure: "Chance reaches farther than long arms."

A simple phone call changed the whole course of my life, my career, my very existence. It was one of those gray dank New York days of December in 1930. I was spending little but time at the Lambs Club, in the Grill Room that evening, tasting the "blends" with some friends and guests, when I was summoned to the phone.

Winnie Kelly, telephone operator of the club, smiled at me. (She had enough on all of us members to cause an exodus of actors from Broadway.)

"Booth Two, Mr. O'Brien—Mr. Hughes calling." The name Hughes alone did not ring a bell in my memory. Mr. Hughes, I thought as I picked up the phone, could have been Rupert, Charles Evans or . . .

"Hello—"

"Pat O'Brien speaking."

"This is Mr. Howard Hughes' representative in New York."

The voice was like velvet—slightly Harvard, with tones of tweed and an old pipe.

"Yes?"

"Mr. Hughes is filming the play *The Front Page* in Hollywood."

"I've heard he is."

"He is very much interested, Mr. O'Brien, in your playing in this production."

I stared into the phone. The neat, polite voice continued. "You played this production on the stage?"

"I did."

"Good. Good! Mr. Hughes wants you."

I fumbled for time to think. "I am rehearsing in a new play that's to open in New York two weeks from now." I was too bemused, frightened, amazed to do anything but sound calm.

The voice did not change its tone. "What is the name of the play?"

"*Tomorrow and Tomorrow*, by Philip Barry. It co-stars Herbert Marshall, Zita Johann and myself. Looks pretty good."

"Well"—a brief pause—"we will be in touch with you again sometime tomorrow."

"Thank you." That was about all the dialogue I could think of. I was puzzled, wary, and wondering.

I returned to the group in the Grill Room and I didn't mention the phone call because it was altogether possible it could be a gag; a rib set up by some of my fellow members at the club. I refrained from discussing the phone conversation as I lifted a fresh glass and eyed my friends; they were robust and often cruel practical jokers.

Rehearsals for *Tomorrow and Tomorrow* were being held at Henry Miller's Theater, a place smelling of tradition, mice dust and the memory of great actors. When I reported the next day for rehearsal as usual, I was met by the producer of the play, Mr.

Gilbert Miller, a proud and solid citizen, admired for his English tailoring and the quality of his productions.

"Pat," he said, fingering his piped vest, "Howard Hughes has been trying to secure your services for his impending production of *The Front Page*. I understand you spoke with his representative last evening."

I said yes, and wondered why Mr. Miller had a pink glow—like Mr. Pickwick in Dickens.

"Pat, old boy—you must make a decision. Mr. Hughes has offered me ten thousand dollars to purchase your contract. I do not want to influence you one way or the other. Mr. Hughes is very rich—oil, inventions, airplanes—and he's been making films. Now while I think we have a hit on our hands in this show—you know the elusive enigma of the success of any play. Plus the fact that this Hollywood venture could provide an amusing adventure. *The Front Page* is a fine play—a smash hit on Broadway. Perhaps it could repeat its success in the film. However—"

"However, Mr. Miller?"

"Despite the generous offer of ten thousand dollars by Mr. Hughes . . ."

"Yes, Mr. Miller?" Was my dream about to burst?

I suddenly felt an unreality about my situation, like the popular conception of Cinderella at midnight at the ball after the pumpkin turned to a golden coach and the nibbling mice to prancing white horses. I was enough of an actor to play it easy and blandly as I tried to sense Mr. Miller's build-up. I felt destiny was waving its magic wand for me. I sensed it, and somehow it could slip away.

I was young; I was harried; I was a citizen of the republic at the beginning of a great depression. So far my life had been the hard one of hunting for work, picking up a part here and there, success and flops in a mixed bag; going into the outer world of sleazy theaters, the darkness of road shows, one-night stands; rolling along in those pre-air-conditioned, Civil War, cinder-spewing railroad trains; appearing in stock companies beyond what New Yorkers thought of as civilization. Mr. Miller couldn't cross me now.

I had been shaken by the Hughes offer—it was beyond all the yearnings of a young actor, all the images I had built up inside myself of what I wanted to be, what I wanted to do. I had no yen to play *Hamlet*, but I felt in myself a kind of stage power that could dramatize a character into more than just living make-believe.

Times were hard in the theater, I knew. Actors were living on their nerve. President Hoover had said, "Conditions are fundamentally sound," but on Broadway venders were offering Relief apples *two* for five cents. Actors owed hotels and landladies $500,000 in back rent. Twenty-five thousand actors were out of work. Roxy, the big plush movie palace, was in receivership. But the Rockefellers were beginning to dig holes in the street that would one day hold up Radio City. I had to get to Hollywood for Mr. Hughes' project.

Mr. Miller looked up from his well-cared-for hands. "Pat, if I decide on a release from our contract, I can't okay the deal until I secure an actor that I have in mind to play your role."

"That seems fair, Mr. Miller."

"When you've given me your decision to leave us, I'll negotiate further with this actor I have in mind."

I politely said, "Thank you, Mr. Miller. It won't take long to make up my mind—but I would like to discuss it with Bart Marshall."

"You do that, Pat."

I felt kind of overloaded suddenly with goodies—like a kid not knowing which Christmas present to open first. I ran across the stage to Herbert Marshall's dressing room and explained the whole situation.

"I need advice."

He thought it over a few moments in calm British composure. "Dear chap—it is not for me to advise you. All I do want to say is that I think we have a hit here in *Tomorrow and Tomorrow*."

"I think so too, and Mr. Miller has the same reaction. So what do I do?"

"Yes, *what?*" Bart continued, lighting an English Oval cigarette. "I know from our various conversations, you have never been to California. This could be very exciting I hear, and the beginning of a whole new career in flickers. If I were in your place and asked to make the decision, I'd say yes—take the gamble, though actually, with a rich Mr. Hughes, it isn't much of a gamble, is it?"

"No, I guess not, and it isn't much of a gamble for Gilbert Miller either. Howard Hughes has offered him ten thousand dollars for my contract."

Bart whistled and said with an old-school accent: "Golly!"

I returned to Mr. Miller, who was sitting placidly in my dressing room.

"Mr. Miller, I'm going to the Coast if you release me."

"Ah, good luck. The actor whom I have in mind to replace you has actually told me that he'd consider playing the part if he can view a full rehearsal from out front."

"I see, Mr. Miller."

"He said he can form his conclusion much more logically than reading the script."

"The sooner the better."

"The company has agreed to a rehearsal for the actor. He's coming down from Connecticut."

I was too taut to ask who the actor was. I wanted to get this over with—and get a train west. The next day the rehearsal began warmly. There were three people out in the darkened theater—Gilbert Miller, the stage manager and the actor who would make up his mind during the progression of rehearsal. We completed the first act in a rush—the first scene of the second act in a glow, and were about to start on the second scene when the actor stood up in a row of seats and said: "Pat, you're on your way to California."

"You'll play the part?"

Mr. Miller said, "Mr. Perkins, thank you."

The actor was Osgood Perkins (whose son Tony Perkins is now a stage and film star). I felt my scalp twitch. Osgood Perkins had starred in the Broadway production of *The Front Page* in the role of Walter Burns, the managing editor. It was spooky.

The final deal for me was worked out, roughly, but the final contract was to be negotiated with Mr. Howard Hughes' representative. I went up to his office on Broadway feeling it was all still a dream—and any moment my ninety-eight-cent alarm clock would wake me. The contract he said was ready to sign. There had been no discussion of money, but I would have signed for $4.00 and a new pin-striped double-breasted suit to get this break in motion pictures. My salary with Mr. Miller had been a glorious $350 a week—more money than I had ever earned on Broadway, and certainly much more than on the hurly-burly torture of road companies. My salary had been $275 a week in the last play I had opened in.

I sat back in a soft, oh-so-soft chair, while the lawyer fiddled with the legal papers. I pretended an interest in the Daumier prints on the wall, and wondered if oranges really grew at the corner of Hollywood and Vine.

The lawyer spread the contract on the overpolished desk.

"This is what Mr. Hughes is offering you—$750 a week with options for five years . . . a $250 raise each six months."

"That seems fair, for movies." I didn't bicker or dally. I signed with the glee of a man signing his own pardon.

"Mr. O'Brien, we have allowed for transportation." He handed me an envelope. "First-class, naturally. The Twentieth Century and the Chief—a drawing room. All right?"

"Of course."

With a hearty handshake, I bade him good day.

My departure was set for the next day. That did not bother me much as I did not have much to pack or a great deal to pack it in.

I was living like Robinson Crusoe on his island, in a little furnished room—death-house décor—on West Sixty-fifth Street. My crumpled belongings could not fill two borrowed suitcases.

At the club, to say my so-long-guys, I found much activity, and the levity was extended far into the night.

16

Laughing and back slapping, it dawned on me that I sure had a beautiful contract, luxury transportation to California, *but* I was flat broke.

"How do I eat on the train? I owe all of you and lots of chits at the club."

"You're a movie star! Don't forget."

"The only coins I have fellas are a few half-dollars and a St. Christopher medal."

"Stop bragging."

Edward Ellis, the sterling old actor, held up a hand. "You have no cause for alarm, my boy. Just call Mr. Hughes' man first thing in the morning and advise him you want a fat advance on your salary. Don't tell them why—just say you want an advance. Let them think you want to make a down payment on a yacht."

"Next round is on me," I said.

The following morning there wasn't any problem with Mr. Hughes' charming man. He wrote me a check for $500. I hadn't had $500 in any of my pockets in my entire thirty-one years. I hoped they had caviar as big as marbles and food I had never heard of on that train, because I was really going to act the way the fan magazines said movie actors acted. I was eager; I was excited—and I was deep down a little scared. But I was ham enough in Grand Central Station to *almost* shout out the speech from *The Count of Monte Cristo:* "The world is mine!"

But was it? And how had I gotten there?

2

How I Happened to Be

Home is where you go, I once heard a poet say, and they have to let you in. My own family's hunt for new roots began when the McGoverns emigrated from Green Galway in Ireland, and the O'Briens from busy Cork, somewhere past the middle of the nineteenth century, when the native American Know-Nothings had a slogan—"Hit 'im again, he's Irish!"

William and Margaret McGovern, after a stormy non-luxury crossing settled in Waukesha, Wisconsin, land of Crystal Spring Water and the Holy Jumpers. Why they chose this, then still half-wild region of the Midwest remains a mystery. They built a log cabin and scrabbled a living farming a few sparse acres. They were a family of nine and their most frequent visitors were rather pathetic, defeated Indians, who were never particularly troublesome.

"They were more curious than vicious," according to my grandmother. "They'd drop by at intervals, seeking a bit of food mostly. Never any attempts at robbery or molesting."

There were many dispossessed tribes and their legacy lives on in such native names as Waukesha, Oconomowoc, Wauwatosa, Sheboygan and the big metropolis, Milwaukee, sixty miles from the farm. As a boy I found the Indian names as exciting as the sound of drums.

The frisky McGovern girls were Mary, Agnes, Katherine and Margaret. The large and active boys were Philip and William. There were others, but as happened in those days before Dr. Spock, they died in infancy. Their facilities for education were only a small red country schoolhouse, the same as the ones that have such nostalgic charm when you read about them. There wasn't any opportunity at all for higher education. There was no money in the McGovern pocket to aid any of the brood to higher education.

"When in doubt, move on" was an Irish motto. With much maternal and paternal words of advice, at the earnest ages of eighteen and nineteen, the junior McGoverns trekked to the big city, the metropolis of Milwaukee. Its population was nearly two hundred thousand. It had gas light, a few bathtubs; some of the sidewalks were still wooden, and strange types called actors (and worse) appeared in things called "plays" full of love, battle, virtue lost, retained *or* defended. There were horse cars, fast buggies and bay horses, beer at ten cents a pail, and hardly any belief in the germ theory, or that a good cigar could cost more than a nickel.

The youngest of this Irish invasion was Willie McGovern, solid, steady, with "a fist like a smoked ham." He went to work as an apprentice blacksmith for the Milwaukee Railroad, and remained there as a dependable man, to become in time the boss blacksmith. There was not much in the way of remuneration, but he learned to love the work of shaping cherry-colored heated iron. He stayed on until he was pushing a vigorous seventy. He was a strong man "and could lift an anvil or a barrel of lager beer with the ease of an ordinary person lifting a kitchen chair." His brother, my uncle, Jolly Phil, became a hansom cab driver and was the last of his kind to hold forth in his station among the rich horse droppings in front of the old Plankinton Hotel.

I remember Uncle Phil saying: "Would ye like a short ride, lad?" At times he would actually let me drive. He kept a neat, attentive horse, a well-swept cab, and wore a cocked top hat at a natty angle on his weathered brow. Uncle Phil was quite a historic town character at the turn of the century in Milwaukee. His greatest boast was of his passengers . . .

"I've carried 'em all, lad—John Philip Sousa, the great blessed John L. Sullivan, James J. Corbett, Harry Lauder. Oh yes, and David Belasco, Lillian Russell (a fine figure of a woman) Sothern and Marlowe, Eddie Foy and oh, the many others."

The McGovern girls went to the Lee House to work at the tables as waitresses. Sara Lee and her husband had the finest eating place in the area and catered to all of the paunch-proud downtown business men. The girls got their "keep"; food and lodging and a minimum salary, and tips—which were meager. Free came the wonderful counsel of Aunt Sara Lee; against evil, entrapment, tight corsets and red cotton stockings. It was a great blessing to Ma and Dad McGovern to know "our brood, the girl contingency, at least, is looked after with such darling care."

The Cork-deserting O'Briens decided to settle in Manhattan. Grandpa O'Brien was more fortunate than William McGovern. He started life in New York as an apprentice architect, became successful, and showed great promise. Grandpa Patrick O'Brien (after whom I was named) came to an untimely and accidental death during an altercation in a downtown family saloon. It was a respectable establishment for the thirsty and social-seeking middle class, but at that particular hour, the cocktail hour (it was not called *that* then) a quarrel ensued between two overexcited customers. My grandfather, a peace-loving man, attempted to intervene, and was shot between the eyes by one of the pistol-waving combatants—and fell dead on the spot. The family felt a great career was nipped in the bud. His wife, my grandmother, had died in childbirth, and there were two children. Billy O'Brien and his sister Mayme were left orphans. The way of the peacemaker and his children is hard. Mayme was "taken in" by relatives in Jersey City, John and Kate O'Neill. Bill O'Brien, her brother (and my father), in his early teens was bundled off to an orphanage in Newburgh in New York. It was a horror out of *Oliver Twist* and he ran away. He was twelve years old, and all the Alger books of pluck and luck were on his side, and a sixth-grade education.

He got a job as cash boy at A. J. Stewart's store. (It was to become Wanamaker's later.) Soon the O'Neills discovered his whereabouts and dragged him over to Jersey City to live with them and his sister, Mayme. Jersey City was practically an Irish city—and jokes about its goats were the nub of many vaudeville gags. But it was warm, fraternal, gay, loud and given to much talk.

Uncle John O'Neill decided to teach Bill O'Brien the dry goods business from the ground up, starting in the cellar packing room. He worked hard, but an urge, impelled by Horace Greeley's "Go West, young man" had its effect on him, and off he went to Chicago, the location just then of the World's Fair. He got a job at Carson, Pirie and Scott's dry goods firm, but something urged him to move on to Milwaukee, eighty-seven miles away by the steam cars. He secured a job at Gimbel's Department Store (dry goods) and from there went to T. A. Chapman's (dry goods). He remained there for over twenty years ("To see if I wanted it to be my life's work . . .").

A new boy in town, he went hunting good, filling food and a well-run eating establishment. The Lee House seemed to be the place. And who would be the colleen to serve him with the choicest piece of apple pie? Margaret McGovern, who was to become my mother.

I am not one given too much to being impressed by the glory of anyone's family background. A man (or woman) has to stand up to life on their own merits, I found out. But I have always gloried in the tough immigrants who were my forefathers. I have avoided all my life being a professional Irishman; not from shame, but because there is something wrong in a man who falls into the false pride of the race nonsense, and thinks one human being is a better human being than one who tilts the godhead another way, has a different color, or likes to cook with garlic or wine.

I did get from my sturdy, life-sparring ancestors a zest for existence, a love of color, a gift of gab, a sense that life is for living. They also gave me God, or He gave them to me; I am not sure which. Ingrained as they were in their faith, its solace, its prayer and its rituals, I have always felt lucky, in a modern world dissolving at times around me, that I do have something that for me has the solidity of hope, grace and dignity as a human being, for all our sins and omissions.

I don't suppose, like most Irishmen, I missed being descended from the old Celtic kings. But then, as my grandmother would say, "Kings in Ireland, now, in them days were as common as generals in the Mexican Army."

I inherited, if not identified royal blood, a mind, a fairly good brain, height, passable decent looks, the ability to enjoy alcohol without abusing it, a knack for standing up in public and being amusing, and if not amusing at least entertaining. I also got most of the aches, fears, doubts, depressions and not-too-quiet desperations.

What drove my grandparents from their own land, be it potato famine, English landlords, the hard agony of failing to find room to breed and brew—whatever it was, it was a lucky day for me. I don't think I could be anything but an American. I don't want to try to be anything else. But whatever genes, spirit, fulfillment of God and destiny brought Bill O'Brien for steamed haddock to Lee House that day, in time it brought me as an individual, and a soul, into the expanding universe.

In this simple way, over a checked tablecloth and the steamy odor of the twenty-five-cent blue-plate lunch, romance came to my parents.

During his daily visits to The Lee House, Bill O'Brien had occasion to meet young men of other lines of work. One was an aspiring young butcher, Charles Schlenger; the other, a salesman of sorts, Charles Taberner, with derby tilted at a fashionable angle. They were giving their undivided attentions to Margaret's sisters, Mary and Agnes. It didn't take long for passion to overcome reason, and soon wedding bells clanged over three weddings; rice was flung, and mothers wept. Margaret McGovern, in proud crisp white, "with a bit of lace brought from Ireland," became Mrs. William O'Brien.

The couple moved to two tiny rooms over O'Donnell's Saloon, on Thirteenth and Clybourn. It was there (and not in a log cabin) I was born as William Joseph O'Brien, Jr. Later I assumed the name of "Pat" in admiration of and in deference to my peace-loving grandfather who had come to such a tragic end through a carelessly handled Colt .45.

O'Donnell's Saloon was, I suppose, on the wrong side of the tracks, but the O'Briens were a practical couple, and for them it was the perfect place to reside.

"Only a half block from the Parochial School and a block from the Gesu Catholic Church."

Their faith was foremost to my mother and dad, and it has been my own cherished heritage for over sixty years.

My earliest recollections are of the pride I had when we moved *uptown*. O'Donnell's was on Thirteenth Street. We moved to Fifteenth Street.

"But it's *across* the tracks!"

My dad rented a little cottage at Fifteenth and Sycamore. It had no room for a bathroom, but it did loudly boast of a W.C., that controversial object referred to many years later by Jack Parr on his "Tonight" show. My mother, however, had a very large tin tub. After the pots of stove water were scalding hot—and I was held captive, loudly protesting I had washed that week—it was poured into the tub, and when the temperature was tepid, I was propelled into the family bath. I have many other memories of that little cottage. My brothers Edward and Robert were born there; they only lived to two years and three weeks respectively. So I grew up an only child with a passionate devotion—and need —for my mother and father. We were a prayerful family. I always hoped and prayed, even as a small boy that the day would come when I would move my parents into a finer house, or at least a larger cottage. I never stopped praying—I learned it at my mother's side and it has always been my solace when I thought my dreams had tumbled and the whole world seemed a mess made of the futility of all human endeavors. But some of my hopes in time were answered, even if *not* always in the way I dramatized them.

The great wonderful days of my childhood seem all wrong for a book.

It is the fashion to write of unhappy, neurotic childhoods. I'm sorry—most of mine was happy as a gig—whatever a gig was, or is. The kids born on the Gold Coast missed a lot—Gold Coast was what we called the neat, dull city blocks where the rich kids lived. We lucky ones learned all of our games on sand lots—*they* had no sand lots, only shrubbery and rose gardens. We skated on ponds— theirs were too far away. We swam in the creeks—they had their indoor swimming schools and their athletic clubs smelling of stale basketball sneakers. We hopped freight cars in the railroad yards— they were miles and miles from any railroad yard. We fought bloody bold battles in the school yards to survive—they didn't have to fight—and never learned to stand up "bloody but unbowed." They would have been welcome to be part of our play, but unfortunately their geographic and social line spanned too many miles. They had their Flexible Flyers—we had just sleds. They had Johnston Racers—we had just ordinary skates. They toasted marshmallows on the beach—we roasted potatoes called "mickies," often stolen—on the corner lot. But as the years moved on, it was natural we would meet on some common ground—higher education blended some of us, and then World War I definitely put most of us on an equal basis, in uniform.

What has become of the games we kids played in those days?

Simple, deadly, muscle-building games, makers of little street wars and rival groups: pom-pom pullaway, duck-on-a-rock, run my good sheep run.

A single skate was the sport car of those days—and odd lumber and grocer's boxes made us all Henry Fords. We were inventive; the improvising of barrel staves for skis to slide down neighborhood hills, hockey in the street in front of the house played under hissing arc lights with a stick cut from a tree and the wood puck carved by your dad.

The hi-fi today and the juke box have destroyed the marble game—mibs, we called it—and one Ol' cat in baseball. Progress is always the answer. Kids must have as much fun today, but sometimes I wonder. There were giant bruises in those times, and a game that didn't promise a bloody nose was for weaklings and for girls. My dad taught me baseball, marbles, and how to play hockey; how to duck, when to advance, and *when* to run. He was a practical realist—except in card games.

The kids of today lack the wild nicknames that were pinned on us by our pals and enemies. "Stuts" Mehigan (later to become senator from Wisconsin), "Wobbles" Harper, "Kinky" Shaughnessy, "Spring Heels" Koehler, "Peeny" Boyle, "Cyclone" Mehigan (ordained a Jesuit priest in the early twenties). There was a rowdy, heady flavor to nicknames. We have become regimented and unimaginative—or more respectable than when every gang had a Gimpy, Cockeyes, Fatso and Mushhead.

My dad's nickname was Tip O'Brien. He derived this cognomen because of a liking for card games in the Knights of Columbus Hall, or in the billiard room at the club, and the attendant was always sure of a two-bit stipend from W. J. O'Brien. And they hung the title on him, Tip O'Brien.

It was an open air world of wonderful Saturday picnics at West Park! My mother would make up sandwiches of pork and corned beef, pickles, pies, and potato salads, the like of which memory hints I have never tasted since. Picnics were the great summer adventure. We would rise early in the morning laughing and howling, scramble into our clothes, shout and dance, observe the sky and scare off the clouds—and make great plans for the rest of the day. Mom had everything prepared in hampers, baskets, brown paper bags stained with rich grease, and we would embark for the park on the trolley for a glorious day of fun, eating, wading, snoozing on the trampled grass, sassing the Keystone helmeted cops; and plan big game hunts among the small animals of the park.

I would carry my bag of marbles among rival groups, sniff back defeat, or crow in victory over sore knuckles.

The men drank beer and undid the cast-iron collars of the day. The women, well shaded against the glare of the sun, gossiped, slapped at children, changed babies, compared confinements, wakes, burials, diseases, lied about childrens' school marks and often had us recite a poem or verse or sing one of Paul Dresser's banal but heart-tugging songs: "My Gal Sal" or "On the Banks of the Wabash."

Near dusk we poured from the park, logy, sunburned, fire scorched; lost children wailing, bad ones getting their heads slapped, and at last the night-smelling drowsy trolley-car trip home —oh long lost country trolley cars now gone from us—and me as a small boy, sandy, itchy, bellyachy, going home with Mom and Dad, in the lost golden weather of my childhood.

I was an altar boy at Gesu Church and how well I remember my first Mass. I was kneeling at the foot of the altar just after the Credo. Father Murphy uncovered the chalice and then waited impatiently for me to bring him the wine and the water. When I failed to budge, he peremptorily summoned me. Still no action on my part. Finally, in exasperation he went over to the table and took the cruets himself. Finally, with horror I realized what I had failed to do, and the enormity of my crime overwhelmed me. I finished the Mass somehow and the rest of the day at school passed in a daze. That afternoon I rushed home to Mother, the held back tears stinging my eyes. One look told Mother something serious was bothering me.

"What's the matter, my darling?" she said. "What happened?"

"Mother, I spoiled the Mass today" I blurted out and then burst into tears.

Mother comforted me and then reassured me that she was sure that God understood and no real harm was done.

A child's impressions last longest of all memories, and no matter where, later, I was, or how badly things were going, I could always depend on the faith I had learned as a child to make bearable in tight corners for many who lived around us. It served my parents in those struggling times when the unendowed workers and the unprovided poor had to live through the panics and depressions of the Republic (that seemed to come every seven years, or more often) and our fathers who left every morning for work wondered if there would be a job that day, or salary that week, or anything to say thanks for that year, but for God's mercy.

Father Murphy was the priest one Saturday night when the church was overflowing. He had been hearing confessions all afternoon and into the night. The line seemed endless, with folks of all ages awaiting their time to confess. Father Pat, sweating and pale, at last opened the confessional door, looked out at the crowd and said in no subdued tones, "All ye mortals stay—and all ye venials go home!"

He emptied the church!

He was what people then called a true son of old Erin, and we kids at the Gesu School loved him. He was also the unstern principal and when we would be sent to his office for punishment for some infraction of rules, he would hand us a chocolate drop, lick his finger, and say sternly: "Don't tell Sister about the candy. Try and be a good boy."

My growing-aware years were the years between 1910 and 1916. There were kid gangs in those days, just as there are now, but they didn't have the hoodlum aura that a lot of the younger lawbreakers seem to be immersed in today—no taint of drugs, school vandalism, molesting, mugging or the sadistic activities now among us.

I remember the names of some of the gangs: the Bloody 64,

27

the Tory Hill Gang, the Tetonia Indians, the Brick Yard Gang and the Sixteenth Street Gang. Our adolescent feuds never involved anything more than panting, shouting hand-to-hand encounters, standing up in the stance of a famous prize fighter and exchanging fisticuffs. Sometimes Irish confetti might have been used. (Irish confetti is the Gaelic title of a flung brick, just as the Irish convincer is another name for the shillelagh.) Till real war came, boys were restrained by the civilized examples of an adult world.

I don't recall any of the combatants being jailed in our gang encounters. The cops, beefy boys with long mustaches, usually let us settle our differences among ourselves.

There was one particular cop who was the nemesis of all the kids on Tory Hill where I lived before we moved uptown. Someone gave him the name of "Red Nose Merrity, the Baby Catcher." But he never caused us any pain because there wasn't a one of us who couldn't run faster than he could, and we usually had a three-block head start when we caught sight of him.

Art for us took the form of saving up cigar bands and pasting them into ash trays, which at that time seemed to me quite the artistic achievement. It *was* rather decorative at that, but for the semi-nude trade marks of burlesque queens that Mom objected to.

"How do they keep from catching their death of cold?"

They used to give away baseball pictures with Sweet Caporal cigarettes, the brand of youthful sinners. We were too young to indulge much in the weed, but the elders in the neighborhood would save the pictures for us. I made quite a collection—Mordecai "Three-Fingered" Brown, "Home Run" Baker, Johnny Kling, Jimmy Archer, John McGraw, Stuffy McGinnis, Connie Mack, Sherwood McGee, Honus Wagner, George McBride and countless others.

Actually cigarettes were not fully accepted as a male vice till World War I. They were called "coffin nails" by the pious and "sissy sticks" by the real men.

Music, not in the canned form of today, formed a great part

of my life. Being Irish, I suspected I was a great tenor; everyone in our neighborhood sang. Years later, I had as a friend Jack Norwood, who wrote the immortal "Take Me Out to the Ball Game," "Shine On, Harvest Moon" and many other hits of my childhood. Jack was married to the very popular singing star, Nora Bayes. Vaudeville houses made us aware of "When You Wore a Tulip" and "Put on Your Old Gray Bonnet" (written by Percy Wenrich, who was also to become a friend later on), "Down By the Old Mill Stream" and "Moonlight Bay." Happy times wallow in corn.

And there was "I Wonder Who's Kissing Her Now," written by Joe Howard. Nostalgia and sentiment pleased us in our shameless years. A group of composers once voted on the most colorful lyric incorporated into a song—a line that would convey passion, the past and deep rooted love. The voting was unanimous on the line "I wonder if she ever tells him of me" from Joe's "I Wonder Who's Kissing Her Now." Too bad yesterday's ecstasy becomes too often today's banality.

The actors I watched from the high peanut heaven of local theaters were David Belasco in *The Music Master* and *The Auctioneer*; James Forbes-Robertson in *The Passing of the Third Floor Back,* and the famous blood-and-thunder productions, *In Old Kentucky* with that thrilling scene entitled "Madge's Daring Swing across the Mountain Chasm," and then the horse race, which was an illusion created on a treadmill by tired farm horses. The road was active then, and the theater flourished.

I never forgot Maude Adams in *Peter Pan,* Ethel Barrymore in *The Twelve Pound Look* with her memorable delivery of the calm, crisp curtain line, "That's all there is, there isn't any more"; Nance O'Neill in *Hedda Gabler* and *The Lily*; Adelina Patti in opera, always called grand opera, and countless other shows. I was infected and didn't know it. Actor's blood boiled in me, but as yet at a simmer. School plays, debates, reciting of red-hot ballads found my changing voice making the scene.

Folk art at its best was the warm, smelly interior of a vaudeville house: six acts and a chaser of flickering movies.

Our family and other families made a ritual of seeing the weekly bill. Good or bad, we cheered and hissed and enjoyed the shows. Later many actors became fast friends of mine on Broadway. Walter C. Kelly (*The Virginia Judge*), Wellington Cross, Frank Fay, Savo and Allen, Margaret Young, the Mosconi Brothers, Bender and Armstrong. There was an act called the Morris Family, a twenty-minute situation comedy sketch. The youngest of the family is today one of my closest friends, Chester Morris, who in silent and sound films played the American hero with the firm chin, firmer than most.

My football career got off to a poor start. I broke my collar bone and it happened in scrimmage, not in a regular game. I spent the season trying to heal the break by carrying a flatiron, ("How can I do your father's shirts?") trying to sleep sitting up ("You'll grow hunchbacked"). The following season I was healed and ready. In the first game my mother witnessed, they carried me off the field limp and pale, and with two broken ankles. I was something of a hero in my agony—a twice-wounded casualty of sports attending a dance at the K.C.s on crutches. My date was Lucille Ziegler, who admired muscle men. I sat out all the dances like a wounded Roman, accepting the sympathy of everyone with great pride.

Some wise guy asked: "What will you break *next* year, kid?"

Being Irish in America was not to me as a kid as tough a job as it had been in my father's day or in my grandfather's time. There was still a carry-over of the cartoon Irishman of popular imagination who had a red fringe of beard, a clay pipe upside down in his wide ape's mouth, spoke in "begorras" and "bejabbers" and Pat-and-Mike dialogue. He wore tight green knee pants, always hunted a fight, swung a black stick and could never resist getting comic drunk. He raised up broods of dirty, sassy kids, kept goats in his parlor and wept at any song that mentioned the green sod, the Irish courage, bogs, landscape and, of course, Mother. This libel was companion to the stage Jew with his derby resting on his ears, an accent mingled with "oys" and other laments, and who would have the gold filling out of your teeth before you could wink an eye. There was also the "comic coon," a racial caricature of the Negro as a flatfooted, lying, mushmouthed lazy loafer who swung a mean razor, was as sexy as a mink farm, lived only off watermelon and fried chicken (stolen, of course). Also mocked by cork-blackened white minstrel men as an ivory-headed moron who could only ask questions like: "Tell me, Mistah Bones, who dat lady I seen yo' with last night? Yak. Yak!"

My father remembers the signs at employment offices reading: NO IRISH NEED APPLY, and in the early days of this country the Irish were brought over in stinking steerage, in herds to become gandydancers (ballast tampers) on the railroads, and in the South, where a good black field-hand slave was valuable and cost over six hundred dollars. It was smarter to hire the hungry Irish to work and die in the fever-wracked rice swamps.

True Irish home life had a charm and warmth and a sparkle. We Irish certainly were a vocal people when I was a boy, and liked to sing and were easily moved to weeping. We enjoyed a bit of the creature and we often had red hair and tempers to match, but it wasn't a comic strip life.

Times were hard and the country was having growing pains. The folk from Ireland, untrained, untaught, had to take the jobs with the pick and shovel, muck the tunnels, cut the rails and drive the ash and garbage carts.

But educate them a bit—as I saw it done—and you had more than just the ward heelers and the political hacks. Add another generation of vitamins and sunshine, outdoor sports and higher learning and you had the responsible officeholders, the doctors and the lawyers.

I was aware of the struggle of the first and second generations, and even of the misery of domestic scenes in the neighborhood, the black sobbing at the wakes, the lamenting when a son went

31

wrong or a daughter got in the family way without the marriage lines.

It was a self-protective community. There were the church and the priest, cheaper and more assuring than the Freudian couch of today. There was the K. of C., and the various emerald-colored clubs where a man could borrow a fiver, be patted on the back and told, "Things will turn up, God willing."

The charities provided a bit when the factories closed, or a political job was cut off, and so did the church benefits and later the bingo games. There was basketball and other sports to keep the lads off the streets, and even a priest who could drop-kick and maybe shoot a good game of pool.

Some of my boyhood friends went wrong—not many. The bootleg days would see a few end up riddled by gang guns in a ditch at the end of a "ride." But in the main they settled down like almost everyone else with a school-days-sweetheart, published the banns, took the vows, raised up their broods as good Americans (who spared a dollar for the I.R.A. and "the trouble" in Ireland).

It was hard to kill the cartoon Irishman, because, frankly, when I was a kid we all enjoyed him. My father would roll with laughter at Mr. Dooley's remarks on events of the day; the wittiest Irishman since Bernard Shaw. On a lower level there were Maggie and Jiggs and corned-beef-and-cabbage humor, and Happy Hooligan, both racial insults, but we kids didn't know it. The "Cohen on the Telephone" on the gramophone, and the desperate mugging of the Celtic prat-fall comics in the Keystone comedies at the movies we also swallowed. It was a more innocent time and the immigrant ships were still bringing over relatives with the thick brogue and the funny clothes and black stick.

An Irish kid soon learned he was different from the other kids if only because he was Irish and they were not. And an Irish Catholic kid soon got to sense he was a lot different. The knowledge came slowly. But suddenly it was there. He heard remarks that shocked him, and then he realized not everyone went to Mass, had holy pictures and crucifixes in the house, believed in the Pope's infallibility, knew what was Holy Communion, the Sacrament of the Holy Eucharist.

For me it was as normal as breathing. I not only accepted faith, I relished it, was devoted to it. To us Irish trying to make a place for ourselves in a land that was new to our parents and grandparents it was the solid rock that sustained us. As a kid I was not lost or wandering. I belonged, really belonged.

Some of the other kids mocked the holy medals we wore, they never crossed themselves when passing a church, they took holy names in vain as a curse, not realizing what they were doing. And if they became vocal with rumors that some bigots were passing on about nuns, priests or the Pope, we had a fight. So in a way my faith kept me in condition and helped me develop a good right hook. Soon, too, these others learned the wisdom of one of my father's favorite sayings: "When Irish eyes are smiling, always hold your left hand high."

We were not, in or out of church, goodie-goodie boys, and the priests and nuns had their hands full with us. And they weren't the holy waxworks, the pious sighers, the films often show them as. They were real men and women, dedicated to renouncing a great deal of what we saw as the joys of life. They may have had some human failings, and could give you the back of the hand as well as lead you to the remission of mortal sin by the Sacrament of Penance and an Act of Contrition. They were pioneers in the faith in my childhood, when Catholics were still not accepted in some places. Their lives were hard and bare and often painful in a material way. I want to recall them here and their work; they remain for me a warm link to my childhood and the boy I was.

In our homes we kids felt a protective warmth in being Irish, being Catholic, and making the Pledge to the Flag each morning in school. It was with pride we said our names were O'Brien, O'Neill, Murphy or Callihan. Later when leaving the nest and going out into the world, I felt a little lonely; the taste of the food and cooking was a little different; the conversations lacked a colorful something in their sparkle, the turn of a phrase was more clumsy than what I knew. But that wore off and today when

I meet the grandchildren of my early gang pals, I can hardly tell them by dress, diet and hobbies from any other American kid. And I don't mind. Except when I remember Ernest Hemingway's remark, "We all have a girl and her name is Nostalgia."

3

Boyhood Years

Strange is the gratification one gets from memory—an almost self-ish pleasure. Murmurs begin to resurrect images out of events that you had completely forgotten. It becomes a sort of self-hypnosis, you are lulled into a dim, yet ever clearing reverie of yesterday. You begin to recall small incidents, and retrospect responds with greater alacrity like a whipped race horse, and colors, sounds, shapes emerge.

The extreme cold of those winters in the Midwest are now leg-end. My first awareness of the frigidity of the world became ap-parent when I heard the wagon wheels grinding shrilly, like cry-ing birds, in the snow. I recall Mom coming into my bedroom to turn on the silver-painted radiator so that it would be warm for me when I got out of the firm embrace of my bed. She would even have my underwear and stockings laid out on the radiator to heat them.

"After all, you have to walk to school."

I shall always remember my first day in school as my personal Stations of the Cross. My mother left me there alone like Robinson Crusoe on his island—worse; it seemed like I was being exiled to Siberia, till a very beautiful nun, Sister Mary Norbert, took my small hand and consoled me in the voice of angels—and things became all right again and I could focus on my classmates, on sharp pencils and things called reading and writing.

I liked hearing the thundering roar of our hard-bought coal cascading down into the cellar bin. There were the red knit wristlets my mother made for me; there were snowball fights, snow men and the snow forts; wonderful sleigh rides, snuggled next to what you'd like as your best girl; hot chocolate afterward at someone's home (stuck for the chocolate and cookies); winters cold and blue—and warnings of careless boys on thin ice pulled out "stiff and rigid as dried codfish, and his poor mother crying her red eyes out at the loss of her poor boy."

The summers came around season after season, with parties, the Golden Lake, rowboating, my dad teaching me how to stroke and sweat at the oars, the smell of clover making me sneeze, the first ride, a horse wide as a barn and a buggy, and being allowed to hold the jerking reins . . . the wonderful hot bread that Mom made and spread with brown sugar.

"Eat and you'll be as brave and strong as John L. Sullivan."

The songs at home were free of radio or television. My mother sang as she did the housework, or prepared the meals: "Don't You Remember Sweet Alice, Ben Bolt," "Come Back to Erin," "Mavourneen, Mavourneen" (this is what caused me to name my daughter Mavourneen). All wonderful corny, gay, vulgar, delightful, happy, pious songs: "When You and I Were Young, Maggie," "After the Ball," "The Rosary," "Macushla." Jazz was still a-borning, rock-and-roll unthinkable, Mitch Miller an unbearded child.

News came to us with the shouting of the raucous newsboys shouting "Wuxtra!" Many a morning I woke shivering to their howls of great disasters: sinking of the Titanic, Halley's comet, the Eastland disaster, the Iroquois fire.

My first train trip was sheer illusion because it was on a simulated train track in the Penny Arcade in Milwaukee, me sitting stiffly—proud but scared—on the observation platform, and some kind of magic lantern effect gave me the illusion of traveling with great speed down a long railroad track.

The Stone Age auto car stank and snorted among us, but we still smelled of the best horses.

In time the family moved further uptown, five blocks, but we did go over two sets of tracks. "Wells Street *and* State Street. We are progressing!"—to a little apartment on Fourteenth and Prairie Streets.

I walked into the apartment and my dad said, "Push the button."

I asked why.

"Go ahead, push it."

I did and the lights came on!

"It's Mr. Edison's electric lamp."

It was a pretty nerve-shattering thing after kerosene lamps and gaslights. We were on the fourth floor and the name of the building was the Elizabeth Apartments.

"Imagine," said Ma. "Naming a house."

We had moved far enough away so I was separated from my old gang, but as we all attended the same parochial school there was no disruption of old friendships along the route uptown.

We started organizing our first baseball team. We were from ten to fourteen years old, and active. There were no Little Leagues in those days. The name of our team was the Bullet Stoppers. The initials B.S. on our sweaters evoked many a snide remark from various youthful and vulgar observers.

We had a pretty good team. I pitched and Irv Mehigan (Senator Mehigan now, as I said) caught my various systems of curves and drops.

"That's the ol' curve—keep 'em coming!"

The football season left us limp and happy. Some of us would get jobs every week pouring whitewash out of tin cans to mark off the lines every five yards on the gridiron. In those innocent

37

days, a touchdown counted five and it took three downs to make five yards, consequently there were a lot of lines to be painted. Our only reward was that we got to the grounds very early in the morning and stayed there through noon, so as to be able to see the game in the afternoon. My dad would come down to Marquette Field and toss a couple of newspaper-wrapped sandwiches over the fence, which assured me of staving off hunger during noon and positively insured my watching the game.

"Eat hearty, son."

"Thanks, Dad."

In 1913 Marquette was playing Notre Dame and I was a boy of twelve. (Thirty years later, I would be playing the life of the man who was playing out there on the field that I had marked: Knute Rockne, who was end for Notre Dame.) I think it was a zero to zero tie, and the sandwiches were hard-boiled eggs and chopped ham.

All the kids usually gravitated to the O'Brien apartment after school because my mother, as my father put it "made the best doughnuts and the best bread of anyone in history." The kids loved Dad. He was always taking part in our games, particularly baseball. Saturday mornings, in worn pants and an old smelly fielder's glove he pulled down some high ones.

I continued altar-boy lessons. This demanded some concentrated study because in those days if you chose to become an acolyte, you were a dedicated kid and had to be on time with clean hands and a handkerchief for blowing. I still serve Mass on occasion. I have never forgotten the Latin I learned as a boy in the old Gesu Church in Milwaukee, a building smelling of candle wax, furniture polish, grace and faith.

Terry Mitchell, (now on the Milwaukee police force) was a close pal and he was really rugged. I was always pretty numb to arithmetic, algebra and math, and Terry always helped me with those delicate and crazy problems of fractions and decimals. (I see him every time I return to Milwaukee, as I do all of my classmates that have survived the years.)

38

Looking at my eighth-grade picture is like looking into a mirror stranger than the one Alice went through. Two small faces are now priests, Father Doyle and Father Fitzgerald; a couple are doctors; some became attorneys, burglars, police and successful business men. None of the faces of boyhood made the banker grade, and I am the only one who chose to exploit his actor's blood. So there, frozen by silver nitrate on prepared paper already fading and turning brown, suspended in inanimation, is the motionless world of memory preserved like bubbles in amber.

All of us Catholics wanted to enter Marquette Academy, but the cost made our parents sigh. No one in that eighth grade had families who had the cash to send us to the school we all had such hopes of entering. There was always the dim chance, by examinations, to obtain a scholarship. That year, the graduates were sponsored by the A.O.H. (Ancient Order of Hibernians). The test was tough and I was fully confident that I could *never* answer the majority of the questions. I hit upon a desperate Machiavellian plan. Emotion, not wisdom might do the trick.

I wrote a vast composition (aided by books from the public library) on the varied and turmoiled history of Ireland, mentioned Wolfe Tone, Parnell. I terminated the paper with a quotation by Robert Emmett. Then I added a text of great praise and many laudatory remarks as to how the A.O.H. had helped kids, like ourselves, obtain that sacred vessel, higher learning. I then tied up the pages with a beautiful green ribbon (from a candy box) and drew, in emerald chalk, a shamrock on the title page.

I gained the scholarship, to the openmouthed amazement of my friends. I shall always be deeply indebted to Robert Emmett and all the other scholars of Ireland. (Years later, when I was held by my heels over the Blarney Stone at Blarney Castle in Ireland, to kiss the face of this cold, germ-plastered monument, I thought then that somewhere in Milwaukee, during my boyhood, part of that stone must have existed.)

I was not yet done roughing up literature.

In my first year at the Academy, I wrote my first classroom essay in the form of a poem and dedicated it to my mother. Yeats, Shelley, Byron or Shakespeare could not have been more sincere —even if *their* rhymes might have been more epic.

> Throughout the years, her love has gleamed,
> Through smiles and bitter tears has beamed.
> Whatever thrill or care
> Was mine—was hers in part to share.
>
> And back in early childhood's day
> From her sweet lips, I learned to pray
> I wonder can I e'er repay, that love
> That blossoms radiant fair, throughout the years.
>
> In mem'ry's book, now tinged with age—
> Engraved on every time worn page,
> Her love stands out—the choicest gift
> And aids my soul its fight to wage,
> Throughout the years.

Later I had it printed and Mom had it framed. (I have it now, frame and all, and it hangs on the wall of my bedroom.)

At school it was announced that the days were at hand for going out for the teams—baseball, basketball and football. You had to give it all you had to get on a team because we were all boys from tough neighborhoods. You had to be solid and indifferent to pain to survive. I made the baseball and football teams, and played basketball, too. (I was usually the fifth substitute. I didn't shine much but I managed to get in a few games and a few lucky baskets.)

The Juniors of Marquette Academy were playing the Seniors in baseball—I was pitching—and Irv Mehigan's brother, Frank, came up to the plate. Irv called for a high inside pitch. I threw it, Frank didn't duck quick enough, and the sound of that ball striking the skull of Irv's brother filled the school grounds. Frank hit the ground like a felled ox. It took time to bring him around. I never pitched a ball again. I played ball, and even play now in some of the club games, but I don't pitch.

A new boy enrolled in the Academy in 1917. We became close pals. His name was, and is, Spencer Tracy.

The world was blowing up, and in our direction, after three years of destroying Europe.

Headlines again; the Lusitania was sunk (Wilson said, "There is such a thing as a man being too proud to fight.") and suddenly we were "making the world safe for Democracy." The bands played, the drill parades started, the Liberty Bond drives were on and Spence and myself and some others left school one afternoon and went downtown to the enlistment headquarters of the Navy.

We were told: "You have to obtain your parents' consent because of your age." (We had mostly just turned seventeen.)

There were tears shed in our homes, particularly mine. I was the only one of the group who was an only child. My parents capitulated, and we all were off to war as if it were just another football game—and the risks only a little higher.

With all of the real, fearful drama of war that followed, none of us ever got to sea. We fought the Battle of the Great Lakes, and worked very hard as gunners, gunner's mate, and other tasks over a thousand miles from any real deep salt water, at the Great Lakes Naval Station.

Somebody has called World War I "The last of the romantic wars." Maybe, but eating navy beans and mopping high-brass offices wasn't romantic or gallant. Yet we were aware of an age ending, of new forces at work. Young women in white with Red Cross collection boxes, selling kisses for dollars; the young pink-faced officers with Sam Browne belts, in tight-collared mustard-colored uniforms; the wounded French officers and English ones too, with swagger sticks, sent over to pep up our war effort. The hunt for German spies, and innocent Dutch pork butchers being called Huns. Air aces in planes of flypaper and match sticks. Cigarettes were no longer for sissies, and the wrist watch was acceptable.

There was a kind of moral breakdown. More drinking, petting in the back seat of the ancient high cars ("I may never come back, honey"). A sense of time was closing in. The movies we saw were full of appeals to flag, country and the hanging of the German Kaiser to a sour apple tree. I often wondered what Hollywood had against apple trees. I expanded, observed and realized I was a green, green kid.

It was a singing war, much more than the next one. We sat on raw pine benches in canteens eating doughnuts and singing "K-k-k-katy," "Smiles," "There's a Long, Long Trail A-winding," "Oh How I Hate to Get Up in the Morning." (I agreed in a fully changed voice.) Irving Berlin wrote "Mr. Zip" ("with your hair cut just as short as, just as short as mine"). But in show business George M. Cohan (I could always win a camp bet he was Irish and not Jewish) gave us "Over There," a tune easy to march to, and it stirred our young blood, even those of us who never went over there.

There was sadness, too, when a telegram was delivered and some mother wailed in agony: *Dead* or *Missing in Action*. There were camp infections, epidemics, and young men died without having lived, their death of childhood diseases not very heroic.

One learned of life, of vice, of comradeship. Of the impersonal cruelty of war, of regulation. Always regulation.

The cynics said, "In the Navy if you can't paint it, salute it."

There were shortages for most, fat profits for others, shortages of sugar, of meat. There were moments when the entire world seemed mad. But on brisk mornings with the lake winds snapping the flag out we young men marching were very happy to be alive and be in this war.

And over there someone said: "Lafayette, we are here."

It was strange being away from home, sleeping with a few thousand bedmates, responding to whistles and bells at boot camp. Home was only eighty-five miles from the Great Lakes station. I wrote my parents: "Be sure to get down next Saturday to watch your son on parade. Secretary Daniels is to review the Navy."

There were by actual count 82,000 sailors marching by, but Mom and Dad were convinced "everyone was out of step but you."

Jack Benny and Walter Winchell were also at the Great Lakes training station at that time, wearing navy blue, but we never met. Playing football on the navy team was a great way of getting liberties for me. I soon learned the score.

"If you engaged in any form of athletics, O'Brien, you became some kind of a fair-haired boy."

Jimmy Conselman was one of the great stars of our Great Lakes football team, as was Paddy Driscoll, and I played hard for Navy, *and* leave passes. I overdid it. Before the Christmas holidays, I had had so many liberties it was definite I could not secure Christmas liberty. Paul Middelton, a Jewish boy went to the commandant and explained to him that Christmas meant so much to me, and as his holiday was Yom Kippur, why couldn't O'Brien have *his* liberty? The brass acquiesced and I was home for Christmas.

I could see the Navy wasn't going to use me in any actual sea battles. The Army was winning the war—and there were signs the end was near.

November 11, 1918, my birthday, came along cold, crisp, the lake waters an icy blue—and the war was over in a clatter of bells, cheers and the sound of breaking regulations.

We were all released from the Navy with neat honorable-discharge papers. We returned home and the decision was to finish high school, and in me the idea of acting grew.

The school had organized an R.O.T.C. unit and all of our classmates were still in uniform. The school head wanted us to don the same garb. We had returned to school in the navy blues, and we intended to wear only that uniform. There was a great school to-do over this, threats of expulsion, but our parents stood by us. We returned to school and in the uniform of the United States Navy. Spencer Tracy went away to a military academy and we lost him as a classmate. The rest of us strode with great pride on to the podium to receive our diplomas on graduation day (still in the blue uniform).

"We went in seamen second-class," I said. "And that's the way we came out."

"Cheers for the Navy."

I enrolled in the university and law school, but my football activities far transcended my devotion to books on points of law. I was not endowed with any Phi Beta Kappa blood. My closest approach to Greek letters was at Kappa Beta Phi, which was known by some as "Kicked by the Faculty." We footballers were not in the good graces of any of the Jesuit faculty. I wore a Theta Nu Epsilon key and was also a member of Alpha Gamma Phi. In those days it seemed a great achievement to be tormented into a fraternity by young sadists. So I joined two of them and learned the horror of listening to amateur saxophone players. The Jazz Age was dawning.

The theater had settled into me as a major love. I played my first important dramatic role in the college production of *Charley's Aunt* as the star, in borrowed skirts. I was adorable. In my kid days I had played various parts—the Prince *and* the Pauper was one—and became involved in elocution contests, but the first big one for me was *Charley's Aunt* at the university.

I didn't neglect sports, but going out for the football team was pretty rough because it meant the best position I could make would be the second-string quarterback. The first position was held by Red Dunne, the first All-American at Marquette. So I didn't get to play very much. That was the year we played Notre Dame, and somehow we led at the half 6–0. The finish was different —it was Notre Dame 20, Marquette 6.

But I had a secret image—throughout the football, scholastics, fraternities, the theater was always hovering uppermost in my thoughts.

How and why I was to become an actor I didn't know. I knew no one, I was unknown. I was no classical scholar of the drama steeped in the craft and the great plays—yet I *knew* I would soon be active on the New York scene.

What makes an actor? I've been asked that hundreds of times and I honestly don't know. Or if I know it's so deeply hidden from me in my subconscious that what I say in public is often different every time I explore the subject. Calling an actor a prancing exhibitionist is too easy—and not fully true.

I had no right to be an actor, I knew, or a would-be actor. I had no rich family to help me. I lacked the polish and the knowledge that some think an actor should have. But I felt dedicated as a nun when I thought of myself stomping across some stage, tossing out fancy words, making love to real, live, good-smelling actresses, standing fakely humble at curtain call, stuttering out a fine little speech skillfully concocted to make it appear I was oh *so* thankful for applause, oh *so* much wanted to please.

I began like most actors as a stage-drugged kid, sitting on moth-eaten seats in high balconies, seeing bad plays, and sometimes a good one; in following cigar-smoking, can-carrying actors, make-up and grease paint still on their faces, their coat collars often made of fur, their spats buttoned over thin but polished shoes. *This* I knew was a race apart. They ate so well, it seemed, and drank so much, and made such grand gestures, and spoke of Ziggy and Dave, and being held over, and sixteen weeks on the road, a smash hit in the tall grass and the sticks.

As a kid I'd try out facial expressions in a mirror. I'd think of myself as a pirate, an Indian chief. I'd wonder how one got to remembering all those words in plays, because at first the words have little meaning. Then came the small school parts and the inner grin, knowing maybe I was just a little better than the rest of the kids. Remembering the names of the popular plays, *Alias Jimmy Valentine*, *Friendly Enemies*, *Three Faces East*, and Nat Goodwin, married eight times in, of course, *Why Marry?*

Impractical, foolish, a hope that didn't seem to have any reason to be fulfilled. Still I saw myself as an actor. Now *how* to bring together the vision and the reality?

4

The Call of the Stage

There was no reason, I kept telling myself, for me to think I could become an actor. My background was not of the theater, and my immature profile and full face in no way resembled those of John Barrymore, Lowell Sherman, or any of the actors called matinee idols in those days. It was a simple neat Irish face I saw in the mirror, but it pleased me, and it pleased my mother and father. It was definitely not in the classic mode, I admitted. My voice was rich, untamed and untrained. I walked normally, unaware of the balance, poise, grace and charm that were the trademark of the professional actor then—just as the itch, scratch and mumble are of the method actor today.

But deep in my still untampered-with ego, I was an actor. I set sights on what Ring Lardner called the Big Town, over a thousand miles away. There was no money in the O'Brien till to get me to New York. My Uncle Charlie (one of the three swains of the old Lee eating house who had married my mother's sister) was by then a successful man by our standards. He managed the Union Club in Manhattan. During the early summer of 1920 a letter arrived from Uncle Charlie for my mother enclosing a check for $300.

"And we are inviting the lad and you too to spend the summer with us here in New York City."

There was great exuberance around the O'Brien household, as if the British had suffered another defeat at Yorktown. Mother and I went on ahead. Dad only had two weeks of a no-salary vacation from Chapman's.

He said, "Don't worry, I'll not come empty-handed. I've been pretty successful at the Round Table in the card room and have set aside a few extra bucks won in pinochle games at the club."

Mother and I embarked for the East in the mood of pioneers facing great adventure. We had a stopover at Niagara Falls (no one took us for a honeymoon couple), the first time I had ever seen this great wet spectacle. I hired a little old man with a horse and buggy to drive us around the falls. I had my two-dollar Brownie camera clutched in my hand to photograph the Seventh Wonder of the World, as the old man called it. I still have a picture of Mom standing at the fence overlooking the falls. She was always to me a very regal person and in the Brownie snapshot she assumes a slightly damp, queenly hauteur. A cousin of mine once inscribed on it: "The Duchess at the Rapids."

For me the entire trip to New York was breathtaking, the service regal, the landscape unreal. For us, our first glimpse of the great city rising in stone and steel from between its two slightly polluted rivers, transcended even my first look at the Taj Mahal when I was in India during the Second World War. It was a wonderful summer and when it came time to return to the Midwest I knew where my future lay. Here in the city, a place still slightly O. Henry's but soon to become Daymon Runyon's and Walter Winchell's. I pleaded with Mom and Dad to let me stay over and let me trot along Broadway in search of employment in the theater.

47

"This means you don't return to college?"

"I guess so."

"Where would you stay?" asked Ma.

Dad said, "Jersey City, in the same place with the O'Neills. I did my apprenticeship there when I left the orphanage at Newburgh."

"Jersey City!" I shouted. "No! New York."

"It's three cents across by ferry boat."

"But living with relatives," I protested.

"Yes, you're lucky as far as expenses are concerned. The only thing actually involved is the fare back and forth from Jersey to New York. Take it or leave it."

I took it. After all, any citizen of Jersey City will tell you he's really part of New York—"only more so."

New York City in the early twenties—still in great part brownstone and nineteenth century—was a focal point of the new modern arts, the excitement of victory, and a postwar madness that followed that noble war that "made the world safe for Democracy." There would never be another war; everyone said so, and Mr. Harding was to replace the sick Mr. Wilson and his crazy League of Nations.

Coming across the bay by ferry from Jersey City, the gulls diving for the rich harbor garbage, the smell of horses and motor cars from the deck below, the wind blowing through my thin pants and my then thick black hair, I felt like a new knight in tight armor going to attack his first dragon, not sure yet which end of the lance to use, or how to recognize a dragon when he saw one. I was raw, country raw, Middle West raw, but with a firm idea I could take that city.

The streets seemed to me heavy with traffic; thick with cars that look quaint to us now; square monsters, hand-cranked, with running boards; most of them still with canvas tops and celluloid curtains and gas headlights; the Model T, the most popular, referred to as the Tin Lizzie, and by college boys as the "Heap."

I wandered the stone streets. The stylish women of Fifth Avenue

48

took my breath away. The first sight of the mangy, worn theaters —pure fire traps—on the side streets above Forty-second Street that was "Broadway" brought a lump as big as a tennis ball to my throat. I stood there in my Midwest tailoring; tight at the waist, belted, narrow pants a bit too short, my socks showing over my punch-holed, brown needle-point shoes, staring at the names in lights. Barrymore, Ina Claire, Cohan, Hammerstein, Mae West, Eva Tanguay.

There had been a great actors' strike the year before: Actors' Equity against the managers for the actors' right to stay alive, breathe, be paid, not dumped a thousand miles from home by broken-down road companies, or rehearsed for months without pay. Sixty shows never opened; thirty-five theaters had been dark. My hero, George M. Cohan, became a strikebreaker, coming out against the actors. The actors, hungry and gaunt, won.

Now there was a raucous peace in the theaters, and I hunted up names of producers I had heard of: Al Woods, the Shuberts, Arthur Hopkins, to see if they really existed. And sure enough their names were up on the billboards.

One was aware that the twenties had opened up with a roar. I could smell the excitement. The war had made many of the young men aware of a world beyond the U.S.A. ("How You Gonna Keep 'Em Down on the Farm After they've Seen Paree!") They had drunk wine, and if lucky enough made love to foreign women with black silk stockings, had seen the Eiffel Tower, Big Ben, the misery and the greatness of a Europe—a civilization battered by wars. They had heard new ideas, new names too. They were just beginning to be talked about at Greenwich Village bohemian parties when I got to New York. Freud, who had rediscovered people were of two deeply involved sexes; Marx, who was dead but who was somehow behind what had happened in 1917 in Russia, had come back to life as Lenin and Trotsky, who were always drawn in the newspaper cartoons as carrying smoking, old-fashioned round bombs. I even heard of Picasso and Matisse,

49

but mistook them for a dance team playing Loew's time with the Dolly Sisters, and McIntyre and Heath.

A revolution in manners had taken place. The women were freer in their speech, wore less, the stockings were rolled to the knees, the hair cut into a short bob or shingle, the dresses became looser and hipless, and there were hints most underwear had been discarded. Soon youth took to smoking through long cigarette holders, calling each other "sheik" and "sheba," drinking bootleg gin, dancing the Charleston ("It's the cat's pajamas") and adoring saxophone players who crooned—Rudy Vallee was just around the corner.

The first speakeasy I ever entered in New York was a pattern for all: bad likker, good Italian food, the blonde crying in the phone booth, the cop mooching a free drink, the fake paper grape leaves on the ceiling, the air hardly permitted outdoors to refresh itself. A setting that was to become a cliché in a thousand Warner Brothers movies, but new and fresh when I first tasted bathtub rye ("Right off the boat, mac—scraped off—ha ha!").

While I honed my courage to tackle the producers' and agents' offices, I became aware of a lot of other young people like myself running about—eager, neatly shabby, with the look of eagles or unemployed young actors; both have that unglazed fanatical stare.

I began boldly to wear a brighter tie, I read the theater notices, I tried the doors to producers' offices, agents' nests, the people who were theater.

After several weeks of prowling and rapping on the agency doors, I heard of a casting rehearsal being held for a musical at Bryant Hall. "Dancers could apply."

My only claim to nimble feet was the Irish folk dances we used to learn from Professor McNamara, back in Milwaukee. I went to the hall practicing my jigs along the way and joined a group of eager-eyed, hopeless-looking aspirants. During the course of the waiting morning, I at last met Bert French, the dance director. He questioned me as to my experience and background.

"I danced at the Irish picnics every year and I look pretty fancy in a green sash."

"A funny fella?"

I had not intended to give a flippant answer, but it was the only thing I could think of to say at the time.

"No, really—I can dance, Mr. French."

He allowed me to audition with the chorus line. Fortunately, the time steps were not too difficult, and I absorbed as much as I could by observing and calmly questioning people in the rehearsal hall. I got the job. I was one of six chorus boys in the front line. (One of them, Donald Kirk, is now in Hollywood and works in television and motion pictures.)

During the strenuous rehearsals that followed I ached and fumbled but I managed to "hip the ballet" almost like a pro. As the days went on, I mastered the routines and the songs. I found out the name of the musical comedy was *Adrienne*. The star was George Bancroft and the leading lady Vivienne Segal. The juvenile, Harry Fox, was to make famous a song called "I'm Always Chasing Rainbows" (an unscrupulous theft from Chopin).

That was my introduction to Broadway, over forty years ago. A hoofer.

I was not a loner, not a solitary. I liked people, crowds, activities, so I didn't stay in dark corners. I made friends. I met Louise and Marion Squire, from the Ziegfeld Follies, through Inez Courtney. They lived with their mother uptown in the seventies and I freeloaded many evenings in their apartment where Mom brewed tea and cut homemade cake. My mother sent me a twenty-first birthday greeting from Milwaukee. We had the birthday cake at Mom Squire's and some of the young show folk came in to share it with us.

Later I reread Mom's letter carefully.

"Dad is pretty seriously ill and although it does not look as though it might be fatal, Dad feels that a thousand miles is a long way away from his boy. He would like you home. So . . ."

It wasn't easy to give in my notice and leave the troupe on what I felt could be (to *me*, at least) an opening to a great career.

However, my parents wanted me, their only child, and I came home to a pale but happy Father, and to Mother.

In Milwaukee I re-enrolled at the university and law school, not as a very ardent student, I must say. But God was good and my dad recovered his health and was back at work at Chapman's.

To keep my hand in theater I wrote, produced and directed a production for the local Junior League entitled, *Fanciful Follies*. We opened at the Pabst Theater and it was a huge town success. George McBride, Hoddy Halsey and Jerry Host, with whom I had been in the Navy, showed that they were endowed with talent. And on the feminine side, Jo Rinehart was assured she could have made another Mrs. Vernon Castle. None of the cast, however, ever went on to show business. The smell of grease paint (and it does have a peculiar pungent odor like none other on earth) made me feel for my lost New York life. It was hard to settle for the studies of torts and briefs in the law courses at the school.

I took on a job to direct a "Pageant of Progress" with a cast of over a thousand. I had bitten off more than I could digest or stage but, thanks to a lot of trustful, helpful people, it was a success. There were weeks of rehearsal for its only two planned performances, but all this time, it only firmed my conviction that I would never be happy until I went back to the real theater. At the end of the school year, I was still concentrating on theater, *theater*, THEATER. Let others be Clarence Darrow, Supreme Court justices—I just wanted to be a happy, contented ham on a stage.

Summer vacations, I had always worked at odd jobs—at the spark-flying blacksmith shop of my Uncle Bill, the American Express Company, or putting in fresh sidewalks for the city, which meant plenty of cement and wheelbarrow work. While working in the Milwaukee Railroad yards, every train whistle kept singing its dirge, teasing me about the city I longed be in—New York, with all of its aches, hungers, earnest young actors and ancient myths.

I heard that my navy pal, Spencer Tracy, had enrolled in Ripon University, in upper Wisconsin. He too was scratching an itch for the theater, and involving himself in theatrical appearances in college shows.

The following year I was back at the university and my folks realized that all of my application to study was worthless. I was unhappy.

Mother, Dad and I finally had a dining-room round-table discussion. Dad got very serious.

"If you love the stage that much, why not go into it with the proper approach? I mean getting basic training in the rudiments of actual acting. So where do you start?"

I gulped. "Outside of the Sorbonne (I have no particular yearning for Europe) the best school is called Sargent's."

Mother said, "It's not a wild place? *These* Protestant schools—"

"No, no, everybody there is very serious about acting. But—"

Dad nodded. "But where would the money come from?"

I snapped my fingers. "Wait. I have it. The state of Wisconsin has passed a servicemen's law. All ex-servicemen can take a choice of receiving ten dollars a month for every month they had served, or education in a college of their choice."

"But it must be in the state of Wisconsin," added Dad.

Mother said firmly, "Our congressman owes us a favor. We've voted the straight party ticket, always. Haven't we?"

Dad said, "Now darlin', politics aren't for women—but I'll see the district leader at the club."

I got in touch with Spencer Tracy and put it to him—would he, too, come to New York with me on the servicemen's enrollment allowance if my dad could swing it? He answered: "Can a shamrock be anything but green?"

So while many, many excellent schools existed in Wisconsin, none of them majored in the teaching of theater arts. With the aid of our political push we relayed our problem to our congressman. We won our point. Spencer and I took off for New York City.

After several nervous meetings with Mr. Sargent and Mr. Jehlinger, we were admitted to the acting academy. I had made it back.

5

Broadway

New York City in the early years of what came to be called the Roaring Twenties certainly earned its reputation—but to a hopeful earnest young actor-to-be the academy days were the highlights of my early manhood. Entering Sargent's School in the already decaying Carnegie Hall building was all I wanted at the moment—and the place was enhanced by the fact that for every male enrolled at the school, there were ten girls. I was pleased at this, having decided for some time the scheme of two sexes was a delightful pattern.

Mother Forbes at the school lives in the memories of all who remember those early days of the Academy. She was a clucking mother-hen type and looked after all of us as though we were small kids still in primary school. She was the den mother to us all in those dusty, splintery classrooms of the school.

Spencer and I rented a mouse-nest of a room at Ninety-eighth and West End Avenue. It was two steep, shaky flights up, but as Spencer said, "It has a ceiling." Our landlady, Mrs. Brown, admired actors and treated us like established stars. But pretzels and water was a frequent diet for Tracy and O'Brien, and I learned to wear my socks from either end.

I had a prized pongee shirt, the envy of all the actor-students. I would wear it proudly for three days and then would rest it in the dresser drawer. Spencer would then put it on and wear it for the next three days. People wondered why we wore so many pongee shirts.

We got a job in the famous play by Capek, *R.U.R.* Spencer and I were just part of the cast of robots—the play invented the word—and our stipend was $15 a week each. After several weeks, Spencer was given a line to read and his salary was raised to $20 a week. This was a definite step up to wealth. It sure aided the exchequer. We were also receiving $30 a month each from the state of Wisconsin as ex-servicemen, and now we could *almost* exist on a near starvation diet.

Spencer said, "I bet they've outlawed steak and onions and we don't even know it."

I discovered that beyond the glittering theater world of lights and color and success, there was another, a larger world of struggling actors, students, and would-be actors. The unknown people of the night, an underworld of yet submerged talent existed, looking for the break, the opening, the chance.

Like Spencer and myself mostly they lived in odd corners of the city near the theaters, in dank little rooms lit by gas, or one flickering light bulb. Waiting meanly, trying to keep their few clothes neat and brushed, moving about on the fringe of the theater world; full believers in miracles.

We were seen at rehearsals, in the lobby of hit plays between the acts. (You could usually, if you fed an usher cigarettes, get in free after Act One.) We stood in line for cheap, high seats, hoped for bit parts, walk-ons. Our club was the bargain basement of some drugstore where our meager orders of coffee were a pass; the phone booths our answering service. We filled up on beans and bread, learned to snatch the biggest portion at the cafeteria, not wait for formal invitations to meals, to add ketchup and the mustard in heaping slops to almost everything we ate—for it helped keep life and blood active; but oh the heartburn!

We learned to press our clothes, keep pants under the mattress overnight, use a shirt till it frayed away, turn the collar, trim the cuffs. Always to wear our aging limp hats with the brim turned down or up at a sharp angle. And act at all times with the professional world as if we had just returned to Broadway from a great success.

We were human, in need of company and compassion, and we huddled together. We fell in love, we held hands, we made up ménages. We fought, parted, made new friends. We shared; our clothes, dimes, friends, letters, news of the theater, impressions of successful stars, the cheap wine, the free tickets. We walked in the rain under raincoats not really waterproof. We tried to keep our shoes shined, and soled with cardboard. We were frozen in winter when the mean gray wind came up Broadway from the direction of Macy's and swirled dust torn newspapers, bird dust at us. We shivered in lobbies, and warmed ourselves in public libraries smelling of wet wool and old feet, and in museums. In summer, in our mean rooms under slate roofs the heat was out of Egypt. But somehow we didn't really mind. Actually we were often very happy.

Discomfort and poverty are not the evils our over-socially-progressed age has pictured them. Lack of hope is the true horror.

Youth is tough—ego can take enough blows to floor a giant. The madness of the idea of being on a stage, facing that great crouching animal, the public, could sustain one better than a plate of lobsters, a bucket of Blue Points and fried chicken at Sheepshead Bay, or a steak at the Waldorf.

I very early became aware of that breathing, panting mass creature out there beyond the footlights: the audience. Every actor, would-be actor in time becomes aware of them or rather *it*, as a unit, and remains in awe of the thing. For no matter how deep in a part on stage or how involved in a drama, one false cough, some strange stirring of that mass sitting in warm darkness and the actor can slip, the play can begin to fall apart.

In his youth the actor keeps a grip on the audience, and if he has that *something*—call it personality, power (he doesn't even have to be a good actor)—he can rule the customers in their seats like a lion tamer his beast with his chair and pistol. Older actors, wary and cunning, slip into mock personalities, as I saw, character parts like well-worn gloves, and get the public to accept them as well-loved memories from their common past. The play, the lines, the part become nothing. The public has come to toss rose petals at an idol.

But I also witnessed those moments when the actor failed, when a bit of business was fumbled, when some hacker set off other coughers, like barking seals; when a child walking for a drink of water, when a prop fell, *or* sadly, when the actor just wasn't up to it anymore. Then came the collapse of illusion, of art, of the theater's own daffy wonderful magic.

Young as I was, I began to understand those actors and actresses who before curtain time poured their courage into themselves from a bottle, just before they faced that yet half-sleeping, dinner-digesting animal out front. Some never did sober up. Some went further, like Jeanne Eagels and others, and took addictive drugs.

The fear came to us all at times—what if we got out up there in front of those burning footlights, and our own flop sweat broke over us, and we froze on a line?

Being young, we looked forward to the challenge, aware, each of us, I was damn sure, that *we* were different, better, more talented, God-touched and unique. We held the future by the short hair.

At the Academy we did *The Importance of Being Ernest*, *The Tragedy of Nan* and other classics. One girl stood out as a vital, high-powered actress. Her name was Dolores Graves and I was pretty daffy about her, but I was daffy about all girls in those days. It seemed a delightful habit.

Spencer was outstanding in everything he did at the Academy. As a young man he was already the personality he became—only brasher. George M. Cohan later, in a play in which he was directing Spencer, said "Mr. Tracy, you are the finest actor I have ever seen." And George M. Cohan wasn't a man to love other actors.

The Sargent's School of Acting and its traditions were inspiring to us all—for from this same school have graduated such theater quality as William and Cecil B. DeMille, Jane Cowl, Edward G. Robinson, William Powell, Roz Russell.

All formative years contain good tasty memories. Ferryboat rides past screaming gulls in the harbor on the summer nights and those beautiful fables one told to willing female ears under a moon. Ocean voyages, years later, were nothing compared to the awareness of life while standing on a ferryboat deck hearing the musical chug-chug of the laboring engines and the rhythmic splashing of the debris-filled waters against the bow while gazing into the New York skyline and dreaming of tomorrow and *tomorrow* and at least three curtain calls in a hit play.

It was in many ways a more patterned age—the war had been far away and prosperity sat on us all—except for young actors. Yet we sensed the surge forward into that daffy second decade of the new century. To be young, as a poet said, was "very heaven." And in love. And it was the emotion, and not the object that mattered.

The men who tutored us in the theater at Sargent's were Edward Goodman and a Mr. Putman and they were good teachers. Charles Jehlinger was the master of the sizzling, sputtering style. Jelli had no peer, we were told, "in the province of passing on to the neophytes of Thespis, the true and profound teachings of a great art." He never professed to teach one how to act, but he was always able to project, in his own way, what he would like you in turn to project from the rostrum.

Later I heard others give their advice on acting. Spencer once was asked: "Mr. Tracy, what would be your initial advice to those of us who plan on the stage as our career?"

"Learn your lines!" Spencer said.

Alfred Lunt said, "Be sure they hear you beyond the first row and don't bump into the furniture!"

My own favorite is "A bad actor can certainly get worse!"

Academy days ended in 1923 and now we were to hit the pavements in search of professional employment. Stock companies were flourishing all over the United States. (Not Wall Street stock companies, but bands of often desperate actors herding together for comfort and protection.) All of us wanted our basic training for the theater to begin in one of these stock companies. They were to be our Harvards and Yales, our small Latin and less Greek.

The problem was, I sensed, as I looked over my fresh academy diploma, *how* do I make contact with the stock companies.

Chamberlain and Lyman Brown were the top agents of that era. But they only represented the established stars. We got a list of the lesser agents, and day after day we would haunt these often sleazy offices. Wales Winter was one of these many flesh peddlers and he was known to be particularly adept in casting stock companies. One day, after wearing out valuable shoe leather, I again stood in line in Wales' office.

An indifferent assistant told me, "How about an opening in a stock company for a juvenile?"

I tried to appear calm. "Where?"

"The place, Plainfield, New Jersey. The company, the Plainfield Players. The salary, fifty dollars a week."

"I'll take it."

"What's your background?"

I did some choice lies about my background. I made sure that the companies I told him I had played with were in the Far West or Canada so he would be unable to trace the truth—at least, not for a few days.

"Well, at least you got background."

"Do I have the job?"

"What else am I talking to you for. You got a wardrobe?"

I had been told that the most necessary items of wardrobe for a juvenile were a blue serge suit, white flannels and a straw hat ("Anyone for tennis?").

I had a blue serge suit and another greenish purple garment not in too good condition, but with the aid of a loan from my roommate, Spence, I purchased the white flannels and was off to Jersey like Alexander the Great taking Asia. Spence had landed a job in a Pittsburgh stock company so some of the Class of '23 was employed.

My courage seeped out as I got near Plainfield—a defenseless, well-named town.

I knew it was going to take a bit of knee bracing to brave the Jersey company. It was with fear and trepidation that I walked into the paint-peeling theater and handed the director Mr. Winter's card and stood waiting at the guillotine.

"O'Brien, we were desperate! This is the first day of rehearsal— the play is *Getting Gertie's Garter* and you are assigned to the juvenile lead."

I said, "So I was told. Where are my sides?"

It was an extensive role and demanded lots of concentrated study. I was frightened as only a semi-fraud with sensitive nerve ends can be.

Somehow those actors that caught on to me only winked, and helped. I shall always remember how kind everyone was to me. World-weary and theater-wise, they realized I was a newborn actor and they went out of their way to make things easier for me; Lozita Valentine, the leading lady, especially. She was my dream girl and I immediately fell in love with her. Also with the ingénue Nora Sterling. I was twenty-three years of age and a not too platonic bigamist at heart. Gretchen Thomas was the third star, a tall, statuesque blonde popular at the period. I fell in love with her too. It seemed the thing to do. Do things by threes. I *thought* I was in love, but actually, the really big, true love of my life then was the *Theater*.

The star was Carroll Ashburn, who later played one of the leads in *Dead End*. The comedian was Percy Kilbride, who years later was to be with me in a play titled *The Up and Up* at the Longacre Theater in New York. Percy was a skilled comedian with a dead-pan rube delivery, and deft in his craft. He was most generous in helping me in my baptism of stock company fire. We became close friends. We played together again at RKO some twenty years later in a picture call *Riff-Raff*. He hadn't changed a twang in his dialect.

Opening night in Plainfield (no champagne), I played the role of Billy in *Getting Gertie's Garter*. In one of the episodes of the play I had to hide in a trunk on stage. On the opening night I was concealed in the trunk. When I tried the lid—panic! The lock had jammed. I was in for good. I was in complete collapse. Fright and claustrophobia set in. I began to move like a trapped eel, and used all of the physical gyrations I could summon up, writhing around bumping the trunk around on stage. The customers began to laugh. I felt the lack of air, the sense of a tomblike doom.

The leading lady, Lozita, with charming improvisation spoke loudly, for all to hear, but especially *me* in the trunk.

"Billy, is that you—or are you a ghost?"

I screamed back from within my confining prison, "No, but it is only a question of time and I will be."

There was a sudden realization that real tragedy must be averted. The prop man appeared on stage with hammer and chisel, broke the lock and I stepped forth, a damp wreck.

This was my opening night. I knew nothing worse could happen to me. The audience had joined in the humor of the whole situation and as they applauded, we bowed, the prop man bowed and the play proceeded. I wasn't even jealous that the prop man had gotten more curtain calls than I had.

In those days actors playing in stock companies were doing four things simultaneously. They were *playing* the play, *forgetting* a play, *studying* a play and *rehearsing* a play. All because each week

61

we did a different production, and in many of the companies around the nation, they did two plays a week. The result was I had some exciting roles throughout those frantic, glorious weeks. We did *St. Elmo, Mrs. Wiggs of the Cabbage Patch, Seventh Heaven, Daddy Long-Legs, East Is West, Buddies, Upstairs and Down, Turn to the Right, Little Old New York*. It was hard, brain-tormenting, bone-breaking work, but gratifying. Weekends, if my studying seemed to be in order, I would take the ferry to New York City to meet fellow actors and express the state of theater affairs in the sticks.

In Plainfield, I lived in a place called Truell Court. It was American plan, "Plain cooking and clean rooms," and run by two spinster sisters, who were characters rather than real people. I was the only actor on the premises, truly a stag in my own domain. I always made it a point to make a grand entrance into the dining room—straw hat, two-toned shoes. As far as they were concerned, I *was* the star, at least in Truell Court. My excuse could be I brought a little bit of spice to the plain cooking of the American plan.

Life in a small American town in summer stock had its charm, and while Mr. Sinclair Lewis had just blasted "Main Street" and all its folk I think he missed its appeal. Thornton Wilder was to capture it better in *Our Town*.

As an employed actor, I would sleep late on ancient mattresses, rise to pitcher-and-towel, mutter over my stage lines at a country breakfast of eggs, ham, sausages, flannel cakes and real maple sauce. Finish off a pint of coffee and clotted cream, light my Stinkerino gift cigar and, donning straw skimmer and piped vest, I would move outdoors under the elms to the adoring eyes of high school girls still showing some baby fat. The drugstore was the town club and I'd ask for the New York papers, while at the mottled marble soda fountain the teen-age crowd giggled and some rash, bold chit would ask for an autograph. There I'd steer for the blind pig or local speakeasy, where the beer was shot full of ether for a bang and called needle beer, the whisky was Jersey lightning and the native white applejack kicked like a trick mule in the circus when it met the liver.

Rehearsals followed on a dusty stage under a work light; the members of the company having already paired off, as chums or sweethearts. (There is the story of one stock company manager, where backstage romances broke into the order of things every year. This season he gathered the company and issued his order. "*This* is a respectable company, a *moral* company. Whomever you start living with when we open, that's how you end up the season.")

Toward dusk we would have a light supper and drift to the non-air-conditioned theater where the citronella spray in the air only excited the local insect life as they dived to their gallant death in the arc lights. There was the smell of old timbers, the theater plumbing, grease paint, wood smoke; the odor of long-ago animal actors that hinted at old mule, horse and seal acts.

The footlights came up; we were casually at places; the red velvet curtain full of historic dust went up, and we were off into some delightful bit of hokum, charm, knee-slapper or thriller. We didn't play Shaw, Ibsen or Chekhov, and would have died of hunger if we had. Today you would call our audiences "squares." But theirs was a better time, and they had not yet become tangled with the morbid perverted world of Tennessee Williams, the slang of drug addicts, the abstract-expressionist philosophies, rock-and-roll sounds, and the terror (between the soap-powder commercials) on every news report that another corner of their world had gone up in smoke. The only fallout they knew was loss of hair, and the atom they had been taught in high school was the smallest particle of matter and could not ever be split. No siree.

After the show, to a few milked curtain calls, we would each wander to his own special group. Either a hard cider and dough-nut party, a spin in a hired car to some local lovers' lane with a local society beauty, or dog-wagon waitress. Or a visit to the speakeasy to rest one elbow on the damp bar and a foot on the brass rail, and watch the glass eyes of the stuffed moose grow glazed as the local town card and sport stood treat.

There was a country club, where sometimes an actor was invited, and the best people played a game called Mah Jong. The banjo player had an electric light in his banjo head, the horn man used a silver derby for a mute, and the band would jam "Livery Stable Blues" until they were stopped and told to play "Dardanella" or "Avalon." There was always of course the Babbitt who tried to stand up and ask for "Melancholy Baby."

On the wide Victorian porches of the club the cigar ends would glow in the dark and the flappers would listen to an actor, and answer: "It's the bees' knees" or "Banana oil."

It's an age now a thousand light years away from us, and the resident stock company is gone with the dodo bird and home-churned butter. Today it's all smart summer theater in modern barns, theater in the round, in tents, straw-hatters, converted mills. With real Broadway stars in the newest hit from Broadway. The sweet little towns view plays about homosexuals, castration, cannibalism, drug addiction, rape, humans turning into rhinos, and all the sad nihilism of the theater of the absurd, and all the dirty words made into off-Broadway art.

6

My First Role

I wonder now how I must have appeared as a young brash, apprentice actor to our director, Earl Dwyer. I am certainly grateful to him and his wife Beth for their forbearance and kindness to me during those puppy days when I wasn't fully housebroken. As for love, I was also smitten with the girl in the box office. She was a darling, so were *all* the women I was in love with that summer.

The best families in and about Plainfield were hosts and hostesses to the actors at times and there was never a dull moment for them when we were on the premises. The parties at the various homes from Plainfield to Scotts Plains are marked in memory as the first of the Jazz Age parties; all the bootleg gin, country club chatter that F. Scott Fitzgerald and John O'Hara were to use as literature.

Spencer Tracy had become a member of the New Brunswick, New Jersey, stock company not too many miles from us. Then he became leading man in the White Plains stock company. During the engagement he fell in love with the leading lady, Louise Treadwell. They were married. It was a fine wedding, we all agreed.

"You next, Pat."

"Now Spence, give me time."

In everyone's life, O. Henry once said, there is always the girl or boy back home. For me too—for all my dream romances among the theater folk. Her name was Lorraine. After weeks of correspondence with her in Milwaukee, in a moment of moon-calf madness, a loss of sense and balance brought on by love, I succumbed to her line of reasoning.

"There's no *real* future in the theater."

I gave my notice and amid gay and beery adieus, said farewell to all of that grand stageful of folks. I loved them all so dearly. Yet why was I on a slow train to Milwaukee? Why had I given up a way of life I loved? Why was Lorraine to me prettier, wittier than the girls in the Plainfield stock company? I couldn't say. I couldn't understand myself. Maybe that Jersey home-brewed beer had affected my brain. I was rushing into everything I didn't want. A non-theater girl, a non-show-biz world, a fine dull Middle West culture, a *job*, a *desk* and in time a *position* in the community.

The job in Milwaukee was with the National Surety Company. That didn't pan out too well so I went to work for the Kansas City Insurance Company. The whole pattern of things was not working out. Every time I'd try to sell double indemnity or an insurance policy, the client would throw a question about the theater at me.

Lorraine simpered and said: "You explain a lot about the stage, but you didn't sell any insurance."

"It just isn't in the cards."

"But we *do* have each other."

"Yes, dearest."

I told Lorraine maybe that wasn't enough—and my parents

(under duress) agreed that I had better retrace my steps and strike out for New York once more. So I did. I had saved some money, and with an advance from Dad I was off again on a train to try to master the stage.

I arrived in New York and hied myself across the water over to Jersey City and to the relatives, the O'Neills, again. They were a big family, but they did have a tiny rain-stained attic room on the third floor full of mouse dust. It was enough, certainly, to give me shelter, if not comfort. My food problem was not a difficult one. Uncle Charlie still ran the Union Club in downtown New York where I free-loaded my meals, and a serge suit lasts practically forever.

I promised myself never to listen to off-stage girls again. Lorraine and her cornflower-blue eyes had nearly wrecked me.

The Plainfield Players had disbanded and the members of the troupe were scattered around the country, like gypsy tents, in various stock companies. Again the rounds of the Broadway flesh peddlers. Haunting the offices, with hundreds of other actors seeking employment, I got news of a friend, Ivia Perine. (I had known her as a high school girl in New Jersey when Mom and I made that 1920 trip East.) She was now actually playing in a musical comedy! After some difficulty I got her phone number, called her and met her after the theater. She had blossomed out. She said she could prepare supper for us in her apartment.

"And I've a tip for you. A replacement part is coming up, for an actor in another show."

"Let's eat first."

We had a charming evening, talking of past and future—actors never seem to talk of the present. I was happy for her success and said so.

"Pat, you must try for that replacement part."

"Tell me about it."

"It's in A Man's Man starring Josephine Hutchinson and Dwight Frye. The role for you is the heavy in the play now done

67

by Robert Gleckler. He has given notice, having signed with Jed Harris."

"What do I do?"

"Readings were to be on Saturday. Go."

"I just barge in? The protocol is to be sent by an agent, present his card, report to the director."

"I know—so skip the protocol, Pat."

"How?"

"Figure out something."

I had been back in New York a short time and had no contacts. Spence was somewhere in the hinterlands and I was on my own. All the academy members I knew were either engaged elsewhere or had left the stage.

Ivia said, "Take a wild gamble Saturday night and go. Go backstage cold."

So I went. The little old doorman was a boyo from the "ould sod." I told him my name.

"*Pat* O'Brien?" It must have rung some kind of a Gaelic bell. I said, "Pat it is."

"Laddie, go through the front of the house and up into the balcony where they're holding the readings. You've come for the readings? Good. Don't tell anyone I told you. The director's name is Goodman."

"*Eddie* Goodman?"

"That is his name."

"He was one of my old tutors at the Academy."

"Goodo."

Eddie had been a pretty rigid disciplinarian, and I was never quite in his good graces at the school. But this was no time for stalling, or fear of any kind. I found Mr. Goodman brooding in the balcony. It was quite dark up there and he seemed exhausted after having heard audition after audition.

"Mr. Goodman?"

He seemed annoyed. "Yes, yes, what is it?"

"Mr. Goodman, I am Pat O'Brien of the Academy. Remember? I'd like to audition for you."

He sighed wearily. "I've about had it with readings. Yes, I remember you. Frankly you were never a Booth nor a Barrymore— but let's go, I'll give you a reading."

"Thank you."

"I doubt it. You can read?"

"I did at the school."

"All right. Come along."

We went backstage to Miss Hutchinson's dressing room. I was introduced to her and Goodman handed me the sides.

"Go ahead, Josephine will read with you."

I swallowed, nodded—and read. After reading about three-quarters through the part, Mr. Goodman stopped me.

"We're moving into the Provincetown Playhouse tomorrow, in the Village. The part is sixty sides long."

I said, "I'll know it by tomorrow noon!"

Miss Hutchinson laughed. "Oh the brash Irish."

It was late at night. I couldn't go back to Jersey City, so I got a room in a dingy little armpit hotel on Lexington Avenue and asked the unshaved bellboy to bring me *two* jugs of black coffee. I was a high spender that night. I couldn't afford it, but it looked as though a career was on the brink of a break. I studied the part all night—I lay down at eight-thirty in the morning and asked the desk to call me at ten. I arose groaning at ten, took another whack at the part. By one o'clock I felt I was ready. I paid my hotel bill, got into the rich smell of the subway and went to the Province-town Theater. None of the cast was in the empty echoing theater. The stage manager had been warned that I was to open that night. He was a nice guy, Jerry Lynch. He offered to go over the lines with me.

I said, "No, maybe later. Is there some place I can lie down?"

"Sure—in your dressing room."

"*My* dressing room?"

"Don't expect the Ritz."

"It will have to do," I said, poker-faced.

69

Of that night I do not remember one image of anything that transpired. It was pretty much of a floating dream. I got through the play with no major disaster because Josephine Hutchinson and Dwight Frye were two firm supports in bringing me through my performance; the confidence of Eddie Goodman too, who later came back to *my* dressing room after the final curtain. He put his arm around me.

"My boy, I'm *proud* of you."

"If you say so."

"You played it *just* right."

"Frankly I have no idea of what actually happened in those three acts. It was as though I was in a different world, you know, and yet didn't seem to be part of it."

"The important thing is you made it."

I called Ivia and told her the worst was over. I had deliberately not said anything to her about my progress until after the performance. She could not have been there anyway because of her own show. Now I raced to her apartment and through tears and embraces, we celebrated what she called "Pat's return to the land he loves, the living theater."

"That I do—I do indeed."

Shortly after that Ivia was signed by a London producer and I saw her off to England, so I didn't have time to fall in love with her. (She is married now and lives in Palm Beach.)

To my ego it was clear that *A Man's Man* with me in it would run on and on. That somehow was not the case. It was a fine play written by Pat Kearney and originally titled *Under the El,* but it was a rather sordid drama and a little too rough for the prosperous citizens, thirty years ahead of its time. We did play for six months, and Eddie Goodman had my name put up in lights along with Josephine Hutchinson and Dwight Frye.

PAT O'BRIEN, in Mr. Edison's electric lights! I hired a photographer to shoot the marquee, had the picture blown up and sent it on to my mother and dad with a note: "Here's your boy in lights. How does it look?"

They wrote back, "It looks just grand. Send more pictures."

During the run of the play I experienced what can only be called the full magic of the theater, even if that sounds too romantic. It did not matter to me that the theater was shabby, the seats creaky, the backstage a tangle of decaying plumbing and dangerous wiring, the dressing room fit only for growing mushrooms. It all existed as sleight of hand, and every night it came alive, opening up, turning for the drab reality of a grub into the two-hour ecstasy of a butterfly being born.

Few have been able to properly express this magic and I lack the ability to do what others have failed at. Yet I must say something about the charmed illusion of the stage as it becomes so much a part of the actor that very little outside of it is as true and satisfying and as vital.

There was first the skilled pleasure of expanding into another's skin; the person standing or pacing on a stage being someone else, so that one lived in two dimensions, oneself and the part that had no true life. Then the glow that came when that mass out front, the audience, moved when you moved, laughed on cue, got the subtle bit of special business, was silent at the right taut moment of drama, shook with delight when a situation worked out.

"As God," John Barrymore once said, "made Adam from dust, so an actor creates something from words marked on paper."

Being an actor, acting was soul-satisfying and the contentment of the comradeship of fellow actors; not always smooth perhaps, filled with little backstage wars, but all united when faced by anything outside our little cardboard and canvas realm.

Coming early, after twilight, to the theater I would stand in the empty orchestra smelling of mothproofing, historic grime, seeing the cracks in the ceiling, the repairs in the curtain. But I knew this would all change under lowered lights. Routine was good, going back to my dressing room, greeted by old friends now; the sputtering drippy sink, the caked mess of make-up, the slightly flawed mirror, the remains of sandwiches, an empty soda bottle, somebody's lost hat. Sitting down to put on make-up was a ritual as serious as a church service; muttering over a line that hadn't played well, hearing other expected sounds; the rattle of the stage door, high heels on a splintered floor, the stage hands moving scenery into place, the reek of their cheap tobacco mocking the NO SMOKING.

The first shuffle of the audience taking their places tingled up my spine; seats were being slammed down. The mutter and polite coughs came as they waited.

Somebody was announcing ten minutes to curtain time.

The actors were gathering around the set, taking places there, or in the wings, somebody telling a whispered joke, one or two actors hung over, somebody giggling. Then our snap to attention as the lights dimmed out front and came up on the set. A quick look into a dark throbbing void where the audience seemed to crouch and dare us to entertain them. The opening line of dialogue, the first bit of business and before I knew it I was on stage in character and banging away as someone else—another person, yet aware of myself as if watching *me*—in the background.

I never became a Method actor, a follower of the Russian Stanislavski school that held as the true faith: "Be a tree, be an apple, be a worm in the apple." I knew I was Pat O'Brien being someone else—a part written down. I always remembered Joseph Schildkraut's story of the great German actor Albert Basserman, who on stage in the middle of a difficult part in some great classic, could still whisper, between the lines of an emotional moment, "Let's hurry it up a bit, my wife has a roast goose waiting in the oven tonight."

When the evening performance went well, even if there was a physical letdown, I felt I had done something unique and done it well. If something had gone wrong, I would try and think how to correct it.

Out front the audience had moved away, talking among themselves. The stage had gone dark, the props and furniture were covered with gray cloth. The dressing-room doors were beginning to bang as actors left for whatever rest or pleasure awaited them. The magic was locked away for a day.

I would leave the theater inhaling that special smell of New

1. Mother in 1888.

2. Dad in 1897.

3. Grandma, Grandpa, Aunt Mame (Dad's sister), and Mother holding me.

4. My brother Edward (left) and I in 1903.

5. At seven years of age, I looked the world right straight in the face.

6. Mother and Dad with me in 1911.

7. As I looked in 1915. My uncle, Guy LePlant, in the center and a boyhood friend, Purnel Griffith, on my right.

8. A light but good fast halfback at the Great Lakes Navy Training Station in 1918. Quite a difference from the picture a few pages later on showing me as Knute Rockne.

9. Sailor Pat O'Brien and several of his buddies at the Great Lakes Navy Training Station.

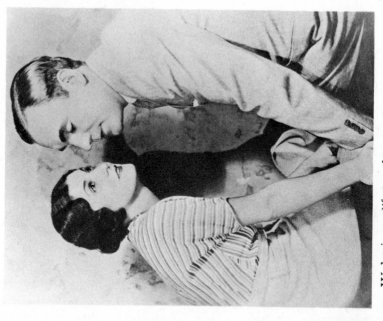

10. The Girl. Eloise Taylor the year we met while both of us were in the cast of the Chicago company of *Broadway.*

11. We begin our life together.

. The well-dressed young gentle-
an in Brooklyn in the early
enties.

13. Here I am in summer stock in
1924 playing the role of Brissac in
Seventh Heaven.

4. A role I was delighted to get
was that of Curly in *Up and Up* in
1930.

15. When Sinclair Lewis' famous
bestseller *Main Street* was made into a movie, this title was changed
to *I Married a Doctor*, with Josephine Hutchinson and myself in
the lead roles.

United Artists TV Inc.

16. Mother and Dad visit me on the set of *Angels with Dirty Faces.*

17. James Cagney and I in the film version of *Boy Meets Girl.*

18. A group of us whooping it up. Frank McHugh, Bob Armstrong, and Dick Powell join me in a bit of harmony.

19. I play the role of a clown in *The Night of Nights.* Roland Young is the ringmaster.

Paramount Pictures

20. The role that changed my life, Hildy Johnson in *The Front Page* with Adolphe Menjou and Mary Brian.

21. A scene from the movie that gave me the greatest joy to do, *Knute Rockne*. Although I was thirty-nine when we filmed the picture, I did not use a double in any of the scenes, and some of the football scrimmages were pretty rough.

United Artists TV Inc.

22. A role that still brings back wonderful memories. I portray Father Duffy in *The Fighting 69th* with Jimmy Cagney playing the role of a wise-cracking kid from the slums of New York.   *United Artists TV Inc.*

23. Father Cavanaugh, then president of Notre Dame, discusses with me my portrayal of Knute Rockne.   *Lionel Heymann*

24. A moment of great emotion. I place a wreath before the statue of Father Duffy near Times Square.

25. Al Smith and I help a milk fund drive.

Metropolitan Photo Service

26. Clem McCarthy, George M. Cohan, and I talk over show business at the Banshee Luncheon in 1940. *King Features Syndicate*

27. Two distinguished race-horse aficionados, Bing Crosby and I, compare choices for the day's racing.

Don English, Paramount Pictures

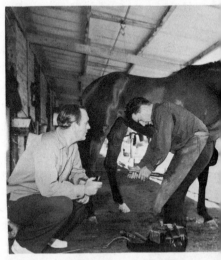

28. As vice-president of the Del Mar racetrack, I keep an eye on some of the operations at the track.

J. M. F. Haase

York City at night; soiled rivers, spilled gasoline, houses and streets left out all day in the sun, the whiff of memories of funerals from a corner florist, the smell of boiling sweet corn from an all-night eating place, pigeon droppings on General Grant, tin cornices.

The sound like a sea shell held to my ear would be the beat of traffic, a tight car brake screaming, tugboats panting on the river, some late feet hurrying to catch the IRT subway. End of an actor's perfect day . . .

A Man's Man ended to sad, despairing, final notices going up backstage, and I was on my own again. During the run of the play I had the opportunity to meet many people and had established what the trade called contacts. I was twenty-four years of age, undismayed and ready to go on.

I had met a woman agent—a rare thing then—backstage during the run of the play. She gave me her card.

"When you're at leisure, honey, phone me because I'm often casting important roles."

I went to see her in her office. She gave me a letter to Gustave Blum.

"He's about to produce a play called *Henry Behave* authored by Lawrence Langner. Give it a try, honey."

"Sure. Who's in it?"

"It stars John Cumberland and features Edward G. Robinson and Gladys Lloyd (that's Mrs. Robinson)."

The Nora Bayes Theater was on the roof of the Forty-fourth Street Theater. It was an unusual little playhouse that held great charm. The role I was up for was that of a blustering, cigar-smoking politician, loudmouthed, raucous and in only *one* scene. This seemed to me a comedown from my name up in lights two weeks previously, with a part that was sixty sides. I said nothing even if I was now to be relegated to a second-rate assignment. But I was young, I figured, and would just keep the action going. The part was a pushover for me—no one else even auditioned for it.

Gustave Blum liked me and so did the cast. The ingénue was

Gail de Hart, and it seemed easy to fall in love, as nights I read *Cyrano* aloud to her.

I told her it was "a compensation for playing a lesser role in a much less important production."

I got $85 a week. In *A Man's Man* I had received $125 a week.

Mr. Blum came to me: "We trust this will be a successful run. At its conclusion, we are planning another production and there is a part made for you."

"A better one I hope."

"An actor's dream."

When *Henry Behave* terminated I went right into *Gertie* as the leading man to Constance McKay. My salary was nearly doubled—$150. I tried to get Gail a part, but it didn't work out. Elisha Cooke, Jr. was in the play and was wonderful in his role. We stayed at the Nora Bayes Theater for over a year and a half. I felt as much a fixture of Broadway as the lamp posts and hot-dog stands.

The secret, and not so secret, dream of every young actor on Broadway is to become a member of either the Lambs, Players, Friars, or Green Room Club. Or, if you were wealthy and lucky enough, *all* four of them. During the run of *Henry Behave*, over a midnight supper Johnny Cumberland asked me: "Pat, how would you like to become a Lamb?"

"I thought you had to spend at least five to ten years on Broadway before this happened?"

"For some. Well?"

I gulped my scotch and said almost tearfully, "When?"

"I'll propose you next week. I'm sure Eddie Robinson will be happy to second you."

There followed some nights of torment, wondering if I would be acceptable. Since its inception years ago, the Lambs Club has had one stringent rule—*one* blackball could cancel you out.

Some weeks later, when I received in the mail a summons to appear before the membership committee of the Lambs Club, I wouldn't have traded it to be President of Ireland, or even the U.S.A.

74

I stood at last in the club, like a soldier awaiting a court martial payoff. Thomas Meighan, who was the Shepherd of the Club read:

"We have before us one Pat O'Brien, a Roman Catholic, proposed by a Presbyterian and seconded by a Jew."

Malcolm Williams (Florence Reed's husband) said in reply, "I move we church the three of them."

Now I was a Lamb! A club man, an actor among fellow actors. At this point in their life most actors bought, or stole a new cane, or put more starch in their collars.

I had moved from the garret in Jersey City, but I didn't want to. It was the cozy home away from my own parental house. But the jaunt by water—New York to Jersey City—was too far for a rising young actor night after night. I got a room at 65 West Forty-ninth Street—third floor back, a good view of bricks and drying laundry, bathroom in the hall. The price was right and the landlord, one Tony, a speakeasy owner, was a dreamboat. His fame and brews were known from one end of the Great White Way to the other. These were the true Roaring Twenties and Tony's basement bistro was popular with all the Broadwayites who could swallow and ask for more. He and his wife Angelique, he often told me, were like a father and mother to me. Their daughter, a tiny baby then, years later married John Huston, the director. Sixty-five West Forty-ninth Street is gone, and memory now—for it is now Radio City, and what was once my room is probably now part of that garish, gay display of what money can buy.

The club reunited me with some people I had admired. During my crazy insurance days in Milwaukee, Jimmy Gleason had opened a stock company at the Davidson Theater and I used to go backstage to lament insurance, and out of the kindness of his heart, Jimmy would let me stand in the wings and watch the performance. I did play bit parts in a couple of the shows and became very friendly with Jim, his wife Lucille and son Russell.

75

Members of the company were Bob Armstrong, Elizabeth Risdon, George Meeker and John Thorne. And now, only two years later as a member of the Lambs Club, I was a fraternal brother to Bob, Jim and George.

"It's great," I said at the bar. "I'm buying."

"Is zat so," said Jimmy, who was writing a play by that title.

When *Gertie* closed, I was at liberty again.

An unemployed actor becomes a different person. His morale sags, he wears a hunted look. The burden of the ages sits on his shoulders as he gossips with other unemployed actors.

There didn't seem to be any Broadway jobs. I went looking for another stock company opening. While on the theater prowl, I heard of an audition for a play, *Women Go on Forever*. I didn't make that one, but a graceful, tough red-headed actor did. His name was James Cagney. I recalled Jimmy as a chorus boy in *Pitter Patter* when I was hoofing myself in *Adrienne* in 1920. Dancers weren't all limp-wristed in those days.

With Broadway parts still pretty scarce, I settled for a season in Asbury Park, salt water taffy and too many fish dinners as the second lead in a stock company. It was another letdown but it was work—it was theater. That, I said to myself, in itself is satisfaction enough. I was lucky; my Aunt Agnes and Uncle Charlie had moved to Long Branch, only a few short miles down the coast, so they had a star boarder again.

A member of the company was James McHugh, one of the finest actors I have ever seen on Broadway or any place else. We latched on to each other and became the greatest of pals. Later, when the season closed, I prevailed upon Jim to share my room at 65 West Forty-ninth. (Tony had promised to save it for me until I returned.)

During this sojourn on the eastern seaboard, naturally I fell in love. I met a beautiful girl, Marie Carton, and felt the emotions stirring. Her father was a prominent attorney at Asbury Park. I was a weekend guest in their home.

Halfway through the Asbury Park season Jim McHugh told me

his kid brother had just returned from London where he had been playing with Bob Armstrong and Jimmy Gleason in Jimmy's play *Is Zat So?* and was coming down on the night train from New York for the weekend. We made great gay plans in our frugal manner, to throw a party for Jim's kid brother. The company all chipped in for the salami and ham sandwiches, the wine and cakes, the local booze, all the things that go to make up a feast. The party, Jim said, went off just great. The kid brother was even greater. He was Frank McHugh, who, throughout all the years has remained one of my closest friends. Oh, it was *a* party. A little crack-skulled but happy. We crawled out to meet the morning sea breeze.

We all hated to see the season go—the closing of the stock company. It had been a delightful experience—two blocks from the boardwalk and me having, like most inlanders, loved the sea, this was a tough parting.

It was a sad gray day of torn clouds, a blustery wind when we closed the theater—the wind, already chilled, drove the white sand across the wooden walks, the guttural geek-geek of the sea gulls was an idiotic dirge. The torn popcorn bags and music sheets fled like ghosts down the curbs, and the small resorts were putting up their weathered shutters.

Suddenly gayness, sunlight and glittering sea seemed lost, lost. And ahead was a hard winter in a cold, indifferent city.

7

Eloise and Chicago

As always the most hopeful situation for the unemployed actor was the touring companies.

Jed Harris sent out a call for auditions for the many road companies planned of the smash melodrama, *Broadway*. Troupes were to be sent all over the globe. Some said everywhere but Latvia and Iceland. Seriously, I have never known so many companies being cast or opportunities for so many actors. Jim McHugh and I joined the hundreds of eager holders of press clippings in quest of employment in one of the road companies.

George Abbott, younger then but already a fast-moving director, interviewed each aspirant. Jim and I made it—not in one of the plush major troupes, but with a one-night-stand company to be sent out through the less civilized hinterlands—the Deep South that H. L. Mencken had just labeled "the corn pone and Bible belt."

"When they say one-nighters, they don't mean two," Jim said. He had nailed the role of Dolph, a gangster henchman, and I was cast as the detective, Dan McCorn. It didn't matter—we would have settled for a company of ghouls playing spooks in the catacombs. Money with us both was on the short side and the meals hadn't been too regular.

Jim and I celebrated. We pooled thin dollars and had an Italian *pasta* dinner in Greenwich Village, with a bottle of wine— $1.50 including the fake label.

There was no time wasted in preparing the tour. We opened in Scranton, Pennsylvania, and played the Main Streets, gasoline alleys, country fairs in Pennsylvania, and Maryland, and Virginia, before embarking for deep into Dixie, with our play of sex, murder, Broadway glitter. Today it would be a perfect period piece of the twenties.

The actor who played the lead in the play spent most of his time on the train writing verses for Christmas, birthday and get-well cards to earn some extra income. It seemed like a daffy hard dollar but obviously it served its purpose because it wasn't too many years later that the young scribbler, John Cecil Holm, with George Abbott, wrote a smash Broadway hit, *Three Men on a Horse*, about a greeting card poet who had second sight about future horse races. As good a theme as any for a farce comedy.

At one performance of *Broadway* in Shamokin, Pennsylvania, the house seemed to be completely lit up with hosts of fireflies.

"Hey—what's that!"

The manager reassured us actors. "It's only the lights on the miners' hats. They parked their picks in the lobby and came in to view the performance. Better be good—they work hard for their dough."

Most of the miners hadn't even washed up from the coal pits, so they were there in blackface, and I had a sense of playing to a minstrel show of Mr. Bones and Mr. Interlocutor. But when they laughed their teeth really showed.

Scranton, Pennsylvania, was a rare treat—a three-night stand. After the opening night Don Kirke, who had been in the chorus with me in 1920, played the heavy in the drama and decided to live up to the boozy characterization. At three A.M. I received a call in high Pennsylvania Dutch from the local jail informing me that Donald was lodged in the pokey. He had been doing a 1926 version of the Twist, only it was the *Untwist*. He had, for reasons unknown even to himself, he told me later untwisted the huge decorative glass globes off the pillars—relics of the Civil War—in front of the post office and was sauntering down the main stem, one under each arm. That crackskull native whisky really was a menace. The local gendarmes put the pinch on Don and gave him a night's lodging in the jail.

I hurried down and was allowed to see him in his cell.

He looked happy but frayed.

He looked at me, and yelled, "Why don't you tin-badge bums let my friend out of here?"

Convinced it was *my* Gaelic tones, the turnkey rushed into the cell and said to me, "Okay, you wisenheimer, *you* stay in with him."

Don said, "You're hanging an innocent man."

The company manager sprung us at eleven A.M. the next morning. The beady-eyed judge fined us $25 each, but relented when Don dug into a pocket and gave him the passes that helped fill the house.

On stage I went on being a cop. The whisky improved as we went south—the manager explaining, "They had more experience making rotgut—they never paid no taxes on their stills, and shot all revenuers."

Our tour extended way down through the Deep South. Corn pone and corn likker were the staple diet in the Dixie way of life and the fried chicken was, for hungry actors, about as choice a morsel as I had ever tasted.

"Why does a Georgia chicken cross the road?" Jim McHugh would ask. "To meet a hungry actor. Pass the drumsticks."

In Birmingham, I got into an old habit—I fell in love with a girl in an act playing the Delmar time on the vaudeville circuit. We were there a week. Romance under an Alabama moon low enough to bite can be joy, even if I was nearly broke during the whole tour. I was twenty-six and the world seemed to belong only to us. I hated to move on, but through the early years, my life was to be a succession of goodbyes and "I'll write." Somehow we never did.

Atlanta, Georgia, was another break—a two-week stand. The stately velvet-hung Erlanger Theater and the white plantation-styled Georgian Terrace Hotel; rocking chairs on the porch, and honest-to-God blooms of the magnolia trees to remind you that here was atmosphere that could exist only in Dixie. Robert E. Lee standing at the bar sipping a planter's punch wouldn't have surprised me. Of course this was all before the South of Faulkner and Tennessee Williams. Writers certainly can change the picture of a culture. Fuzzy Woodruff was the local dramatic critic and he loved the show and everyone in it. On the Saturday that University of Georgia won the football game against Alabama, the entire squad marched down the aisle and onto the stage and took over at the end of Act One. It was their show from then on.

Jim said, "They are getting even for Sherman's March to the Sea."

Everyone joined in the celebration and the South rose again that night, bottle in hand, "Damn Yankee" on its lips.

The next morning I received a telegram from Jed Harris, the producer of the play.

LEAVE SHOW AS OF SATURDAY NEXT JOIN CHICAGO COMPANY OF BROADWAY REPORT SELWYN THEATRE EDWARD CIANNELLI STAGE MANAGER YOU WILL ESSAY SAME ROLE AS NOW REPLACING JOE KING WHO IS TO GO INTO NEW PRODUCTION THE ROYAL FAMILY REGARDS JED HARRIS

I was soon packed and it was an actor's farewell to mangy hotel lobbies full of hound dogs, cotton blossoms, magnolias, black-eyed peas, chitlin's, Mountain Dew corn whisky, black faces waiting, waiting, and a sense of a lost past that never really existed for the South. I hated to say goodbye to that grand troupe, but actors' partings are emotional and painless, most of the time.

The road as it existed then was a hard, grueling life for actors. The body, the mind, the nerve ends had to be able to take punishment. Long train rides in rolling stock with which Grant must have taken Richmond. Cinders, holes burned in one of our few suits, cast-iron sandwiches and battery-acid coffee in crossroad stations, where cows and a plow and Sears Roebuck catalogues were big business. Small-town inns, big-town decaying hotels, but all with the same damp gray sheets, the bathroom a credit to Queen Victoria if it worked, and a Rube Goldberg puzzle of repairs when it didn't. The feeling of termites eating away the very floors under our feet. Yet the people were kind and excited by the theater and they were good hosts, good company, and the shotgun and the bull whip in certain cases for anyone who tampered with a daughter's virtue.

The towns all had the same look, the same mud-spattered Model T in front of the same movie houses, the Bijou usually, showing William S. Hart; the young girls in their cotton summer dresses parading arm in arm, being gossiped about by the drugstore teen-agers; the elders chewing and discharging tobacco, sitting under wooden store awnings on chairs with only the back legs on the ground. Lazy hounds beating fleas out of their tails, big talk of coon hunting, fox runs in the misty mornings under the slashed turpentine pines, big lies about catfish and bass, and a feeling with horny thumb of kegs and bales of tobacco and cotton.

The local tin-badge sheriff mooching free passes, the trouble with the scenery to make it fit, the filling in of parts when some actor didn't make it, the hasty packing of hotel towels and ash trays. And on to the smoky train breathing hard at the depot, and actors off to the next playing date. Sleeping sitting up often on the tickling grimy plush smelling of coal gas and ancient journeys. A crap game in the baggage car, worn cards played on a suitcase, the jokers wild. The tipple was the local white corn of the South, often drunk from a quart mason jar. The train whistling at a crossing where a Negro on a patient mule waited—and cows and horses stood along a rail fence watching the actors pass.

Cold morning, hot days and humid with not even a mud turtle stirring. The big towns were still often merely the small towns grown up. But there maybe the plumbing worked; real *hot* water for washing up.

Chicago in December 1927 resembled its dirty mean cruel legends. It was Capone's town and everybody knew it. The mayor was busy promising to punch the King of England on the snout if he ever came to town—and if Eliot Ness was around I never met him. Every day bullet-eaten bodies were really found on the streets. There was no law south of the Loop.

The place—the Selwyn Theater, backstage by the door. Enter a beautiful girl in flapper outfit, helmet hat, long, long wonderful legs.

Me: "Hi!"
She (not too enthusiastically): "Hello."
Me: "Just joining the company. Better with the southern troupe."
She: "I'm just joining, too. I've been with the New York company."
Me: "How do you like Chicago?"
She: "I don't know yet."
Me: "It's a tough town for a girl alone."
She: "You'll protect me, Mr.—?"
Me: "Pat O'Brien. I know a reasonable speakeasy. Good food —a low tab—Miss—?"
She: "Eloise Taylor. Where's the company manager?"
Me: "It's a date?"
She: "We'll give it one run through."
Me: "Let's go find the manager."

I sensed at once that Eloise had turned me on as no girl ever had so far. I was aware of danger, and I knew there was no retreat.

83

Backstage seemed like the interior of the Lambs Club in New York. First to greet me was Wally Ford, soon to star in John Ford's great film *The Informer*.

Wally was playing the lead in *Broadway* and he had suggested to Jed Harris that I be brought to the Chicago company. Bob Strange and Jay Wilson were two more Lambs on scene. Allen Jenkins, the character actors' character actor, played Scar Edwards. He and I were to make many pictures together. But all I could think of, as actors bragged, compared notices, told gags and paired off, was the girl I had met at the stage door. During the run of the play I kept a Scotland Yard eye on every move that Eloise made. My side-mouthed warning to everyone backstage was "Don't take her—she's mine."

It wasn't easy to keep other wolves at bay. Everyone who met Eloise wanted to romance this doll from Des Moines. She had a svelte body—the perfect model for the magazine covers of the period, definitely not the housewife type. I knew I was trapped; like the fox held in the trap by one leg I was sure I could get out of it. But I found out I didn't want out. I was deeply and truly in love, and in Chicago, city of mugs, rackets, rub-outs and terror. It was to be a stormy, lengthy courtship full of pain, agony, lovers' quarrels, mutual misunderstandings, separations; also of ecstasy, compassion, lovers' meetings and tender partings. It wasn't easy to sustain Eloise's interest in me alone. The competition was tough and it was a struggle for me to stay in the running with a road company actor's bankroll. However, I faced the challenge —what else could I do—and held to positive thinking at all times —and my adoration did not falter along the way.

Even the mob boys adored her. I am not condoning crime but I've noticed that mobsters and the hoods seem to have a respect for the acting profession. I often wonder if they too were not actors playing out their sinister dramas on a stage where the props were real and deadly.

The twenties of crime and conflict in Chicago have been so exploited by movies and television and novelists that the reality of anyone who was there is tainted by too much exposure to the fiction. The reality was dreadful enough, but it was grimmer, more cruel in a casual way than the legend. The gangster, the hood, the gunsel, as I saw him, was not romantic or glamorous. He was usually small, short, underfed, pimply, most likely diseased, and except for a few men at the top, rather stupid, and in his stupidity he was deadly and dangerous. The real menace was that the law had often gone over to his side.

Chicago ran wide open. In the dives the real jazz men were still playing. Louie Armstrong, King Oliver with his one eye, and the Chicago school of Bix Beiderbecke and Benny Goodman were the new thing. The clubs, the roadhouses, were big, airless, crowded firetraps, the saxophone music loud and the alcohol deadly. Faces were white with lack of sun and the rich came to gape at the romance of the underworld. The getaway car, the tommy gun, the tossed pineapple were by-products of a revolt against law and order, but the average citizen, unless he got in the way, wasn't bothered. For him life remained what a philosopher called a "quiet desperation" just reading his comic strips ("Andy Gump," "Nize Baby," "Boob McNutt") keeping up the installment payments and saving up enough to see our show on a wedding or birthday anniversary.

The city impressed me as being dirty, cynically corrupt, and that was saying something after the wonderful era of nonsense under dapper Jimmy Walker in New York City.

The lake front was impressive with that big body of water really blue, pounding at the base of the apartment houses and hotels; and the beautiful girls in their short skirts, short hair, clipped morals and slang moved in and out of the revolving doors, to be caught up in a flurry of silk by the lake wind and exposed like items of a harem for sale.

The theater was very active then in Chicago; there was a literary movement that had produced Carl Sandburg, Ben Hecht, MacKinlay Kantor; and the sound, smoke and the odor of the stockyards (when the wind was right and ripe) made it a city of character, often sinister, a place of muscle and power and a feeling; where had it lost control of events?

Protection was mostly what the gangsters sold. If an industry or an individual didn't buy protection the risk of a cement overcoat was great. A few of the small fry of the underworld attempted to intrude into the actors' realm, offering protection. Various performers received telegrams:

YOU ARE ON OUR HONORARY LIST TO CONTRIBUTE $100 FOR THE SENATOR'S DINNER

"What senator?"

"Senator Holdup."

Collections would be made at the stage door. Some of the actors panicked and left for New York without notice or their laundry. Others paid. A few notified the police, which was silly. The big shots had the police in their pockets.

One individual, the late "Bojangles" Bill Robinson, met a caller for $100 at the stage door and held out, not an envelope with the cash, but a freshly honed razor on the ready. Exit collector! The man with guts enough to meet this penny ante was then playing at the Palace as a dancer. When the sound of this petty racket reached Mr. Big, Al Capone's orders were given to the mob muscle to stop the pressure. Reports were several hoods were liquidated. The $100 actors' racket never repeated itself.

Al is said to have mumbled, "Some people don't just know how to stay neat."

That year a dear little man, a close pal of Eloise and mine, the comic Joe E. Lewis, was fearfully slashed, his throat cut, and left for dead in his hotel room by mob boys. His humor had innocently offended some racket boss and the assault on him struck new terror in the entertainers' ranks. Joe didn't die—some miracle saved the sewn-together mob victim.

I'll never forget the wonderful night Joe walked into the Comedy Club after weeks in the hospital, his badly scarred head and throat still swathed in bandages. We gave him a tremendous ovation.

He laughed. "I hereby serve notice on the entertainment world I will be back before long. Somebody give me a glass."

Today Joe stands out as the great master of the ad lib in any supper club. This shaggy pixie of the saloon circuit, an ace hatchet man for all hecklers, is a living sample of how real and evil Chicago was in those well lost days and nights.

Our play was a big hit in Chicago, not alone on its merits as a drama. *Broadway* was a realistic play about the American underworld. Nightly it attracted many members of the local mobs in great numbers. They would always buy out the first six or seven rows. They came at show time elaborately groomed, frequently *over*-elaborately, especially the molls. The men's armpits swelled with hidden artillery and the ladies were also supposed to be armed. In tux and beaded dress they politely enjoyed the play. They were a very good audience.

One evening, twenty minutes before curtain time, a well-known young tough man, Frankie Lake of the Big Boy's entourage, entered my dressing room. We were pals. He sat down, opened his coat. In full view (glimpsed in the mirror) was a grim .45 in a shoulder holster. To put it mildly, I was somewhat concerned.

"Hey, Frankie boy—what the hell?"

Frankie smiled, "Don't panic, pal—I'll park the Lady from Bristol"—pistol in Cockney rhyming slang—"behind your mirror."

"B-b-b-b-b-but why, Frankie?"

He cut me off. "Hell, pal, I can't tote a rod in the theater—they'd think I'm a gangster! I'm leaving the roscoe here—just put it back of the mirror like a nice boy."

I finally emerged out of shock. "Tell me, Frankie, what makes you boys so nice to actors? You guys go out of your way to give the actors a break."

Frankie thought it over, leaned forward. "Patty, I figure it this here way—you actors are getting away with murder, and so are we. . . ."

The buzzer sounded. "Frankie, there's the curtain call. See you after the show and don't forget to pick up your Lady from Bristol."

"I'll do that little thing."

I liked Frankie Lake and I'm sure he liked *me*. (And for this I was glad.)

There were all names to give a man the shakes—besides the Capones, Ralph and Al. There were Tommy O'Connor, Terry Druggan, Bugs Moran, Machine Gun Kelly among the Irish brigade.

Between my hoodlum pals, an ardent courtship and a play that was overpaced, I led a fast life.

Mother and Dad came down from Milwaukee to see our show. When I made my entrance in the first act, Mom couldn't contain herself, and she cried for all to *hear*:

"That's my boy!"

Applause. Up to that time, I had never gotten a hand on my entrance.

Later I said, "Ma, you shouldn't have done it."

"They liked it—you heard."

Dad said, "I think there are *two* hams in the family."

Eloise took to them and them to her, but I wasn't making any premature family announcements.

Chicago was a good show town and I broadened my friendship with many actors. Ted Healy was working in Chicago. He had the original Three Stooges with him; they had a resurgence of popularity in later years. Ted, loose, not neat, nor a tea drinker, was one of the all-time comedy greats. Some of the present day comedians couldn't carry his suitcase. Later, Ted and I appeared together in the MGM film, *Blonde Bombshell*. I played opposite the gorgeous, strange, exciting Jean Harlow. The film was one of the first of the inside dramas about the movie business.

We met one of the best supper-club entertainers and one of the first great ad-libbers, Jack Waldron. (Of Alexander Woollcott he said, "He has delusions of gender.")

Mike Fritzell was a king in his own right in the after-dark semi-underworld of the Frolics, and Chez Paris. He staked me often to courting money and always said, "You'll make it some day, son—I'm not worried."

Like in the story book, I had the opportunity to repay him his kindness in later years.

Chicago saw Sophie Tucker, Joe Frisco, Ruth Etting, Duke Ellington, Rae Samuels, Margaret Young and others. My own personal drama was of low lights and soft music with Eloise. We had a time. I found out you can't press your girl's hand any harder over a $60 check than a $6.00 check. On the night of the Big Equity Ball, one of my competitors beat my time for a date with Eloise. I watched, miserable all evening, from the balcony, begrudging every minute they were dancing. Two days later the man took his own life. No one ever knew why, but Eloise suspected I got a voodoo doll south of the Loop in the Negro section and stuck pins in it. I didn't; I've never played with dollies.

8

On the Road

Chicago began to fade for us. We closed our run at the Selwyn and had progressive bookings for a week or two week stands, interspersed with a few hurried one-nighters. We played three one-night stands in Ohio at Zanesville, Newark, and Lima, and a three-night date in Toledo. In the little town of Lima was a stock company and the leading lady was Mrs. Spencer Tracy (Louise Treadwell). Porter Hall, later a film heavy, was also a member of that company.

"How's Spence?"

"Acting, acting. Aren't we all—if we're lucky?"

Opening in familiar territory, Milwaukee, for a week's engagement was an event.

HOME TOWN BOY RETURNS WITH GREAT FANFARE

A sticky situation arose on opening night. Wally Ford swears to this day I planned and maneuvered it. The role of Dan McCorn that I played was that of a hard-boiled detective, very soft-spoken, almost Chesterfieldian in manner. Near the final curtain the night-club girl, Pearl, has, in full view of the audience, killed someone. McCorn is aware of this, but in his book the rub-out was justified and as she sits in the sleazy night-club set, beaten emotionally and mentally destroyed, McCorn walks by. He gives her a casual look.

"Pull yourself together, kid," he says.

This particular scene as played out, no matter who did it, always got a rousing burst of applause. Reading the line in type fails to explain its stage magic.

The line was also the warning cue—it gave the stagehands ample time to prepare for the final scene, with Wally dancing out on stage with the complete girlie ensemble. It gave Wallie a very flashy tag at the end of the play, and an actor likes to insist on this kind of a curtain. This time a numb stagehand picked my line for the end of the play and pulled down the big curtain, ending the show. The girls and Wallie felt cheated. The air backstage was blue with Wally's curses.

All the stage manager could say was: "On stage everybody for curtain call." Wally screamed, "He paid that guy off to ring down the curtain on his line! What a dirty Irish trick."

I stage-whispered, "Listen you! I couldn't pay off anyone. I have more relatives in Milwaukee putting the bite on me than there are barrels at the brewery!"

These people, my relatives, all assumed that I could get as many complimentary tickets as I desired. This of course was not so. I was given only two comps and they went to Mother and Dad. I had to pay out of my own pocket for any other tickets I wanted. With my many relatives, and my deflating salary, it was a few weeks before I drew a full paycheck.

We did good business in Milwaukee, an achievement in itself. One of the old adages of show business is: "The three worst weeks in show business are Christmas week, Easter week, and a week in Milwaukee." However, the show got rave reviews and fine local support.

After Milwaukee came Cincinnati for a two-week run, and here we ran into censor trouble. The flesh of our show girls excited some of the male bluenoses in town.

Our troubles in Cincinnati were silly. Some randy, overly zealous city fathers and some holier-than-thou smut hounds gave us orders.

"The play cannot continue after what we have seen in the opening night's performance, unless all the girls in the chorus wear stomachers."

It was a word none of us had ever heard before.

"A *what*, dearie?"

"Sounds like a pot holder or a rump doily."

For the remaining performances in Cincinnati, the girls donned something like a tea cozy and they looked rather silly.

After Cincinnati, St. Louis came in for two weeks. The reviews were grand and resulted in a successful run. I was making a not too unsuccessful hit in my personal life.

Eloise was not a Catholic. One Sunday morning in St. Louis as I came down into the hotel lobby, I found her—much too early for an actress—sitting there reading the morning paper.

"What are you doing up this early?"

"I was wondering if you'd mind if I went to Mass with you."

"No, honey, I don't mind. There's room for everybody in my church."

"I've never been there."

The priest seemed to sense our mood in the course of his sermon. He was most vehement in reprimanding his parishioners and all others who were guilty of intolerance.

"Get it out of your heads that only Catholics can enter the gates of Heaven. This sermon is on tolerance. All religions had a proximity with God and the one thing that Catholicism would always preach would be tolerance and love thy neighbor."

I felt a hand steal over and grasp mine. Eloise had been raised a Methodist.

There was about her a deep seriousness on any subject that interested her. And I could sense that much that puzzled her about me she hoped to clear up by understanding my faith. It was the "crazy Irish" side of me she didn't fully trust. I think that Mass showed her I did have a moral dependable background.

After the services, we walked around St. Louis, had a splendid breakfast and spent a wonderful afternoon visiting the sights and smells of the zoo. There was no mention of the little priest's admonition to his people to be tolerant and love one another. Yet I sensed the new understanding a firmer bond between us.

The *Broadway* company closed its lengthy road tour in South Bend, Indiana, the home of Notre Dame, Knute Rockne and Studebaker cars. The company disbanded and shook off parting tears and the usual show business farewells of eternal devotions. It had been a great run and the patterns of some of my future life were becoming clearly visible. I was no longer the earnest apprentice, the man who fell in love with every girl.

I had managed during the play's run, despite theater tickets for relatives in Milwaukee and the low lights and soft courtship and music tabs, to save a thousand dollars. *A whole thousand dollars!* Never, in my wildest Monte Cristo–Rockefeller dreams did I envision having that much money for my very own. I felt like Young Prince Midas and took a room at the Lambs Club. Eloise went to live with one of the show's girls up on Eighty-first Street. She and I kicked that thousand dollars around with a very happy abandon, feeling life was for living, money for spending. It wasn't long before it was all gone and we were close to a doughnut and coffee diet. I had been showering Eloise with proposals of marriage; being broke and unemployed didn't stop me. But her reply was always pretty much the same.

"I love you, Pat," she'd say, "but you're a pretty crazy Irishman. Let's wait and see—to coin a phrase—what the future holds for both of us."

A practical girl is not easy to answer and I soon saw she was as practical as she was beautiful. "Pretty but dumb" didn't fit her at all. At the moment of my most ardent romancing she would break the mood with womanly logic.

"It's inevitable, Pat, that as actors we'll be separated for long

93

periods of time. Manhattan may have nothing to offer us in the theater, and we're going to look for a stock company engagement."

"Aw honey—think of something happy."

A week later she was hired as leading lady in a stock company in Worcester, Massachusetts. I continued to stalk the casting offices alone waiting for that eternal dream—the big break. One day at the Lambs Club I latched on to Lester Bryant, who announced he was organizing a stock company for Baltimore, Maryland. I never left his side till he had his company: Edna Hibbard, male actors Spencer Tracy, William "Bill" Boyd (not the Hopalong Cassidy Boyd, but the star of *What Price Glory?*), Frank McHugh *and* Pat O'Brien.

Before entraining for Baltimore there was a general tap-out of the various club members to stake us on our trip.

"Come on—we need traveling money."

Even so, none of us had any extra funds upon our arrival in Baltimore, a very solid town with lots of history, and a love, we hoped, of the theater.

We opened in a play called *Tenth Avenue*, a bit of period realism. But Baltimore audiences were not stock-company-minded, the manager told us. "They're road-show-conscious and as a result, we are not turning them away at the box office." During our first dismal week, a musical comedy road show, *Boom Boom* starring Jeanette MacDonald, Frank McIntyre and Lynne Overman opened at the McLaughlin Theater, right next door to our auditorium, and didn't help our business. There was a young man named Archie Leach in the troupe of *Boom Boom* who impressed me as quite a stilt-walker, being very good on the high wooden forms. At that time it was his only claim to fame. Today he calls himself Cary Grant.

We managed to survive, but we were not a roaring success. The natives seemed to prefer their soft shell crabs at Miller's, and the dreadful home-brewed beer, to our show.

We all lived at the Kernan Hotel and agreed it was a real trap.

Our most printable label for it was the Bear Pit. It did have a wonderful pungent oyster bar and so we signed for all of our meals, hoping for the owner's sake we might be fortunate enough to have an extensive engagement and be able to pay off our debts. Oysters, terrapin stew and lobster as a steady diet is not amusing.

Christmas Eve in Baltimore all the faithful attended midnight Mass and then returned to the dismal hostelry to have a feast of sausage, rye bread and beer. Christmas Day, surfeited with sea food, we gathered at the festive cloth of Mrs. Sparrow's Theatrical Boarding House. ("Guests will not wipe off stage make-up on our towels.") Her name will ring a bell of memory in any actor who ever played the Maryland circuit.

All that was missing that Christmas was family, girl and a chance to hang up my stocking on Mrs. Sparrow's gas-log fireplace.

Eddie Sherwood ran a Baltimore night club on a roof garden. We could sign our tabs there. Eddie loved actors more than money. We had a fairly good run in Baltimore after all, and as Eddie had been such a good host and creditor we decided to chip in and buy him a watch as a memento of our Baltimore engagement.

"For being such a wonderful all-around guy and pal." We picked out the watch after much haggling and gave the money to our stage manager, Lester Bryant, to purchase and engrave the timepiece. We then presented it to Eddie on a Saturday night after the performance.

"You've earned it, Eddie," I said as spokesman.

He was greatly moved, tears falling on his stained dinner jacket, and expressed his gratitude in histrionic terms.

"I'm gonna cherish the watch for the rest of my natural life."

Later Spence said, "You know Eddie Sherwood had to lay out the money himself. Lester Bryant never made the purchase."

"The chiseler!"

"Please, Pat—don't spoil Eddie's pleasure."

"You mean we don't expose Les?"

"That's right, you hotheaded mick."

95

"Who you calling a mick, you mick."

It was near the end of the engagement that some very stage-struck housewife in Baltimore had a huge shaky lemon meringue pie delivered to the Kernan Hotel. "A small gift for those actors who had given me *so* much enjoyment." (We never did discover just who the joy-givers were.)

The pie arrived on a Friday evening and a committee of us decided to save it for the following day.

"It looks too beautiful and regal to consume at midnight."

On Saturday, between the matinee and evening performances, we decided to divide and enjoy the pie. There was some confusion in the cutting with a backstage scissors, and a lot of beefing as to size and shape, and sudden angers and grabbing of slippery pie both as food and a weapon. The result in our hands was something of a series of damp heaving battles.

It became a pie-throwing contest.

I wiped my face and said, "It's the first time in hotel history, I guess, that wallpaper decoration is pure lemon meringue."

Spence removed crust from his hair. "I suggest we write the dear lady a joint note of gratitude for her thoughtfulness and tell her how much we enjoyed her baking *and* sundry goodies."

Little has been written about the eating habits of actors, or their digestive system. I soon developed the stomach of a goat and a carrion vulture; the ability to eat at two in the morning, swallow tar-distilled coffee, fight food poisoning and country germs with the aid of a little bourbon, remembering the motto of the potato famine years in Ireland—that "anything you could bite through was food, and whatever didn't eat you, you ate in turn."

The true noble success story of many a famous actor was his cast-iron stomach. Lots of dainty, pretty little actresses, sweet as dew, could devour a two-pound steak and a pint of tipple and go on and give the performance of their life without a burp.

Spence had received a call from Boston to replace an actor in a show headed for Broadway. The money was good and it was an important booking. Naturally he succumbed to the offer, even though our business had picked up somewhat.

"Still," I told him, "there's no assurance we can run for more than five or six weeks more at the most. Who you replacing?"

"A fellow by the name of Gable, Clark Gable."

The following week, Boyd and McHugh also got offers from other companies and soon they were on their way.

This left Edna, the leading lady, and me the lone survivors of Baltimore's "Custard's Last Stand and Pie Fight." We freely admitted we had no offers—for us only Mrs. Sparrow's iron rations for dinner each night. Edna and I offered to save the play, to survive the blitz and stay on.

"With a cut in salary, how's that?"

The management in an iron derby hat wasn't optimistic.

"I can't go along with your offer. The company closes."

Edna said: "Same old story—back to Hopesville and Dreamstown down on the Hudson."

"You're a great trouper," I said.

"You're a fine liar, Pat. But thanks."

I had sent a letter to Eloise, who was still leading lady in the Worcester stock company. I earnestly poured my heart out in my best overripe prose. I repeated all of the amorous declarations I had made so fervently in the past. The letter was loaded with quotes from *Cyrano* and Elizabeth Barrett Browning. The entire document was designed to end with a definite proposal of marriage.

Days, weeks passed and I received no answer. I was profoundly disturbed and heartsick. I couldn't understand her not acknowledging *this* letter. An actor in agony lamenting his aches is almost a compounded felony, and I certainly showed my scar tissue; and an actor in pain suffers like anyone else, no matter how much ego protection he has piled on. The raw wounds ache, the nerve ends scream.

In New York at the Lambs in their cheapest room, I also carried the burden of unemployment.

Why had I not received an answer to my letter? I swallowed pride and took a chance and phoned Eloise (collect).

"Hello, it's Pat."

"Why haven't I heard?"

"What about the long long letter?"

"I don't think you ever wrote the letter."

I exploded into the phone system. We shouted, moaned, wept. In time (reversed charges) she felt maybe there had been a letter.

"Darling, all right, there was a letter, even if you have no proof."

(It took the United States Government to prove I was not having a dream about the letter. I still have their proof of my vindication, certified by the United States mail: the envelope of my letter salvaged from an airmail crash, somewhere between Maryland and Massachusetts. The letter itself became ashes, wafted away somewhere over the dark hills.)

"Will you marry me?"

"I'll let you know soon."

The days went on after that in the same old Broadway infantry patrol, day after day, in search of what seemed to be the unattainable: a job. Frank McHugh's show was successful, Spence was still in Boston and I was waiting for a girl to make up her mind.

One dark dank night, that F. Scott Fitzgerald had identified as, when "it's always three o'clock in the morning," at the Lambs Club, Bill Boyd came up with a hot idea.

"Vincent Lawrence wrote a helluva play that had had a fairly successful run on Broadway a few seasons back. Starred Arthur Byron and had only three characters."

"What play?"

"*The Ghost Between.*"

"So?"

"I've got a real sixteen-jewel idea. If somewhere we could get a copy of the play script, we could change the title and you and Edna and me could get it booked." Bill enthusiastically winked. "What do you say, feller?"

"What would the new title be?"

"Hell—I don't know," he replied, "we'll have to think one up."

"It's stealing."

"Don't *ever* look at it, Paddy, like that. Call it borrowing."

"Borrowing?"

"That's it. We're keeping it alive, aren't we?"

"A work of mercy, Bill. Pure mercy."

"That's it."

"What about a director?" I asked.

"I've already mentioned it to a guy I've worked for and he's all for it."

"We could pay royalties."

"To hell with royalties. Don't spoil our luck. If we change the title, who's going to know?"

"Who?" I echoed, like the chorus of a popular song of that title.

Bill somehow got the script and changed the title to *The Door Between*. We went into rehearsal and opened the purloined play at a small theater in Brooklyn, then we took it into the Bronx Opera House. Bob McLaughlin booked us into Cleveland for two weeks with an added week each in Columbus and Pittsburgh, and from there into the Hollis Theater in Boston.

There was only one set—inexpensive (in those days) to put together. Bob McLaughlin had backed our little project, unaware I'm sure of what we hungry, unemployed actors had done.

We arrived in Cleveland on a Friday and were set to open on a Monday. We settled into the Winton Hotel. Bill introduced himself to the manager.

"Now, sir—our production and our potential opening at the Ohio Theater looks just great—yes sir, just great. But we are overwhelmed by details, so would you bill us at the end of the month?"

It wasn't much in the way of a hotel—in the downtown district, but the manager looked like a gambler; he had the W. C. Field's stare and a steely eye.

"Well, now—"

Bill Boyd, loaded with charm and personality, waited for an answer. Edna was a beautiful little thing. She batted her eyes.

I chipped in with a bit of the Gael: "The local Knights of

Columbus speak highly of your place. You're Irish yourself, I see."

"No."

"The Irish," I said "welcome you."

The manager beamed. "I tell you what I'll do. I'll set up a salesman's sample room for you—I see you're broke. I'll put in three cots and you can hang a curtain between you."

"It may be a little like circus quarters," Bill said.

"At least you'll have a roof over your heads."

"At least," said Edna. "*And* a strong curtain."

The manager who was our salvation in this situation is today one of the biggest hotel men in the country, Robert Christenberry. He became the manager of the Astor, then the head of a chain of hotels. A few years ago he was candidate for mayor of New York.

("Lucky I lost," he told me when I saw him recently. "Who would have taken care of the hotels?")

So roomed like sample dresses or notions, fed and sheltered, we opened the stolen play.

We received good reviews in Cleveland. We went on to Columbus and could have stayed an additional week, but we were already booked elsewhere.

Edna's husband joined us and we prepared for a big Boston opening. They went to the Copley Plaza, and Bill Boyd and I signed in at the Ritz-Carlton.

I nearly had a stroke in the lobby when Bill spoke up.

"Your *best* suite of course."

"But of course, sir."

When I got a look at it, I said, "We could ice it over and have a hockey tournament—it's that expansive."

"It sure is, Paddy."

"How'll we ever pay for this, Willie?" I asked weakly. "We haven't got a quarter. I just gave my last one to the bellboy."

"We'll worry only when it's necessary," Bill grinned. "Right now, just sit on your duff and relax! I'm a big man in this town, Paddy boy. Louie Wolheim and I were a smash hit here in

What Price Glory? I could run for mayor, only Curley is a pal of mine. A drinking pal."

"Bill, you're my kind of guy—whatever you say is okay with me."

Bill was a great favorite with the local critics in conservative, cold-nosed Boston, and though the play was just a simple little vehicle, it was well fortified with laughs throughout. The critics were enthusiastic in their reactions to our snatched production.

"We are on our way Paddy and in all probability we could take the show on into Chicago. I'll buy a Packard roadster with gold-plated headlights."

"Maybe I'll get married."

"Keep this talk cheerful."

"Willie, I'd rather have a girl than gold-plated headlights."

"You can afford *both*."

Of course it couldn't last. The fourth night at the Hollis Theater, Bill and I were in the middle of a scene. I looked off stage and saw four hefty cops. I felt, *this is it*. At the completion of the scene, Bill made a wary exit. Edna came on. At the end of our scene, the curtain rang down on the first act. I rushed back, avoided the cops, and made the dressing room.

I said to Bill, "What's the score—what happened?"

"Nothing much," he replied calmly, tossing legal papers at me, "except Vince Lawrence, that writer feller, caught up with us. They've attached the scenery, the play, our salaries."

"No jail?"

"Not so far."

I looked around backstage. The cops had departed and there really wasn't much to do but go on to finish the play. The management coolly informed us: "You are closing as of Saturday."

Bill shrugged. "Well, that's that. But now, how to pay for the suite and get our fare back to New York?"

"I have no suggestions, except we *could* steal another play."

When we dragged back to the Ritz-Carlton, Bill called a bell-boy and ordered him out to find some chili and beer.

He turned casually to the boy. "Oh son, by the way, tell the

Transportation and Reservation Department that Mr. O'Brien and I will be running down to New York for the weekend. Meeting of the Pulitzer prize play committee. We'll be leaving on the midnight train and be back Monday. Just put the whole thing, tickets and all, on our bill."

"Yes, sir."

"Paddy, give the lad a half dollar."

Bill Boyd and I left the theater Saturday night, train tickets in hand, and went to see what Bill called "the choo-choo cars."

That was in 1928. Somewhere in the corner of some dark store room of the Ritz-Carlton Hotel, in Boston, sits a forlorn actor's trunk that had trouped with me all through the hinterlands. Now it belongs to the ages, and the stockholders of the Ritz-Carlton.

(Years later, when I went to Boston for the première of the film *The Iron Major* I told the manager what had happened twenty years before. But we did not go down to look for my trunk.

"The managerial staff, Mr. O'Brien, has changed hands many times during the years and there is nothing to do but laugh loudly about the incident."

"I fully agree.")

9

Between Calls

Again began the eternal turning of the wheel of the New York actor's life; looking for work. Eloise had closed in Worcester and signed for another engagement as the leading lady in a stock company in Duluth, Minnesota.

"Twenty below zero, darling—and the natives say this is mild weather."

She played there for some weeks and I was forced to accept from her a short loan from time to time during my jobless days.

A casting call went out from the Chamberlain-Brown office on a play called *Danger*. George Nash was assigned the lead.

He told me, "I can get you a small role in the production, but the salary is silly."

"Never mind the silly salary, I have a silly eating habit," I told him. "Just get me the part. Anything, just so it's work."

On George's recommendation, I got the part. We opened in

Greenwich, Connecticut, for three days, and then rolled on to Hartford. The play wasn't much, I sadly saw, and we closed down for two weeks to revise the script and make changes in the cast. I would have been fired in the cast change with four others, but George Nash intervened and I stayed on.

"Better a flop play, Pat, than *no* play."

"I wonder, George."

We opened for some demented reason in the Bronx Opera House the same place we had opened in *The Ghost Between*, I mean *The Door Between*. The title of the play, *Danger*, was too easy for the sourpuss critics to resist, one of them writing, "The play *Danger* opened last night. Its title is indeed prophetic—there's danger of its not being a success."

We closed.

"But at least this time," I told George, "there is no railroad fare involved."

All the actors did was to limp back to the Lambs from the Bronx. There was no fatted calf waiting for us, but the ham sandwiches were welcome.

Spencer Tracy was in a play (also with a one-word title) *Dread*. It had opened in Brooklyn and they were preparing to take it to Atlantic City for a week's tryout.

We were gathered at the Lambs one night listening avidly to the gloomy wit of Ring Lardner as he tested alcohol. He had himself written a play, *June Moon*. Ring turned to Spence. "What are you up to, my boy?"

Spence replied, "I'm going to Atlantic City next week, with *Dread*."

Lardner looked at him sorrowfully with those fried-egg eyes of his: "Spence, I don't blame you."

Dread never did make Broadway.

Georgie Jessel, who up to then had confined all of his artistry to singing, writing and acting, decided to try his hand at producing. Georgie can do anything. He prefers mostly to escort beautiful women. He isn't beautiful himself, but he has great wit and charm, and as the kosher Don Juan of our time, his reputation is legend.

Georgie purchased a play from Willard Robertson called *This Man's Town* and went into production. Just prior to opening, the young actor playing a reporter in the play was taken seriously ill. The call went out. I got the nod and opened in the play. The playwright, Willard Robertson, did the lead in the show. I still think it was one of the finest plays with which I have ever been identified. We opened in New York and we were blasted by the critics. Not too seriously—they didn't give us both barrels. But the show could not survive and Georgie's night-club pallor grew paler. There were two people playing bit roles in it who became stars later—Sam Levene and Marjorie Main.

Many of the actors along Broadway, I was aware, were heeding the call of Hollywood—and hunger—and trekking westward. Talkies had not yet come into focus but it wouldn't be too long before Al Jolson would belt out a few songs in *The Jazz Singer*, the first film with sound sections. I had no intention of gambling with the strange medium that Ring Lardner called "the leaping snapshots." A lot of actors took off for the Celluloid Heaven, but the majority failed. I began casing the casting offices and putting in bids for a stock company assignment.

Bob McLaughlin, the man who backed us in our ill-fated Vince Lawrence rape, was organizing a company for his theater, the Ohio, in Cleveland. The plans were to operate on the stock-star system; assemble a group of competent players, do top Broadway shows that would be in stock domain, and bring in a top name star for a two-weeks run. In this way we hoped to run a full-season stock company.

Three of us from the Lambs Club were picked by Bob for the project; John Gallaudet, Lloyd Nolan and myself. That stock engagement gave me one of the great thrills in my theatrical career, when Helen Hayes came on to play *Coquette* and I was privileged to be her leading man.

Helen is tiny, pixy-like, warm, with a mysterious charm—

beautiful in her own special way; a scene stealer and all the talent in the world. I shall always consider these two bewitched weeks the highlight of my days in the American theater. It was the beginning of a friendship that has continued up to this day.

I kept saying: "The theater's First Lady, and I am the lucky guy to be her leading man!"

One line I read to her was: "'Honey, I love you more than all the houses and trees and everything!'"

In case you haven't heard, another famous line that she inspired was created by Charles MacArthur, who later married her. During courtship he handed her a bag of peanuts and said: "I wish they were diamonds."

(Many years later I was playing in *The Front Page* in Palm Beach, Florida. Helen was in the audience with her husband, Charles MacArthur, the co-author, Eloise and Mrs. Ben Hecht. At the end of the play, I delivered a short unabashed curtain speech and looked across the footlights.

"Ladies and gentlemen, tonight, the First Lady of the theater, Miss Helen Hayes, has graced us with her presence. Helen dear," I added, addressing her, "do you still recall the line I read to you in the Ohio Theater in 1928?"

She fired back: "'Honey, I love you more than all the houses and trees and everything.'")

Charles MacArthur had written *The Front Page* in collaboration with Ben Hecht, and as I've said, it was my first film and the turning of my career.

The Duluth stock company—as companies go, it went; it closed. But Eloise went on to another stock company in St. Paul, Minnesota.

At the conclusion of the Cleveland run, I had put aside a few dollars, not many, but enough to stave off the most greedy creditors. Eloise finished her stock engagement and returned to take up residence in a little brownstone basement apartment on Eighty-first Street.

I was back at the Lambs. Now Eloise and I, elbow to elbow, could beat the pavements together, going from casting office to casting office, always hoping . . . hoping . . . hoping, and teasing the thirty-five-cent blue-plate special and worrying over shoe leather. My hopes now went beyond just getting a job.

My girl still had not said yes on the marriage question.

Summer in New York, even though funds are low, can be a lover's holiday. Coney Island, Sheepshead Bay for steamers and lobsters, ferryboat rides to Staten Island, bus rides on the old double-deckers on Fifth, trolley cars on Sundays with visits to Battery Park, the Metropolitan Museum, long walks in Central Park, still free of muggers—dreaming our tomorrows, but she still would not say yes.

Coney Island was our Palm Beach.

After a wonderful day in Luna Park and on the beach, we once dined on our merged meager funds. By mid-evening, the cash between us was $1.70. There was a full soft yellow moon. We decided to play the scene to the hilt. I engaged a rolling chair on the boardwalk and we shared a king-sized bag of popcorn. The weathered old gent who was pushing our chair would whistle at intervals to disperse the teen-agers who were milling on the walk. At one point, near the merry-go-rounds, when he whistled, a group of teen-agers bowed low and in mockery and one said: "Make way for the rich folks!"

Being actors we smiled, bowed sitting down, and became "rich folks" for the crowd. We gave it a fine reading.

That night in Coney Island, to quote *Cyrano*, "The moon hung like a gold watch from the fob of heaven."

Eloise merely dusted her fingers and said: "That was the best bag of popcorn I have ever eaten."

During one of these soul-wringing, nerve-destroying excessively hot summer weeks (that one can only encounter in gasping New York) I received a call to do a filmed theater commercial. This was a new field for me but it paid thirty-five whole real dollars for a day's work.

"Where is it?" I asked.

"In the Fulton Fish Market downtown, in Al Smith's old neighborhood."

"Good—let it smell."

The director was Eddie Buzzell, for whom I worked later in a Columbia picture, *Hollywood Speaks*, playing opposite Genevieve Tobin.

Part of that $35 that Friday went for the most impressive bouquet of lilacs. I also bought a tiny string of pearls.

I rehearsed a speech. "If this isn't the finest necklace in New York City, I got cheated out of twenty bucks."

I arrived at Eighty-first Street with gifts. (I had stopped first at the Lambs Club for a two-hour shower to get rid of the fish perfume after a day's work at the fish market.)

Eloise prepared a wonderful dinner of tuna and rice, a most popular actor's jiffy meal on days of short bankrolls. She said the lilacs were beautiful (she still has the $20 pearls).

"The lilacs and pearls should certainly serve, honey, as a springboard—or a weapon—to get that long awaited yes."

But she still kept me in her special category.

"You're still a crazy Irishman. Not a person to settle down. Want the gifts back?"

"No. Any more tuna left? It's my fish day—three ways."

Eloise got a job in a vaudeville act that broke in on Pantages time and went on to Chicago.

Once more, like in a bad movie, we were separated. I answered a casting call from the Chamberlain-Brown office for a play called *Laugh That Off*. I got the part but on the fifth day of rehearsal, I saw the producer ambling innocently down the aisle. Intuitively, I smelled bad news. I was right.

"Pat, you're being replaced."

"In short, I'm fired."

"It's a matter of words. I got another actor."

I was disappointed too because the leading lady, Shirley Booth, was a doll and had been kind to me throughout rehearsals. She was, and still is, a great comedienne and in those few days of association with her I learned a great deal about comedy timing.

She never lost that talent and is an actress who can play either comedy or drama, and play them well.

Back to the Lambs Club—and Eloise far away at the Majestic Theater in Chicago. Sorry for myself and being a romance-cursed Irishman, I sent her a wire:

DARLING JUST GOT FIRED IT'S RAINING BUT I LOVE YOU THE CRAZY IRISHMAN

But I did have a place to go. No matter how many disillusionments and hard knocks during those formative, crystallizing years, there was always the compensation of the laughs and the pals at the Lambs. Ring Lardner usually collected the biggest crowd. The club pest once approached Ring's table and started reciting a poem about "A Little Yellow God," which was deadly from the start. Lardner sat through it numbly, listening with a long-suffering mien.

The balladier finally finished.

"Mr. Lardner, the author of that classic is now deceased."

Ring, with that same faraway gaze asked, "Did he write it before he died, or after?"

Speaking of his play *June Moon*, Ring said: "During our try-out in Atlantic City, Pat, people would accost me on the boardwalk. One wise bird said: 'Ring, your first act is great, but the last two acts need a lot of bolstering.' The next expert said: 'Mr. Lardner, I would say you have a good first act, but your second and third acts really need a lot of work.' A salt water taffy friend added: 'Great first act, Mr. Lardner, but you'd better do some surgery on the last two acts.' Then I ran into a baseball umpire who hadn't seen me in some time. 'Hello, Ring—what're you doing in Atlantic City?' What could I say? I said: 'I'm down here with an act.'"

Once Ring told me he was returning to New York from Los Angeles, where he had been vacationing a few weeks at a movie studio, sneering at a producer. As he boarded the Chief, near by was a woman seeing her husband off on the same train. She recognized Lardner, and in an excited whisper told her husband,

"That's the great Ring Lardner—you know, the famous raconteur —the wit—every word he says, I hear, is a bon mot."

"Huh?"

She instructed her husband: "Strike up an acquaintance with him. Stay near him and remember what he says. He's the greatest."

Ring, with his trained Indian ear, overheard the wife's commission to her husband. For two thousand transcontinental miles, all the way to Chicago, Ring might have been a mute. The husband tried to tail Ring all through the trip. He sat next to him in the club car, hunted out his table in the dining car, got off the train whenever Ring did at the ten-minute stops. The poor stupe tried his best to generate some great witty conversation, but a "Yes indeed" or "No, thanks" were the only words the cluck could claim from Ring Lardner. He didn't give up. He stuck by stoically. When they changed from the Chief to the Twentieth Century at Chicago, he was still doggedly on the listening post, but nothing came in. The next morning, together they walked up the ramp at Grand Central to the taxi stand. As Ring climbed into his cab, he turned to the sucker.

"So long, pal—and don't take any wooden nickels!"

"I suppose, Pat," Ring said to me, "it could have been worse —I might have said to the chump with the creepy wife: 'Twenty-three Skidoo!'"

Ring Lardner was a strange and sad genius. One of the greatest and most original of American short story writers, his biting acid depression hinted at a man who saw only the darkest side of life. He had begun his career as a sports writer, had created in *You Know Me Al* a series of baseball yarns of the ivory-headed baseball player, a world that for the first time in print actually reproduced the fantastic talk and life of the professional big-league ball player and his "World Serious" language. Successful as a playwright, columnist, wit, a major literary figure, he did not cheer up at his well-deserved progress.

He had a family of fine sons, a good wife, a comfortable home in Great Neck, many devoted friends. But in the deep dark night of his depression he would sit in the Lambs Club absorbing alcohol at an alarming rate, get to his feet at a late hour, hunt for the elusive sleeves in his topcoat and mumble. "I've got to get home now. It's the kids' night off and I have to sit up with the maid."

He died long before his time, worn out by a bitter view of the world. Of his four sons, one died in Loyalist Spain, lynched by Moors; another was killed reporting World War II. John, a writer close to his father's abilities, was suddenly carried off by a heart attack. Ring, Jr., a Hollywood screen writer was blacklisted he claimed because he was one of Hollywood's "Unfriendly Ten." Some of Ring's corroding picture of destiny appears to have seeped into the lives of his family.

There seemed no clear explanation to those of us who knew Ring so intimately at the Lambs Club, for his burden of agony, his dark view of existence. He was one of those forlorn, gifted God's creatures, who somehow could not submit to any faith or a hope in mankind.

10

Life among the Lambs

The life of a touring actor is often little better than that of an isolated lighthouse keeper far out at sea, a forest ranger on his tower, or the prisoner in a solitary cell. True the actor is in human company with fellow actors, but on a long tour the kindest face by too long intimate exposure can take on the mask of a monster, and old friends can part over something as serious as a pair of lost socks, or the loss of a worn-down grease stick.

The touring actor has no anchored home life. He, for short periods exists in strange rooms, like a Kafka character, among furniture that age has not turned into antiques. He is a stranger, who visits towns where the natives often still think the earth is flat. Other villages have not changed much since the last Indian was shot and buried. The inland big cities have their charm, often their special beauty. But for people who have seen New York, usually everything else beyond Hoboken is the sticks.

So the actor is left to his own lonely resources. Romance and booze seem at first the answer to everything. But as a steady diet, except to those who enjoy punishing themselves, these, too, reach a point where you'd just as well read the sports pages.

Stars, the top layer of big names, can carry dogs and often a kitten on tour. The rest of the cast gets little but the fleas as companions from animal life. In youth, it doesn't matter too much. There is always the big gold ring to be won for stardom, fame, money, coats with real fur collars, the ordering of fancy food without looking at the price column first. With middle age, hope begins to fade out, the lighting begins to change, as wrinkles appear and there is a rebellion against time which often leads to ruin. In old age the actor has often become a kind of caricature of himself and his profession. He usually talks only shop and stage business; where he first played with men and women who later, by accident, by luck, by certain theater tricks, rose above him.

The loneliness can be cut down by visiting the local gin mills, the bars, and places that were *then* still called saloons.

I remember playing with Bill Boyd a cold winter week at the Nixon Theater in Pittsburgh, before going on to Boston. One night after the theater, loneliness and desire in our bones, Bill and I went on a popular local saloon safari. One place was a chaos of birdcages and birds. The proprietor told us about his pet hobby, no pun intended.

"Me pet hobby is birds. I am the proud possessor of sixty canaries and am really devoted to them."

Bill said, "Noisy little swine, aren't they?"

The birds sang lustily from their respective cages.

I said, "Never have I heard a more harmonious group."

Bill said, "I'd like to see 'em on top of ladies' hats."

I said, "I'll buy the next round."

A goodly crowd of two-fisted imbibers joined me in the offer. The birds sang far into the night.

I was feeling hazy but happy. I bargained with the owner of our fine feathered friends.

"Mac, I want to purchase one of the canaries."

"It's like selling a child. No."

"You have *so* many."

Along about sunup he weakened, and we closed the deal over a last cup of brew.

"Six free ducats to our show Mac, and thirty-five dollars, and that includes the cage."

"You're taking advantage of me," said the barkeep, "but I'll toss in a box of free birdseed. Take good care of Serena."

Outside in the chilly wan Pittsburgh dawn we stood. Bill, myself and me carrying the bird Serena by one finger hooked in the top of the cage.

"Now that you've got yourself an eagle," said Bill, "what the hell are you going to do with it? It's too small to roast."

"I'll tell you what I'm going to do," I answered, lonely for home and kind faces, "I'm going to send it home to my mother in Milwaukee."

Bill shivered and buttoned his coat. "You shouldn't have had that last saucer of sauce, my Celtic friend. It's sixteen below. That bird can't be shipped over a thousand miles and live. You're the killer type, Paddy."

"Bill," I replied smiling, "I've been talking to Serena. She loves the cold—and she's never been out of Pittsburgh and wants to travel. Don't you honey?"

"I hate talking birds—and drunks who converse with them."

It was cold and Serena looked at me with beady eyes as if to ask *who* would bring a lady out on such a day?

"Feathers are very warm," I said.

Bill shook his head sadly. "That canary is turning blue."

At the hotel, Serena sang us to sleep that morning, never the worse for the chilly trip from its native saloon.

The following day I packed and shipped the bird on to Milwaukee.

Mom wrote me: "It arrived, dear son, safe and singing. I have never had a bird before and I call him 'Lindy' because it had flown so far. It's not a girl, but a boy bird, Mrs. Callahan next door tells me. She should know—she's had twelve children herself."

Lindy stayed with Mom and Dad for a number of years and sang gloriously right up to the last summer or winter, hot or cold.

While on the road I always dreamed, not of birds, but of Eloise, and of New York City. When I came off a tour jobless, I was happy to be back even if fairly broke. To any actor New York is the only city that really matters. Broadway the only street (actually the side streets *off* Broadway—there are few theaters on Broadway itself for anything but motion pictures).

The smell of subways, freshly printed newspapers, the interiors of old lobbies, the hint of cooking over Sterno cans in furnished rooms, the smell of the streets after a sudden rain, the perfume of refuse trucks—all are the scent of New York, and of his world, to an actor.

I went back to my familiar shelter at the Lambs. Eloise had also just come off the road. She was at the train to greet me, looking like a Tiffany window at Christmas. She had, she said, prepared dinner in her Eighty-first Street hideaway.

"Tuna and rice?" I whispered to her.

"You're a mind reader, sweetie."

Later we walked down to the Actors' Chapel at St. Malachy's on Forty-ninth Street and said some earnest prayers for all of us poor and wonderful wretches in show biz. It made us feel less alone, and a shared prayer is the best kind. It has the power to keep you warm on a cold night, and it's better than adrenalin for heart and courage.

At liberty, living at the Lambs Club nearly made poverty glow. Its rowdy and colorful members were hardly ever at rest.

Al Phillips, who had the role of General Grant in *Abe Lincoln* on Broadway, once came out of the theater and hailed a cab. Al was so immersed in the role of the great Ulysses S. that he enacted the part in all its nuances, at all times, on and off. He walked like Grant, he talked like Grant. He did not stress the hard drinking—he was too faithful an actor to spoil it by working drunk. The cab came to the curb. Al stepped in.

The cabbie turned and asked, "Where to?"

Hal Skelly, who was starred in *Burlesque* with Barbara Stanwyck up the street, was passing by and overheard the cabbie's question. Leaning into the cab Hal said: "Drive the General home to Grant's Tomb."

Frank McGlynn, in the title role of *Abe Lincoln* at the time, also adhered to *his* characterization on and off, nearly taking up rail splitting. On matinee days, between the afternoon and evening performances, Frank, in full Lincolnian attire—shawl, top hat, and frock coat (he grew his own whiskers)—would stroll from the theater up to Central Park and back again. His treks always took him past the Palace Theater, where, in the lobby of the famous vaudeville house, many of the employed and unemployed vaudevillians gathered to exchange gossip. After the sixth week of McGlynn's twice-a-week promenade wrapped in professional gloom, Joe Frisco, the inimitable wit whose stammering was the trademark of his art, remarked as Frank strode dramatically by, as if to a cabinet meeting in the dark days of the war, "You k-know t-t-that ham won't be ss-s-satisfied until he's assassinated."

Joe was small, full of spirit and devoted to horse racing; he cocked an ironic eye on the world and deflated it with a few loose-strung words.

Joe was a remarkably quick wit. Once when arrested for jaywalking, he asked the policeman, "How-w fast was I-I-I going?"

Joe Frisco, for all his huge repertoire of jests—I have been in his company a lot—never told an off-color story. At no time in his career did he ever have to use "blue" material. Once he and Esther Williams, the swimming star, were appearing on a variety bill together. This was a new kind of show business for the well-built Miss Williams, and it was mighty strenuous doing four shows a day in a tank. Her act demanded that she be very active in very little in the pool during the show. After a few hard times she remarked to Joe, "This is a pretty rough deal doing these three or four shows a day, especially with my swimming act."

Joe remained dead-pan. "Why d-d-don't you f-f-float the s-supper show?"

One night at the Friars Club, Joe—a historian of odd events—was telling us about a newspaper popularity contest, with entries submitted from all over the world.

I asked, "Who won?"

"The r-r-returns j-just c-came in. W-w-winnie Churchill f-f-first . . . B-b-bing C-c-crosby second."

"Who was third, Joe?"

"Cardinal Spellman ran third and paid four-sixty."

We used to see Joe at the Del Mar racetrack. Eloise asked Joe once who he had in the race just finished. He mournfully tore up his ticket, looking like Tiny Tim with no goose in sight.

"I j-just b-bet on a horse called Venus de Milo. She's s-s-supposed to be that dame with n-n-no arms, but she ran with no legs t-today."

Once Joe bet a horse that was involved in a dead heat. He rushed earnestly up to the clubhouse to look at the photo finish. On his return to his seat, Bing Crosby asked him: "Well, Joe, how's about it—how did the results look to you?"

"T-talk about a dead h-h-heat. Those two horses looked j-just like the D-d-dolly S-sisters!"

Joe, during most of his career was unemployed. He could get work but refused to lower his price for appearing on stage after the depression of 1929. As Joe put it: "Why should I take a cut? Did H-h-hoover?" He devoted his life to horses.

One evening at the old Keen's Chop House, Ring Lardner, another horse-playing patsy, was dining directly under a huge painting of three galloping equines in full stride coming hell-for-leather into the finish. You couldn't have split a hair between them, it was that accurate a dead tie. After hours of gloomy gazing at the picture, all during the rather dismal dinner, Ring turned to me. "You know, Paddy, that one in the middle isn't trying."

Ring liked to make surrealist remarks about things.

There was a bad play running at the Belasco Theater. Ring sat through it, and left a message for the management: "Dear Sir: Your play has no plot."

In the cloister of the Lambs Club, Ring liked peace. One of the members was conspicuous for his wild hair, which stood on end. Lardner looked up, viewed this horrendous waving apparition, grabbed the hairy ape by his lapels and pulled him down to his side. "*What* do you look like when I'm sober?"

But life wasn't all wit—it was hoping for work on stage.

Henry O'Neill and I got a call from the Chamberlain-Brown office to report to Bryant Hall to read for the play, *You Can't Win*. There were two parts—brothers. Henry and I got the roles. The show opened in Great Neck and then came into the Frazee Theater in New York.

The critic Alan Dale, without even making a summary of the contents of the production, wrote one paragraph: "The play opened at the Frazee Theater last night. The title was *You Can't Win*. My comment—it won't." It didn't. It went off to Cain's warehouse and I went to the movies to think things out.

The talkies were beginning to make their ominous lisping threats in the world of entertainment. The trek to the Coast had begun. I told myself I wanted no part of it unless I had a real contract. Actors who did embark for California were always given this admonition by Willie Collier, one of the senior members of the Lambs: "Don't buy anything out there you can't put on the Sante Fe Chief."

Hollywood was dangerous territory. I was told the heartaches of Broadway had their replicas in Hollywood. "They got a mouse that talks out there, and the two biggest stars are Rin Tin Tin and Rex the Wonder Horse."

"Those animals eat well," I said.

Money was so short with me, it was getting harder to buy tuna fish and rice to bring to Eloise to prepare. She was the proud possessor of a historic diamond ring that had once belonged to the famous actor, James K. Hackett.

"There is no alternative," I said firmly.

"All right, Pat, I make the decision and you make the journey."

I took the ring to Simpson's, at the sign of the three O's. ("Everything," Ring Lardner once said, "has been hocked there but the lions on the Public Library steps.")

I received a pretty good chunk for the ring. It bought a lot of tuna, ferryboat rides and trips to Coney Island.

When there was no money for dates, I stayed home at the Lambs and listened. Once there was a religious discussion. They were always deadly. God goes by many names, but men have died for changing a letter in some ritual. It never got *that* bad at the Lambs. The debaters were pretty equal vocally. The question came up: Was "Thou shalt not commit adultery" the sixth commandment or the seventh? The King James version holds to seventh place, the Catholic moves it up one to sixth. *Our* seventh is, Thou shalt not steal. The discussion became warmer, with hand gestures. Some of the rebuttals were heated. Wilton Lackaye looked over the scene and played it in just the right tone, with all of his powerful eloquence.

"Gentlemen! Never let it be said that members of the Lambs were ever at sixes or sevens over adultery."

Fred Keating once came into the Lambs at two A.M. He had an ocelot on a leash. It was pretty frightening to the unsober, to say the least. Fred put the snarling leopard on top of the bar in the Grill Room. The bartender said, "Jaysus-Mary-save-us," and took off. So did all the members. Keating had the Lambs Club to himself that night for as long as he could hold that ocelot.

Later I was involved with a full-sized leopard.

I was in a play, in South Bend, Indiana, with Wally Ford, Martha his wife, Eloise and I. We were invited to a dinner party given by Joseph Stevenson, owner and publisher of the local newspaper. We were to be served a twilight dinner because of our evening performance. I went to an ornate gold and marble bathroom to wash my hands. I came running back breathlessly into the living room shouting:

"*Don't* go in the bathroom—there's a *leopard* in there!"

119

Wally, pale green, turned to me. "To hell with your leopard—a *monkey* just bit Martha!"

Eloise rose with a worried look around. "Let's all get out of here before a gorilla serves the cocktails."

Our host came in, in the midst of our nervous hunt for our hats and coats.

"It's too wild here, Mr. Stevenson."

"Oh, my creatures. I have a collection of pets, among them a tiny monkey and a cute baby leopard. They are both harmless. The monkey *bit* Martha? I assure you he was just making an affectionate gesture."

Martha said with wary words, "Fortunately it's not *too* serious a wound."

We all settled down and dinner was served.

Wally looked up from his plate. "Would you like to guess what we're eating? Moose!"

Martha said, "That's better than the leopard eating Pat."

It was like eating a sautéed basketball.

Later I heard Mrs. Stevenson convince her husband that rare animals were not conducive to making their guests feel at home.

The big break seemed to have come for Spencer Tracy in *The Last Mile*, by an unknown playwright. He was given the lead in the new play that was to open in Hartford, Connecticut. An all-male cast, which to me seemed a little dangerous at the time. I recalled Broadway had had few if any productions without the girls. Tracy returned glum and sagging from the break-in in Hartford. He was a pretty disconsolate guy. We were sitting at the round table in the Lambs Grill.

"Boys, I'm in one helluva flop! I'd like to pull out, but I have a run-of-the-play contract."

"What do you mean pull out? Stay with it."

"It's to have a week of doctoring and then open on Tuesday."

"Maybe you'll get a break and the theater will burn down."

None of us saw much of Spence during that week of revision and rehearsal.

He pleaded with us.

"Don't see the show—I've got no confidence in it."

I bought a gallery ticket on opening night and witnessed a one-man performance of amazing power, of near-greatness— Spence as the condemned man. At the final curtain the audience stood and cheered. There were salvos of applause. They could have taken curtain calls until five in the morning. It was a spine-tingling production, the first of the powerful prison yarns. All the actors were fine, but Spence was an overnight sensation!

It was his springboard to Hollywood, when John Ford, the director of *The Informer*, saw Spence's performance and had Winnie Sheehan, then head of Fox, sign one Spencer B. Tracy to a long-term contract.

Spence had been honest when he told us he was in a flop. The Hartford tryout audience had been anything but responsive. "Their receptivity was as cold as the Yukon." Spence thought he was in a bomb. John Barrymore once said, "The theatergoing public is enigmatic—and that's putting it clearly and mildly."

When John wasn't so polite, he was hardly fit to print. Once in a theater full of coughers, he stopped the show to call the audience "damn barking seals." Then he went back to the play.

Arthur Treacher, who is familiarly known to his friends as Pip, remembers our hard times. He tells an old story of our Lambs Club days. Pip, his accent thick as Devonshire cream, will say: "You know, this Patrick here is a *frightful* man. Years ago, when Pat and I were jockeying about the Great White Way, seeking employment in the theater, I drew an untimely suspension from the Lambs—thirty days, for non-payment of dues. One sad hour, as I was strolling up Forty-fourth Street, very low in the mouth indeed, Patrick emerged from the club, cheerful as a Piccadilly beggar. He said, 'Well, Pip old boy, good to see you. Come on in and we'll quaff a few.' I answered: 'My dear fellow, aren't you aware that I am suspended from the Lambs?' This frightful Celtic troll replied: 'Don't let that bother you, Pip old boy. Come on in, I'll get you a two-week guest card.' You know, by this old dodge, helping other actors, we nearly cut the active paying membership dues in half!"

One of the inebriates of the club, Ben Burt, a song writer, had been at alcoholic play for hours at the bar. As he left, passing the bulletin board, the suspension list of those in arrears was being posted for all the miscreants to view. Ben gazed at the list for a long time, realizing his name was included. In somewhat inarticulate tones he recited sadly: "Thirty days hath September, April, June *and* Ben Burt."

I don't want to appear to say that the keen, penetrating wit of that era does not quite seem to have survived; but if it hasn't, there may be a logical reason. The theater has changed. Various new low-level entertainment forms have swamped this generation. We all whisper that the theater, that fabulous invalid, will survive, come what may—pay TV, feelies, smellies. The theater had its inception before Christ and will continue, we assure each other. It has heartaches, disappointments, broken dreams, grime, greed, all the faults of man, but where in the world could you meet such people as actors, singers, designers, directors, bred in the atmosphere of music and laughter, and a world of make-believe? If this thinking seems corny, a hell of a lot of us have survived on its philosophy, and at times on little else.

The Lambs, while mostly populated by people involved in the theater, also had members like James J. Walker, mayor of New York City (and a pretty good popular song writer). Jimmy was a very loyal Lamb. Dry times or wet, the bar of the Lambs was never raided. We had political power. Jimmy was gifted with wit, and was never at a loss for a retort, whether it was in the political battling in Albany or the banquet tables on the Continent.

I recall F.D.R. asking Jimmy one time, "James, why is it whenever they ask you Irishmen a question, you invariably answer with a question?" And Jimmy's soft answer: "Do we now?"

Jimmy had the Irish love of sentiment. At the Sports Writers' dinner, presenting an award to Joe Louis, heavyweight champion of the world, Jimmy said: "I am not going to make a speech. Joe, all I can say to you tonight is, you have placed a rose on the grave of Abraham Lincoln."

The life of an unemployed actor followed a pattern to help nourish life and preserve wardrobe without too much wear on body and cloth. If there was no morning call for a play reading, or whispered gossip about casting to follow, you slept late. This preserved the vital body warmth and also did away with the decadent need of breakfast. Rising about noon, one thought of all the best expensive places in town to eat, and then either lunched simply with a luckier fellow actor, some visitor to the town, or decided that bread and milk was the Spartan diet to build a firm body without any of that revolting extra fat. If one had not arranged for the eternal cold cuts or tuna and rice dinner, with one's girl, there were some who would wash dishes or serve table for their food. But I never did any of this; the brothers at the Lambs would not let one get too lean in the chops if they were able to lend a green note. But pride among young actors took off more pounds than free loading, and long hair was fashionable and saved barber fees.

There was always entertainment if one didn't mind missing first acts. Someone in the theater, advertising, designing or painting was usually celebrating in flat or studio, in rehearsal hall or dance palace. Red wine and meat balls and *pasta* was as available as heartburn. One could keep social contact without too much loss to a shrinking bankroll.

The wardrobe of an actor was a miracle of packaging. He always seemed well dressed; his face was shaved (even if the razor blade had been resharpened on the inside of a drinking glass). The overbrushed hat could be worn at all angles, the brim snapped in various ways, and no matter how thin the crown, always sharply tilted. Shoes shone, even if the sole was thin enough to tell the head from the tail on a stepped-on dime. (Look at the back of the heels of an actor's shoes; if they are dull back there, he is shining his own shoes.) Shirts were a problem, frayed cuffs were trimmed with nail scissors, and the utilitarian colored sport shirt of today was still only worn by half-wild native guides in Hawaii. Shirts called for heavy starching, but the detachable reversible collar was making its last stand, and was a boon to the actor short on clean linen.

There were various ways of keeping the knife-edge creases in one's pants; one was to walk around in one's underwear in one's own room. Some actors carried small portable electric irons to do their own pressing. So steam leaking from a room could mean anything from getting a wardrobe in order, to boiling a plum pudding. Actresses were experts in steaming worn-down velvets and laces and other clothes in front of showers, sending up clouds of steam to bring life back to crushed outfits. Sewing and basting and spot-cleaning was part of an actor's education. Some took nearly as much pride in a neat patch as in a good two weeks in stock in New Brunswick, New Jersey.

Contrary to what one would think on our glamorous skid row, there was not a great deal of stealing, only a great deal of borrowing; one's best shirt could have been to Hong Kong or on stage in London without one. Nor was there among earnest, hard-driving professionals much con man's byplay for cash. All professions have their weak-willed lunatic fringe, but actors are eccentric mostly about their crafts and skill. A girl might view a show with a visiting gentleman with that "Oh you kid" gleam in his eye, and explain how to dissect a large Maine lobster with him. But he usually ended up with his nose against a just-locked door. To accept gems and rent money for what the tabloids called "a love nest" showed a girl had no backbone for success on the stage. That there were exceptions only proved that there were the accepted conventions in the first place.

As for life and love among themselves, actresses and actors were just like other people. In their youth—romantic, eager and hot-blooded; in their prime perhaps greedy and spoiled; in old age given to taking a stimulant against the mean battling of the world. In the main, we were, as human beings, far from *Peyton Place*, and not exactly type-cast for Pollyanna.

Only in looking backwards was being unemployed, setting oneself up against a city, anything to remember cheerfully in too much detail.

11

More from the Lamb Fold

The Lambs Club, through the years, had members who became legends to the theater world. As an often unemployed actor I had time to cultivate the most colorful specimens.

High on the list was George Nash, with whom I appeared in the play *Danger*. He was known at the club not so much for his salient wit as his eloquent pronouncements; all declaring in golden booming tones that there just was nothing vocational or sporting he couldn't do just a little better than anyone else. He was not at all adverse to demonstrating at any given time if challenged. Strangely enough, George would always prove his skill by acting out perfectly the demanded deed. He swore he had rarely played billiards in his life. One evening he was an interested spectator at a furious game of billiards between two eager-cued club experts. Came a long wait in the ivory-ball encounter. One of the players studied the upcoming shot religiously from all angles. He walked slowly around the ornate teak table, stood back, gazed with the penetrative eye of General Meade at Gettysburg at the ball in question; pondered like Einstein how he was going to accomplish the seemingly impossible. George Nash rarely had a billiard cue in his hand in his life (with the possible early exception of defense in saloon combat).

He strolled leisurely over to the player, took the cue, bowed affably to the players.

"Now let me see. Oh *yes*."

He proceeded to make the impossible shot that would have gotten hot applause from the great Mosconi himself.

George Nash would declame at various times his prowess as a fistic combatant. He would assume the various hoky poses of the ring champs of the past and with articulate detail—shadow boxing —tell of his sparring matches with Philadelphia Jack O'Brien, Tom Sharkey and James J. Jeffries. He was never, at any time, mean or malicious. I often think that he was aware that we knew he was a fine liar, even in spite of the billiards episode. Shouted down, he rose more fanciful than ever.

One evening one of the great masters of magic *and* a card manipulator, the great Leipzig, was a guest at the club. After witnessing a demonstration of skill, George asked, "May I borrow the cards from a visiting performer, and proceed to prove I am a master of the deck. Or as we pros call it, the 'Devil's Prayerbook.'"

We all gathered around and waited. George, with a flourish, spread the cards over the bar, explaining, "The origination of this particular trick I learned in Bagdad."

For twenty minutes he went into a great explanatory spiel—the chronological background of the trick. He then said: "I must be excused momentarily. Nature."

He *never* came back that night. There just wasn't any trick. George had left his audience, walked gaily out of the door, up Broadway to his favorite bistro.

Now every time I enter the Lambs, I'm sure that somewhere up there in the Great Infinite, is the late George Nash, instructing the angels *how* to adjust their wings and jazz up their harp playing.

There were many great hoofers around (a term dead as the word "flapper" or the term "drugstore cowboy"). Boyle and Brazil, William Holbrook, Doyle and Dixon, Tom Patricola, pint-sized Pat Rooney and Marion Bent, the one and only Jack Donahue. In the minstrel field was George Primrose, king of the soft shoe (Ed Sullivan lived too late for most of them).

Ring Lardner once said, "Tap dancing must be easy—so many do it so damn well."

A little dancer who was later to become my lifelong pal was James Cagney. He and his wife Billie had an act, Cagney and Vernon. Billie even today can get up and hoof and really fly. Jimmy was in a class all by himself as a dancer. Had he wanted to, Jim could have been a great ballet star. His dancing in *Yankee Doodle Dandy* was only a small sample of his skill.

Jimmy in those days was thin and bouncy with the flaming hair, the arched iron chin, the clinched teeth seen through the menacing smile, and that machine-gun-staccato talking that his imitators think is the man. He could speak perfect Yiddish from his boyhood days on New York's East Side. He worked as a package boy in Wanamaker's, a page boy at the Friars, and soon, ready for the show world, picked up dancing and a partner and parts in shows. As an actor he had a driving vitality that seems very real, and something to stand in awe of. In those days, short and slim as he was, Jimmy could, in a play or movie, take on any big brute in a fight, and the audience believed he could actually beat anyone to a pulp. He often could, for Jimmy was all India-rubber muscle, steel-faced. He accepted his roles, but he knew it was only a facet of himself and his talent.

In films he came through at once in *Public Enemy*, the first and best of the gangster films. His direct, clean action, his ability to make a line bite like acid, gave the impression here was a tough kid who wasn't playing around. In film after film he was the hoodlum, the Robin Hood with the gat, the con man, the spiel artist, the slim kid with his eye on the big chance. Later he played G men, and other parts. But to the world he was tough and mean.

Women found him a new fascinating type, and the studio had

him in films where he would grind a half a grapefruit in a girl's face, kick another across a room with a perfect drop kick, manhandle them like a trainer of a new tiger, from Jean Harlow to Ann Sheridan. And nobody protested his savage courtships too much. As the years passed, Jimmy grew wider and more solid. He is today nearly Mr. Five-by-Five, but the hard-eyed vitality is still there. The thickening body contains inside it still for most of us one of the great legendary images of our youth. With Babe Ruth, Jack Dempsey, F. Scott Fitzgerald, the early Stutz Bearcat car, the last of the beaded speakeasy hostesses, he was an image in the American scheme of things; of the Roaring Twenties and the Tepid Thirties, of the dust bowls and the bread lines and gang wars. He is the saga maker of the hard kid who couldn't be pushed too far. In real life, Jimmy is a gentle man, who draws and paints, reads, raises prize cattle, farms, is happily married, has much family. He still grins that crooked mick grin that made him famous. He'll even lift his fists at you for a mock blow, but he was never the Jimmy Cagney he imprinted on so much film stock— just a dancer gone wrong.

When Jimmy went out to try for picture fame, the Pat O'Brien income, like the nation's, was still pretty much depleted after 1929. I got a small windfall acting in a two-reel film. Arthur Hurley was doing these two-reelers in New York City. One day at the club he asked me: "Want to pick up a few fast bucks?"

"Anything *nearly* legal, yes."

Along with Lyle Talbot and Vivienne Osborne, we got a two-day stint in a rapid celluloid adventure, shot with the speed of an Indian arrow. I don't know where it was ever shown.

"Probably," said Lyle, "in band pavilions, Mississippi steamboats or a phone booth."

I never heard of it after we made it. I got $250, which paid my Lambs dues and boosted Eloise's grocery department away from tuna. I sent her a few more lilacs, but I laid off buying her pearls. "After all, there's no use spoiling a girl you're courting with costly jewelry."

128

"Try me, mister, just try me."

But I spent less time at the Lambs.

It wasn't all buddy-buddy at the Lambs. One of the really great fistic encounters was a bout between Louis Calhern and Walter Catlett. Louis played heels, sneering heels best—and his manner often carried over into public life. However the thing started, I don't remember. *Where* it started, I recall vividly.

They started roundhouse swinging at each other at the bar, swapped hard punches all the way to the front door of the club, down the steps, arms swinging, out on the street; they battled from Forty-fourth Street to Columbus Circle.

When they got that far uptown, still trading punch for punch, they breathlessly agreed on a draw.

They got into a cab, returned to the club bar. Arms around each other they drank and sang far into the night.

As the dawn came up the argument started again. Walter and Louis were swinging again—out of the bar—and out of the door. But not for long.

At last they sat battered, bruised and boozed on the Lambs Club steps and at peace with the world and each other, watched the dawn come up over the skyscrapers of New York City. The epic battle had ended in a draw.

A character in the club was Joe Miller, who was not really an actor, but a "patron of the worldly arts." He was a high-class bootlegger—an "interior decorator"—and in those days, it wasn't too difficult to cultivate a clientele. Joe, wide, ugly, *nearly* human, at no time in his career won any beauty contests. Yet once, upon his return from a European trip, (to bury his money) he affected a monocle. Ben Burt took one look at the monocle.

"Joe, with that monocle in your kisser, you remind me of a stained glass window in a Bowery men's room."

I enjoyed going to baseball games with Ring Lardner, Frank McIntyre and Frank Belcher (a cigar manufacturer of fairly good stogies, and a close associate of John McGraw, the masterful leader of the New York Giants). McGraw used to delight Ring and his friends with the story of a young rookie that had come to him from the hinterlands. "It was Memorial Day, see, Ring, and the kid—with one of them shaved-in-the-back haircuts from Kansas, a first appearance in the Big Leagues. Just come up from the minors and this day was what you big domes call the baptism of fire? First inning, a fella from the other team hit a long single. The kid outfielder made a running leap, like an upstream salmon for love, but misses it by two feet. Two runs score. A couple of innings later, an opponent hit a Texas leaguer. The rook comes running in and collides with the man on second base. Two more runs score. In the ninth inning, a long ball is hit into center field. The rook misses it completely. The ball falls about fifteen feet away. All during this fiasco when this guy returns to the bench, I am ignoring him, not a word do I say to him. The game is over and the team is going into the clubhouse. The kid hurries up to me.

"'Mr. McGraw—it's that wind out there. You just can't figure that wind.'

"'I know,' I say, 'it's the trade wind, kid—you go to Toledo tomorrow.'"

Another baseball fan was William (Bill) Frawley (who was the Frawley of Frawley and Louise, in the vaudeville era, and a hit since in the "I Love Lucy" show and "My Three Sons."

Bill's stage performances snared him an early film contract. He was called to make a movie test at the Paramount studios on Long Island. The casting director, a neat type, prevailed upon Bill to don a "skull doily" (hair piece or toupee) for the test before the cameras. Bill got the job and figured to hell with the head rug. On his arrival at the Hollywood studio, he marched into the producer's office without his wig. The producer, a Hungarian, who had seen the test, greeted Frawley.

"Happy to have you out here, Mr. Frawley. However, I rather expected to see someone with hair."

Bill boiled over. "Well then, why the hell didn't you test a lion!"

With Hollywood success, Bill became an easy touch.

There was a panhandler who cased Bill every time he was in the vicinity of Hollywood and Vine. Willie, always a sucker for a soft story, could never turn the panhandler down. He invariably slipped the moocher a buck or more. After two years of "Can you spare a little coffee money, Bill?" Bill asked him: "Listen—what in hell do you *really* do with this money I've been giving you all this time?"

The bum said proudly: "You're so damned curious, I'll tell you! I buy a drink with it—that's what I do with it!"

"You're so damned honest, I'm going to *buy* you a drink. What do you think of that?"

He took the bum into the Brown Derby. They were seated at the number one table, this horrible-looking tramp—a four-day beard, unkempt, shabby, in gamy rags, a real bindlestiff.

Bill, expressionless, signaled the maitre de, "Bring two double scotch-and-sodas." The bum looked at the maitre de and shouted, "Make mine the same."

Frawley rose and took a punch at the bum right across the table.

A member of the gang of actors was Frank Fay, who in the heyday of vaudeville was called "undoubtedly the greatest single act that ever played the Palace." He had a debonair style and a sophisticated easy charm. The Palace audiences were always hep suckers for the Fay material. No one in his field could ever touch him as an M.C. or a stand up comic.

When Fay appeared in the play *Harvey*, he was a smash hit. Frank was a problem to his friends. He was fanatical about his religion, intolerant of other creeds, and given to loud, denouncing talk that offended people. He was a very devout Catholic. He was two hundred per cent for Franco in Spain's fearful Civil War, and he was vocal about it in liberal New York. He frequently overstressed his religious philosophy by seeking to influence his fellow players to embrace the Catholic faith. Unfortunately for Frank, he attempted to bring converts into Catholicism by browbeating them. Never did he utilize the intelligent or tactful approach, or try to attain his purpose by an easy indoctrination.

It was news one day in the Lambs Club that one of the cast of *Harvey* had become a Catholic. A bystander at the bar said, "Probably a run-of-the-play Catholic."

With his unorthodox methods of missionary zeal in trying to bring converts into the Church, Frank was always ready with a caustic barb on any discussion about his faith. One day, Bert Wheeler, while lunching with Fay at the club, rebuked him for not attending Mass any more at the Little Actors' Chapel at St. Malachy's on Forty-ninth Street.

"Gee, Frank, now that you're such a big hit on Broadway, we never see you in our little chapel any more. You always go to St. Pat's now. How about that?"

Fay casually answered: "Tell you what I'll do, Bert. I'll be at the twelve o'clock services at St. Malachy's Sunday, providing they announce it at all the earlier Masses."

There was more casual tolerance in those days before World War II. Ralph Murphy, one of the Lambs, now a Hollywood director, attended services at St. Patrick's Cathedral with his wife, who was not a Catholic. They arrived early. It seemed an endless time before the priest made his entrance to the altar. They waited and waited. Finally Mrs. Murphy whispered to Ralph: "When are they going to start?"

Murphy whispered back, "They don't dare start till Fay gets here."

Wherever Frank is in Heaven, I hope God has given him a small parish of his own.

12

The Longhair Mob

At any dark moment it is often best to sit back and wait for a change.

Wally Ford, the leading man in the Chicago troupe of *Broadway*, came to me brooding over lunch one day at the club.

"Paddy, I just bought the rights to a play, *The Nut Farm*."

"It must be about actors."

"And I've found an angel to stake me and I'm casting now—McLaughlin will let us break it in at his theater in Cleveland."

"Cleveland is certainly my omen of luck."

"I'm lucky in securing the services of a great comedienne—Josephine Hull—and you, Paddy."

We broke the show in at Cleveland and were then booked into the Cort Theater in Chicago. The reviews were very good and we had a comfortable run for some twenty-six weeks, with hopes of a booking for the show in New York.

Two weeks before closing in the Windy City, I lost my voice completely. One minute I was talking, the next—not even Donald Duck sounds. I signaled desperately for help. After a cursory examination by a doctor who was summoned in haste to the theater, I was told, "You must have a tonsillectomy."

I was forced to leave the show. I chose to go home to Milwaukee for the operation because, as I told my parents, "After all, I'm not a child—I'm in my late twenties. But I want the family doctor at my side—more important, I want to be in my *own* home."

Mother said, "Stop playing a deathbed scene."

It was a rough operation for me. I sustained a violent hemorrhage in the middle of the night. I heard, far off, Mother call out to Dad, "Get the doctor immediately."

Then I also recall her saying, "Never mind the doctor—get the priest."

I was too shocked and weak to wonder which one I needed most. My mother was not one to yell, "Wolf, wolf," needlessly.

Lying there between heaven (I hoped) and earth, I don't recall now who arrived first. However, the hemorrhaging was stopped, the last rites postponed. I missed the New York opening and naturally, it was a letdown—*another* near-success. I had the hovering solace of my parents, and Eloise came in from New York to hold my hand. After a short convalescence, we returned to Manhattan and I got involved with the beatniks of those days.

A writer, Christopher Morley, the Big Daddy of the intellectuals had discovered beer and a hunger for art in New Jersey—what he called Hobohemia—and it became fashionable to go to Jersey for fun and pretzels.

I never thought I'd play *Broadway* in Hoboken, New Jersey, for thrill seekers, but I did. A week's stand. Arty bohemian salaries were as short as the run, but it was grocery money and helped buy the tuna and rice. I switched roles and played the heavy, Steve Crandall, instead of the cop, which I had played in the Chicago company and on the road.

I got on well with the bohemians, who like our later day beatniks, didn't bathe too often, and who sat around on floors, in sandals, taking on the problems of the world. They used to talk of Freud, Marx, Virginia Woolf (who later became a play title) Einstein, Noel Coward and Proust, Matisse *and* bull fighting. (Hemingway was setting the fashion.)

Hoboken became the place for the smart folk to go. The tails-and-white-tie crowd came, those that read *Vanity Fair*, and went also up to Harlem to say what great artists the Negroes were. There was a big black-and-tan vogue at the time, and one of the most entertaining evenings I ever spent was seeing an all-Negro cast at the Lafayette, playing *The Front Page*.

The Village downtown was the hangout of many of the intellectuals who came to Hoboken, and they invited us to their studios, not yet called pads. Rents were low then. Now the Village is only for rich advertising copy writers I hear, and TV writers, photographers for *Harper's Bazaar*.

They drank the red ink called wine, and wound the *pasta* on forks, listened to the early jazz of Louis Armstrong and King Oliver.

It was the age of protest. Against morals, conforming, going home to the family feed store in Idaho or the Ford dealership in Azusa. A lot of them were going to Paris to sit in front of the Dome, and I guess I heard the first Gertrude Stein recited about this time. To me it was as clear as it ever was, that it was nothing piled on nothing, alas, and sense is sense is sense to me.

For two paying weeks there I was in the full swirl of the fashionable *avant-garde*, with the pretzels and beer, listening to rehashed D. H. Lawrence among muddy Picasso colors.

After that engagement for Christopher Morley, I began the job trek once more and was given a script to read, *The Up and Up*, a race track yarn about a bookie, Curly, and his problems, trackwise and with his girl, who held no great affinity for his occupation as a bookie. I was offered the role. Howard Lindsay was to direct, his wife Dorothy Stickney to play the feminine lead. In humble glee I went off to St. Malachy's Actors' Chapel to pray for the success of the horse track enterprise going into rehearsal at once.

It was an exciting, slangy, nice hard-guy script, and I learned more from the inspired direction of Howard Lindsay those four weeks than from any theatrical wizard before or since. When casting was completed, there were two old friends playing major roles: Percy Kilbride from the old stock company in Plainfield, and Sam Levene, who had appeared in *This Man's Town* with me.

"I pray you boys will be good-luck omens."

Sam said, "I'll break a matzo for success."

Percy, an economical New Englander, merely sighed through his nose.

People not of the theater like to ask, "Why don't you know if a play is good or bad *before* you go into it?" The fact is there has never been any science perfected that can tell about a play's future. I saw some of the best plays ever written die in fearful agony on opening night. I could name—but shall not—a dozen or more examples of dreadful tripe that ran and ran and ran on.

The truth is that the theater is a strange art, *not* a science, and a mystic art full of obscure ritual, strange dogma, and lived in surroundings a man wouldn't raise a pet dog in.

Yet those infected by theater, like victims of some strange dancing sickness, love it. I know that a first reading of a new play on a dirty stage, with broken chairs and the chill in the place cutting to the marrow, and the dust so thick it smells of the War of 1812, will thrill me. The old sets stacked along the wall are sleazy; the few work lights makes us all look as if painted by Van Gogh in a most yellow and mad moment. Someone has a cold, someone coughs, the half-eaten corned-beef sandwiches smear mustard on the piano. The actress's little dog whimpers under the dying palm in the brass pot. Someplace in the front of the theater the money men, the director, the producer, the various agents—the flesh peddlers—are talking in whispers; it's like the night before a desperate *putsch*.

The director stands up and says casually, "Let's just read it through. Anyone missing? Well, you on the end there, double up on the bit parts. Don't punch it, let's get with the mood. Act One. Scene One. Entrance. Speech."

A cold reading. Typed sides are held in the dim light, the star, the lead is unshaved; the heroine has her hair in curlers under a blue cap. The comic has the king of all hangovers. Someone is blowing his nose.

The reading goes on. Sometimes an actor asks *how's* to feel in *that* situation? Sometimes the director asks for a *different* approach to the line. "Don't telegraph it." Someone firmly says the author should rewrite the act here. The thin pale voice from the third-row seats is the author's; protesting to what is being done to his priceless prose at Dramatist Guild percentages. No one pays him any attention. No one ever will unless it's one of the fancy big-name authors.

Day after day, faster, more pace. Cuts, added lines from the screaming author. Cuts in his great scenes, he shouts. Now more chalk marks for places, now wardrobe fitting if needed. Talk of the scenery, talk of the play—through exits, entrances, timing. Then the dress. It couldn't be worse, all agree. Laughs in the wrong places. An hour too long. Everybody dragging tail or rushing lines. Cues misplaced, lights wrong, the bits of business lousy, the blue spot where the yellow amber should be. Too slow a curtain, too fast a tag line. The agents hint, "A dog—a turkey—not three weeks even." And that last hot moment when you stand in places, and the customers crouch out there, taking off their overshoes, waiting for you to dare to entertain them.

We opened in Asbury Park. My memories are of salt water taffy, wet bathing suits and sea food dinners. The local critics—someone said they were fishermen in the daytime—were kind with their texts, but not too enthusiastic. However, we were booked into the Biltmore Theater, New York City.

It was what Ring Lardner called the "oldest story in show business, two great acts, but *no* finish." The consensus of the reviewers agreed. But my reviews were grand. I was in. I thought the play would go. Maybe. However, Helen Menken gave a wonderful after-the-theater party at her apartment. It was gay, like the night before Waterloo, from the French side, or Noah on the Ark aware of what the weather report would be in the morning. Eloise seemed to be far away from all the excitement, staying in the background all evening.

During a lull she came over. "Paddy, you are a *big hit* tonight—everybody loves you and that's not hard."

Fake modesty aside, I seemed to be a hit. We would be on Broadway forever. But it didn't happen that way. The juvenile left the show. "I'm cast, forgive me for saying it, in a better role in a better show," he said. They closed after ten days and we were still running. We had to replace Don McDonald, and the replacement was John Cecil Holm, later to be the co-author of *Three Men on a Horse*.

Then Dorothy Stickney was taken ill and was replaced by Sylvia Field.

It wasn't all I had hoped for, this little play, but Lewis Milestone, the Hollywood director, had seen me playing a fast-talking bookmaker. This, as I've told, did help change the whole course of my life.

We moved to another theater, the Longacre; we all took a salary cut in hopes the show could survive. It couldn't.

On closing night a play script was delivered to my dressing room with a note: "*Please* read. The producer will contact you at noon tomorrow."

At the play's wake that night, in a friendly speakeasy, I told the actors all about the new play I was going to read and sincerely hoped there would be parts for everyone. We didn't cry in our beer, or laugh through our tears, but we could have as we toasted the future, hoping for the best to happen. Actors are blatant sentimentalists, I long ago decided, because otherwise they could never survive the lack of hope, food and security in their lives during their formative years.

I read the play the next day, *Overture*, written by William Bolitho, a now forgotten "literary genius" of his time, and famous as a firecracker reporter on the New York *World*, a beloved newspaper. He had died of old World War I wounds, and the production was to be produced by Bela Blau, a little gesturing, strutting Armenian. He had the greatest confidence in this posthumous play (that was one of the first to study the menace of Communist power in the world). My part was Maxim, a Communist leader, ruthless and cunning, a fanatical egotist. Colin Clive had been brought over from England where he had appeared in the surprise success, *Journey's End*. He had been a big hit in London and now he was to make his American debut. He was what the trade calls "a beautiful actor and a grand guy." (*How* can an Irishman say such things about an Englishman?) Barbara Robbins was the lone female in the cast. She was a doll. We opened in New Haven and I was thrown for a surprise loop when, after opening night Professor William Lyon Phelps asked me to address the Drama Department at Yale.

"This is a pretty far cry from the kid who was locked in the trunk in *Getting Gertie's Garter* in the Plainfield stock company," I told the press agent.

"Make it Shaw's *John Bull's Other Island* when you tell it."

We opened at the Longacre Theater. It was like a homecoming. Marxism was the intellectual fashion and the play looked at it with a cold, hard, searching eye. Marc Connolly had taken over the direction. The reviews were solidly on our side. (Maybe we lost the *Daily Worker*.) Everyone in the cast did beautifully, but most of all, the posthumous play; William Bolitho's drama was received with great respect from the critics.

As the producer sadly admitted: "A dramatic success critiquewise, a financial failure."

"A mystery to me, because it's a fine play and after the enthusiastic receptivity of the opening night and the response of the Fourth Estate, hell, I was sure we had a success on our hands."

"But Paddy boy, they aren't buying the tickets. Maybe the play was too far out."

The closing notices went up. This was to be the story almost of my entire life on Broadway. Close, damn close, but never *never* a long long run.

During the production many of us used to herd up at a place called King's, a little bistro over in Hell's Kitchen, to sip a mixture of beer and ale concocted by the Irish proprietor. All of us, Spencer Tracy, Henry O'Neill, Frank McHugh and myself would sip and sneer at Hollywood which had just swallowed up Jimmy Cagney. Around a scarred black table in the back we'd pick apart and brag a bit about our respective productions; how big the house was, how many laughs we had received, how many we had lost, how many laughs we had recovered.

One night I was delayed at the theater and the last one to get to King's. I stopped at the bar to chat with the barkeep about the ball scores before joining Spence and the boys. A tall, gaunt, ghostlike figure at my right, something out of Edgar Allan Poe, very unkempt, tapped me on the shoulder.

"Pal, you've never met me and I know you only casually from the various evenings you and the boys come in here."

"So?" I asked the ghost.

"If I had fifty bucks, I could make it to California."

My reaction was complete astonishment. "I've never seen you before in my life! I don't have fifty dollars."

"But you have friends—I haven't."

I don't know what prompted me. I said: "Wait a minute."

"I'm not going anywhere."

I went back to where the boys were seated and told them I was going to give the stranger fifty dollars, or get it from the bartender.

"I want to stake him."

They looked at me as though I were a complete idiot and Spence said, "Are you out of your shamrock-picking Irish mind? Giving *him* fifty bucks?"

I nodded and went back to the bartender. "I've got fourteen dollars in my kick, but it has to add up to fifty dollars for this rag-bag there. Give it to me and put it on my tab as a special favor."

He looked at me as though I was a complete nut.

"Well, it's no skin off my rear *if* I get it back."

He went to the till and handed me the money.

I turned—with a gesture of King Midas, I hope—and gave it to the stranger. "Good luck, mac."

"This, sir, will get me to California. I don't know if I will ever see you again, but if I *do*."

"Don't borrow from me again."

We shook hands. I returned to my pals, who greeted me like I had just returned from the loony bin.

"That moocher is an artist, a real artist," Frank McHugh said. "That dirty make-up—a real artist's job."

Spence said, "That was no make-up, that was real dirt."

I said, "We'll hear from him."

"What's his name?"

"I forgot to ask."

Fate was to bring us together again in a dramatic encounter only two years after this incident.

With *Overture* blacked out, I was actually steeped in despair. The play, a fine one, had been wonderfully received by the New York critics, I had been praised. But to what end? I began to wonder just *how* could you make it on Broadway on just talent.

It was a black week and then Philip Barry, the well-known playwright, called me at the Lambs and made an appointment for lunch. Over the cocktails he said, "I've seen *Overture* and was very much impressed with your performance. I've written a play titled *Tomorrow and Tomorrow*. Gilbert Miller will produce. Herbert Marshall and Zita Johann have been signed. But *don't* get angry—I want you for the role of the butler."

"A *butler!*"

"A good secondary part."

"No!"

"Read the play and I'll call in the evening."

I read. *Butlers* come and *butlers* go, I told myself, but *this* was the super-butler. I had Philip Barry on the phone before sundown and said yes. I called Eloise and told her the news. Off we went to St. Malachy's to say our prayers again to St. Genesius, the patron saint of actors, even for the part of a butler. "At least I'll get fitted for a new wardrobe."

During the first week of rehearsals, Father Leonard of St. Malachy's called me at the club. "Pat, tell me what time are rehearsals concluded?"

"We usually finish around five, Father—why? *You* don't need a butler?"

"No. Would you do me a favor and come over to the Actors' Chapel this evening?"

"Is it important?"

"Yes. A very good friend of mine is being converted to Catholicism and I'd like you to stand up for this neophyte."

I told him I would be happy to. That evening I walked over to Forty-ninth Street and back into the sacristy. *There sat my girl, Eloise Taylor!* I did the world's greatest double take.

She just said simply, "I've been taking instructions since the time I played in Duluth, where I decided to embrace your faith. I wanted to be very sure so I went to see Father Leonard."

I said to Father Leonard, "*This* is your friend I'm to stand up for?"

"Yes, Patrick, this is she."

Eloise looked earnestly into my face. "I wanted to become a Catholic, not only because of my love for you. I want to embrace your religion."

Father Leonard coughed politely. "My son, besides the instruction she received from the priest in Minnesota, she wanted added assurance from others who had knowledge of the faith of our fathers."

So for me it was a glorious moment to see Eloise enter the faith. In no way had she even hinted that she might ever become a convert. Actually, I must admit at that time, deeply in love, I had never asked her to become a Catholic. I would have married her if she were a cannibal! Eloise was my girl. Yet, looking at her, after all the accumulation of questions and answers that had preceded her decision, there are no words, even now, to describe my ecstatic joy as she embraced my faith.

The ritual of being received into the Church is always inspiring and rewarding. I had a lump in my throat and could barely hold back the tears. Eloise glowed with love and the awe of the moment. I took her hand and in somewhat of a daze walked out of the church with her. I blurted out the first thing that came to my mind.

"Darling, if I didn't have to rehearse tonight, I'd take you to Coney Island."

The following night we chose the bus ride rather than Coney Island, and under one of those fat Manhattan moons, we talked. This was our nightly routine—bus rides, trolley cars and ferryboats. But the plot was that always somewhere ahead was the future. Not a very original observation.

Then it happened—the phone call at the Lambs about the movie, *The Front Page*. The negotiations of a Hollywood contract with Howard Hughes. All as told in the beginning of this book.

Parting from Eloise was damp, with a tear or two—taut, and something so personal I can't put it down, even now.

I said from the moving train steps: "This is the real beginning for us."

The trip in itself was uneventful. Fields, then more deserts than I had ever heard about. But I was in a dream world the entire three thousand miles. Only my first sight of the orange groves through the train window was pretty shattering as we climbed down to the coast from San Bernardino. Now I believed orange juice really was often made from fruit.

The conductor brought on the Los Angeles papers in San Bernardino and I immediately turned to the theatrical page in the Los Angeles *Examiner*. My eyes bugged out almost on stems at a bit in Louella Parson's column:

"Howard Hughes' 'The Front Page' production gets under way tomorrow at United Artists Studio. They await the arrival of a young actor who, I must say, I have never heard of, and, I wonder if most of my readers have either. His name is Pat O'Brien. Well, we shall see what we shall see."

I laughed, feeling my throat go tight. I had a contract in my possession, so I wasn't too concerned, or was I? *We shall see what we shall see* . . .

My first sight of Los Angeles was through a deluge of rain. I expected the Ark to show up; this was the grand-daddy of all rains, but I was met at the train by a brace of United Artists representatives and rushed off to the studio.

"How do you like it, Mr. O'Brien?"

"I do." It was heartwarming to see that on the cast sheet of the production the names of some old New York pals: Frank McHugh, Walter Catlett, Freddie Howard. The list of the cast was a long one—most of whom I had never met.

As we entered the studio gates I felt, in the dismal rain, like a condemned man entering Sing Sing. I'm sure you've seen *that* scene in lots of pictures.

13

I Become a Movie Actor

A slim mop-headed young man extended his hand to me in a small office. Outside it was still raining.

"We've been waiting, Mr. O'Brien."

"Me too."

"I'm the director. Come see the set."

Lewis Milestone ("Milly" as we became better acquainted) made me feel right at home on the wonderful ratty set of a Chicago press room of the twenties in the Criminal Court building. Realism went as far as functioning spittoons. The director explained to everyone the picture would be shot at night and there would be four or five weeks' rehearsal before he turned a camera.

"I want it done as in the theater. Our New York actor is more accustomed to working at night rather than during the day and this will be the procedure."

"I don't want to put you to any bother," I said.

"Nonsense—no bother. Meet the cast."

I was introduced to Mary Brian, Edward Everett Horton and that wonderful character, Louis Wolheim, who was to play the managing editor.

Milly informed us: "Rehearsals start tomorrow. Take the rest of the day off."

I left to register at the Roosevelt Hotel. I couldn't believe any of it. I didn't have one toe dragging in reality. I was in the middle of a montage of train sounds, orange trees, studio interiors; shaking phantom hands. I don't know how I ever got to sleep. I tossed and turned like a hula dancer, wondering what it was all about.

I reported the following day shaved, pressed, jumpy, expressionless, and worried I hadn't asked for a round-trip train ticket. Rehearsals began. At one point during the reading, the director turned to me.

"Pat, when you hid the murderer Williams in the desk, did you lead him from the window or carry him all the way across the stage?"

Everyone respectfully waited for my answer.

I said simply, "Neither. Because I never did play the Hildy Johnson role."

A dramatic quiet hit the set. I felt near panic. Milly screamed, "You never *what!*" As calmly as I could, I replied: "No one ever asked me if I did the play in New York—so cool off, Milly. I played the part of Walter Burns, the managing editor, and I only played it in a stock company, in Cleveland. The only thing they asked me in New York was whether I played in *The Front Page* on the stage . . . nobody asked me *where*, or *what* role."

"So what do we do?"

"I've got a contract and it looks like you're stuck with me!"

Somebody laughed; there were some hearty chuckles. Milly sighed and put his arm around me. "Let's go, Hildy. I think we have a helluva picture going. Places! Sound, camera, *action.*"

Three weeks later tragedy struck. Louis Wolheim, playing the role of Walter Burns, was suddenly stricken and died within a week. The production was in real trouble. It was a terrible personal shock and it left a pall of gloom a foot thick on all of us. I heard again that old frightening adage, "The show must go on." It never sounded more foolish or heartless, but in time I found it does take one's mind off many of the problems of this world. The question now was, who would replace Louis Wolheim?

A stranger myself in a new land—Lord, how I missed the Lambs Club—the guys, the bar games, the old well-worn jokes—I felt lonelier with this tragedy. I was deeply grieved by Louis' death. He had shown many kindnesses to me, such thoughtfulness to a beginning film actor. He took on the role of a mentor, showing me all the different approaches in this new medium. He gave me so much counseling. I had lost a great new friend, one I had known less than a month.

The film business is practical (at times) and fortune consuming. A replacement had to be found, and at once. There began a great trek of agents—flesh peddlers, talent hagglers, theater touts—into the studio with suggestions of names to play the role of the managing editor: Richard Bennett (Joan's, Barbara's and Constance's father), Arthur Byron and many more mostly from the New York stage. No one suggested Perkins, the original actor in the part. I didn't myself dare deprive Mr. Miller of another actor.

Milly tossed a bomb on the company of waiting actors one day.

Our rehearsals had continued, functioning only in those scenes in which the managing editor was not involved.

"Carry 'round," Milly said, addressing us with a bland stare. "I have signed the actor for the role. Adolphe Menjou will play Walter Burns!"

"He looks like a repainted Rolls-Royce!"

Consternation hit the set—actors, crew, everybody. Adolphe Menjou we all knew and loved; the sleek Don Juan of films, the debonair Lothario with silk hat and tails—Menjou, the great lover in *Woman of Paris*. It couldn't be! I felt this must be one of Milly's high-geared gags. But it was true.

"Tonight's the night we meet Mr. Menjou, Wolheim's successor."

It turned out to be some night. While we were waiting, twelve of us were shooting craps, all of us down on the dirty, grimy floor of the stage.

"Oh bones," said Frank McHugh. "Come to papa."

"Roll 'em *way* out."

"Four to five he doesn't make his point."

Someone looked up and there was the debonair Mr. Menjou himself, standing with great aplomb, impeccably groomed as always.

"Hi, suckers," he said. "Save the introductions for later—I await my turn at the dice."

He knelt down (in that beautifully tailored suit with the knife-blade creases in the pants) and joined us in the wildest crap game that has been yet seen on any set. Near dawn he counted his winnings, dusted his tailoring and said: "Bring on some real plungers."

That was our introduction to Dolph. He proved a great guy, wise, alert, careful of his money—and an actor of rare, low-down power as the editor. He went on to continue a great career. Accolades were bestowed on him by the critics for his performance. I continued to hold a deep affection for him and a tremendous respect for his artistry. But in all the decades, since we only did two more pictures together, neither Dolph nor I were ever lucky enough again to have wonderful powerful roles such as we had in *The Front Page*. (He died as I was working on this chapter.)

He once said, "Great parts make great actors. Yet where is there a statue to a writer in this town?"

One evening, a strange little figure wandered onto the set, a sort of tough Jewish leprechaun. He looked a little high as he turned to me.

"Who's your agent?"

"I haven't any."

"You have one now, sweetheart—but I won't take a dime from you until I improve your present deal."

I said, "You've got yourself a deal, whoever you are."
"Selznick, Myron Selznick."

That was the birth of my actor-management deal with Selznick-Joyce. A great team of studio screen makers: Myron Selznick; driving, demoniacal, self-destructive; and Frank Joyce, shy, quiet, the proverbial smiling partner. They were the first agents to demand huge salaries for actors, the pioneers of special deals, the makers of respect for talent. They both died too early. I had for them a friendship I shall treasure throughout my life. Myron was an exciting man—and a sad one when his partner Frank Joyce died.

Myron helped me see the real Hollywood, the sunkist Pompeii, the dreamboat coast, the strange and fearful politics of the studios, the manipulating of actors, stars, publicity. Hollywood had just gone through a sound and song revolution a few years before. In 1927 the four Warner brothers, on the edge of disaster, had released a film of Al Jolson in *The Jazz Singer*. It was *not* a talking motion picture as people think, but rather a silent picture with a musical score, and few, very few, talking scenes, and Al's voice on blaring recordings. It broke the silent dam. An actor's tonsils suddenly were worth their weight in gold.

Swept away was the golden crazy era of Tom Mix and his solid silver saddle and *real* longhorn cattle horns on his Dusenberg roadster; ended was the fabulous era of drink, drugs, scandal. Spanish-castle-building ended, and everyone was aware of a depression just beyond the orange trees.

Steinbeck's Okies trekking from the horrors of the Dust Bowl were being beaten by the police just outside of the dream town; Marxism became a popular parlor game, and theaters were trying to lure customers in with Free Dishes, Bank Night, Bingo, and A Free Live Baby (suckling pigs).

I had come out to Hollywood too late to share the early marble swimming pool age, the kingdom of Mary Pickford and Douglas Fairbanks, when custard pies first flew, and Mack Sennett's Keystone Cops brought the Model T into film art. I would often see a shabby D. W. Griffith, inventor of American film storytelling, lonely in a bar hoisting a few, forgotten and neglected, and Charlie Chaplin was becoming more and more full of social protest. Saddest sight was F. Scott Fitzgerald (another Irish boy) the hero of the Jazz Age of the twenties trying to write screenplays; you would find Scotty numbly staring into the sunlight at the Garden of Allah Hotel with cronies Bob Benchley, Monty Woolley; all promising each other they would *soon* go on the wagon.

I was not a glamorous person, and it was just as well. The age of glamor was over as the nation's bread lines grew.

They were teaching Garbo to talk and John Gilbert to bark, and Louie Mayer at Metro said the famous studio chicken soup would *not* be adulterated. Bing Crosby, was, like myself, hoping to make it big in the studios and everyone in films who could was moving west: To Beverly Hills, to Westwood, Brentwood, and to the sea.

Myron Selznick refused to let me become impressed because Marion Davies held a mortgage on the Pacific. She owned the most beach front.

"All the big talk and a nickel will get you a cup of coffee."

Myron was a drinking, gambling, carousing man, burning himself up and seeming to enjoy the warmth of his own flames. Like the poet, he burned the candle at both ends to get a pretty light. I was one of his pallbearers. His eulogy was written by the Hollywood Boswell, a reformed reporter, Gene Fowler, and read by William Powell; one of the most moving I ever heard. Its substance was the sad retelling of: "There was a little boy who never grew up . . ."

Milly continued to direct *The Front Page*, and we all knew we had a new kind of picture—a bit of rugged satiric Americana. I found out how I actually got the job . . .

In the golden days, Millie told me, William Randolph Hearst, the press lord and aging playboy, used to take a group of his and Miss Davies' friends to Europe in some very fantastic caravans. A group of Hollywood people would be summoned, as if by royal command to make a trip to the Continent. They would spend a gay week or ten days in New York, all as guests of Mr. Hearst, seeing the current shows before they embarked. On one of these nights when Milly was along, Hearst had purchased a block of seats for *The Green Pastures*, playing at the Mansfield Theater. When the time came for the distribution of the tickets, there was one short. Lewis Milestone said he wouldn't mind missing the show—he would go across the street to see the play there.

"The title intrigued me, Pat—*The Up and Up*, and it starred, it said, Sylvia Field and Pat O'Brien. The role of the bookmaker, the part you played was one that you did in a staccato, rapid delivery style. One particular scene impressed me. You were on the phone taking bets and giving the history of the horses in a sustained breath, while making love and trying to explain why you were staying in the bookmaking racket."

"It wasn't easy, Millie."

"In *The Front Page* when Hildy appeals to Walter Burns to come over to the Criminal Courts because he has the murderer locked in the desk and simultaneously explains to his girl on the other phone he's going to be late on the evening of his honeymoon, I saw the same kind of scene. That is why I told Howard Hughes you would be able to play the role."

"I'll write Mr. Hearst a letter of thanks for not being able to count."

Those familiar with the plot of *The Front Page* on stage know it had an explosive curtain line, used by the editor on the phone to keep his reporter from leaving town with his girl. "The son-of-a-bitch stole my watch!"

Menjou said to Milestone, "Just seems criminal that we can't use the line in the film."

Milly answered, "Who said we weren't going to use it?"

Menjou's famous eyebrows stood at attention. "But can you use *that* epithet on the screen? The Hays Office would run us all out of the picture business! They even frown on 'bum.'"

"Look, when you pick up the phone from the desk to make the call, just before you read the s-o-b tag line, plant your fanny next to the typewriter. As you say that word, nudge the Underwood, so the carriage will release itself and ring the bell."

"You think it will work?"

"Sure. No one will hear you actually utter the word—the bell will drown it. But the audience will be fully aware that you have said it."

"You think so?"

"We'll do *take* and *retake* until the synchronization is perfect." It was. After a lot of nerve-fraying takes.

I might add here, for the historians, that the original Hildy Johnson on Broadway was played by Lee Tracy, whose stirring performance in the original production should not be forgotten. I had, in New York, told Lee of the contracts that had been offered to me by Howard Hughes.

Lee had cocked his hat and winked. "Tell them nothing, kiddo. Even if they had wanted me, I'm under a two-year contract to Jed Harris. So grab it—and I'll give you the sides of *The Front Page* that I had for the part, and some pieces of business *not* in the script."

"You sure you don't mind, Lee?"

"Look, Paddy boy—I remember with Fred Allen about California. 'It's a great place to live—if you're an orange.'"

I must have the nature of an orange, I sometimes think, until I remember the *color* was not a favorite of my grandfathers', both of whom came from Ireland wearing a bit of the popular shade of green.

The Front Page was completed and the première was held. (Wilson Mizner called a première "a bloody Indian raid in top hat and tails, and the Johnstown Flood without water.") We liked it.

14

Under the Palm Trees

The bells rang. To those people on the sound stage, it meant the scene was over—lunch time. But not for me—the bells were ringing for me and my gal! This was the day—this was the hour—the hour that would see the fulfillment of all those dreams on the boardwalk at Coney Island under that big yellow moon—the culmination of all those wonderful plans we made on the ferryboats —stargazing through murky Manhattan fog. After four years of a stormy courtship involving lovers' quarrels, misdirected letters, heartbreaking separations of miles and miles, Eloise in a stock company in Minnesota, I in a troupe in New Jersey—four years of hoping and dreaming that someday the culmination would be the right one—how could either of us visualize that California would hold the pot of gold for our particular rainbow's end?

Yes, this was the hour—two short hours given us out of a busy shooting schedule when Eloise would become Mrs. Pat. No fancy invitations to tell everyone of this great event—no grandeur—no pomp—no rice—no old shoes—no organ pealing "Here Comes the Bride"—and, our respective parents two thousand miles away! And, it was *raining*. I remembered too, in 1928, another day when I had been fired from the show, *Laugh That Off*. It was raining that day, too. And now, it was again raining as I placed the tiny ring on her finger and Monsignor Kennealy pronounced us man and wife in that dear St. Monica's Church by the sea.

And so we were married. The brief ceremony was ended and Pat O'Brien went quickly back to the studio to resume filming *The Front Page*—the picture I was in as a result of mistaken identity. But we had our own Front Page—yes, a page one—a brand new beginning that was to bring great happiness to us both and through the coming years, the maximum reward of four wonderful children, and, of course, what followed—grandchildren. *Let it rain!*

Eloise found a little apartment in Hollywood that came complete with sunlight and house dust the day after we were married. She did all the cooking and we never had tuna and rice *too* often. I bought a little yellow Ford car and said, "Think of it as Cinderella's pumpkin coach."

"I've never driven a car."

"That's a hot lot of news, honey. Neither have I, except a little old Model T I had at Asbury Park, all a foot job. I hope our instructor is patient."

He was, and so were several trees and one wall. Soon every morning Eloise would drive me to the United Artists studio for work on my first film job.

Our apartment was close to the Blessed Sacrament Church. Often we'd go there for silent prayer in the cloister of that beautiful Jesuit church.

Eloise, one evening, had just cooked a wonderful dinner, and we had eaten it. We were sitting listening to old jokes on the radio. The doorbell rang and Eloise answered it. Standing in the doorway was the tall, gaunt, somewhat emaciated Edgar Allan Poe figure who had touched me for fifty dollars in New York.

His opening remark was the laugh line, "You don't remember me, do you?"

It didn't seem true. Was it a rib?

Before I could reply, he said, "Do you mind if I come in?"

"No. We're just sitting here by ourselves."

"I'm the guy who borrowed that fifty bucks from you in that tavern in New York. You remember?"

"I remember," I said, watching my wife's eyes go out on stems.

"Unfortunately, I can't repay you in money, but if it's any compensation, I would be quite honored to paint a portrait of your wife and you."

"You a good painter?" asked Eloise.

"The world's greatest."

"You don't look like Picasso."

"That bum. I'm John Decker."

Which then didn't mean much to us. Or the world.

We acquiesced. The fifty dollars was lost. John Decker, who was to be acclaimed in California as a pal of John Barrymore, W. C. Fields and Gene Fowler, was a sort of road company Van Gogh. He could paint—when sober. Eloise's portrait hangs above the fireplace in our Brentwood home. Mine is upstairs. Decker became one of that rowdy clan of Errol Flynn, Thomas Mitchell, Milt Gross, Sadakichi Hartmann and Wilson Mizner. Stories told about them made up a modern Canterbury Tale.

According to art critics, Decker's masterpiece hangs in the lobby of Chasen's Restaurant in Beverly Hills; the subject is W. C. Fields as Queen Victoria, bonnet and all.

Southern California in those days was not a breeding place of culture—and perhaps never will be—and its native genius went in for inventing cheeseburgers, and lies about the weather. So this cluster of self-proclaimed bohemians around John Decker, some of whom had actually walked in sandals in Greenwich Village, and a few of whom had mooched drinks at the Dome in Paris, were written up in the local press as "the God-warmed artists among us." Hollywood was not yet on a cultural kick, but there were signs of it coming.

155

John Decker lived a fast, hard life, and like most of the crowd, slid away to Forest Lawn. His work is collected now mostly for the personalities of film and theater he recorded so brilliantly on canvas. His painting of John Barrymore (owned by Talullah Bankhead) is the best likeness of that unhappy actor, showing the man of the sorrowful profile; half fawn, half self-devouring demon. In his late years John was a pitiful sight around the studios; ill, rather shabby, the mind going so that his lines had to be written out on sheets of cardboard and held up for him to read out of camera range.

Milt Gross was a delightful clown; he had made a world-wide reputation with his "Nize Baby" cartoons and texts in New York. But in Hollywood his satire did not fit the banal comedy needs of the town. Often I'd see Milt, D. W. Griffith and F. Scott Fitzgerald talking together on some Beverly Hills street corner; three men for whom the word "genius" was no press agent term. Herding together, rejected by the town, living on its fringes—they who had given America a sardonic art, perfected the art of storytelling in pictures, one of them the golden boy of the Jazz Age, all looking prematurely old and fishbelly white in the merciless sun of California. I soon saw this was no place to come to create any new art forms. Rejection had led them, and others, to a bitterness and a cynicism about life that was not natural to me, and of which I wanted no part. The actors like Errol Flynn and Bogart, who were drawn to this bohemia, I think suffered from it; it cut them off from the actual reality of the coast, and a saner way of life.

So I was not a regular of this royal John Decker rat pack. They claimed to be intellectuals, and yet their conversation was often about their victories over women, and their expensive ways of life.

Spencer Tracy had gotten a contract with the old Fox Studios, but was not too happy with his scripts.

"I'm playing telephone repairmen, or the hero's best friend who always gets the Dumb Dora blonde."

Irving Thalberg, MGM's pint-sized wonderkind, realized the great potentiality in Spencer Tracy and signed him to a long-term contract. The rest is film history for three decades.

Edward Everett Horton, who played Bensinger in *The Front Page* entertained us at his beautiful estate in Encino. He had countless antiques of great value. His wonderful mother lived to be a hundred and two or four—according to how Eddie felt when he quoted her years.

Eddie himself goes on forever, touring the last twenty years with a play, *Springtime for Henry*.

One of the entertaining pixies in the picture was part of a dynasty of early Hollywood characters. Matt Moore, one of the three famous Moore brothers, played the lackadaisical reporter in *The Front Page*. He was a great tennis player and Eloise often spent afternoons at his Santa Monica court, taking instructions, and wound up swinging a mean racket.

We loved all the three Moore boys. Owen had been married to Mary Pickford. Tom in his later years was a dialogue director at Fox. They all enjoyed drinking and never denied it. They are all gone now and still remind me of James Joyce's famous line: "There is no such thing as a *small* whiskey to an Irishman."

After I finished *The Front Page* we drove down to Palm Springs in our little yellow Ford to spend a belated honeymoon. Howard Hughes' office had said: "Stay as long as you like at the Springs, and when we have an assignment, we'll advise you."

This was something new for me, drawing a salary check every week and basking in the glamorous sun in the desert. Palm Springs—Milt Gross had called it "a gentile sand box with palm trees." It was still to become fashionable. The days went on and our vacation became more and more the fulfillment of a dream. We spent days riding horseback, hiking, and in memory of those starving days of Broadway we would seek out a little church in Palm Springs to give thanks again for the fulfillment of our desires. The desert is a lonely and wonderful place and like living on the moon.

The phone rang one day.

"Mr. Hughes' office calling," said an office voice.

"Good."

"Return to Hollywood. Everything will be explained upon your arrival."

I presumed it was a new vehicle that Howard Hughes had purchased. In Hollywood, his office voice told me, "Mr. Hughes has no vehicle at that time. He has loaned you to Paramount in New York. You go back."

"What is the picture?" I inquired.

Mr. Hughes' representative, the office voice, gave me a clue. (There was *always* a representative. As a matter of fact I only saw Howard Hughes three times during the time I was in his employ.)

"Be in New York next Tuesday. You play the lead opposite Nancy Carroll in a picture called *Personal Maid*."

I thanked him and turned to relate the news to Eloise.

Howard Hughes is an enigma—I think even to himself. A hermit, as the years pass he is seen less and less. His official voices do his business. Once Jerry Wald waited three years to hear from him. At last Wald was told Mr. Hughes was on the phone. "Yes, Mr. Hughes." "Wald, what time is it?" "Eleven-twenty, Mr. Hughes." "Good. You're fired."

We had great fun in planning our trip that Mr. Hughes was paying for. We were traveling top-drawer, with our own money in the bank. We boarded the Chief the following Tuesday, feeling like Monte Cristos. I handed the porter ten dollars.

"This is our first trip back to New York, and just because we are so happy—here's another ten. We look forward to your best service!"

"And you'll get it!"

It was better going East, a success, than going West with a leaking bag of hope.

When the Chief arrived in Chicago, the porter, with moonbeaming countenance, happy with his twenty-dollar tip, bowed low and said, "Mr. O'Brien, it's been a pleasure serving you and it's been a pleasure watching you on the screen. Man, you can sure ride a horse, and I knew your pappy when he was chief of police in Frisco! Yes sir!"

My wife said, "*This* is news."

My chin dropped to half-mast. He thought I was *George* O'Brien, a popular cowboy star. I was tempted to ask for at least ten dollars back. These are the little things in an actor's life that are so cooling to his ego. Later, I met George O'Brien and told him about the incident.

"George, if anybody ever tells you you once acted a hell of a great reporter in *The Front Page*, just give him twenty bucks and say: 'Gee, thanks.'"

In New York we were nested at the St. Moritz overlooking Central Park; a beautiful suite, filled with flowers and a crisp polite note from Howard Hughes' New York representative: "Order any theater tickets you wish. Miss Nancy Carroll has requested a rewrite on the script. You will be notified when the shooting schedule begins."

Miss Carroll dallied with the script for three weeks. We did Broadway to the hilt, dining, dancing and the theater. I swiped a few nights off for big gay reunions at the Lambs with old pals. Eloise entertained all her girl friends in the plush surroundings of the St. Moritz. The boys at the Lambs mocked my attire, sun tan, tailoring, and suggested I talked now like Ronald Colman. A few drinks aided in my regaining their respect.

Finally the picture was ready to start. At the Long Island studio I met Nancy Carroll. She was a charmer, and her wide-faced candy-box beauty was the dream of millions of men. The blond boy playing the juvenile lead was called Ray Guion, but he was really Gene Raymond. Later he married Jeannette MacDonald, who (in films only) carried on a fabulous affair with Nelson Eddy—*who* today, in his sixties, is still cracking lady's hearts in concerts in Australia.

The picture had a six-week shooting schedule, and ran over into nine. In those days a director who didn't run over was suspected of not being a genius.

We went back to Hollywood on one of those old-fashioned trains, returning to California as if riding a magic carpet. Three to four days—no air-conditioning—today replaced by belching jets that hurl you along with the speed of an agent's lie. Maybe too fast.

On our trip we kept asking ourselves, "Will it last? How long can a dream sustain itself? Can we stay lucky?"

The disasters that hit most actors around us who make the grade in Hollywood is actually not often their fault. The leap from a dingy bedroom and a life of avoiding the landlady and eating out of paper bags, to a five-acre estate in over-fancy Bel Air, and your choice of cars in any color, with hothouse romances, flattery and a host of parasites as hard to shake as the mange; all these things have destroyed a lot of fine young men and women.

I like to think it was my upbringing, my faith, that kept me from destruction. As a Catholic, and a husband, I had a solid marriage, and I might say I didn't mind getting on my knees and reciting: "Hail Mary, full of grace, the Lord is with thee, blessed art thou among women, and blessed is the fruit of thy womb Jesus." I had the humility to know I was one of those living in God's mercy.

Those who lacked a faith, or whose intellectual arrogance felt no need of God—I saw them often sink into the sterile philosophy of mere negation. I don't want to sound the preacher but it was the rootless sterility of success, the lack of some balancing morality that ground out the scandals that plagued Hollywood from time to time.

They wrecked themselves in expensive cars; they doped, thrilled and were destroyed. They died young often, and left the remains of a beautiful body. It was the banal tragedy of studios needing glamor, exploiting good looks, some kooky personality; people without the hard, disciplined life of the stage years, the long way coming up the tough years, so that when success came most of us who had toured and stood in lines, and hunted jobs and worn out shoe leather, could sit back and say, "Wait a minute, nothing lasts, nothing goes on forever except the bushwah and con game of press agents." It was all hard to resist; that publicity that we read about ourselves. It was so charming and so flattering to the ego of an actor. And an actor without an ego is as rare as red hair on a Chinaman.

It was my home and my church that saved me in Hollywood. The cigars may have cost more, and the clothes fitted better, but when I was in church, I joined in the prayers, with a little private one added to the others. "Let me be as I was, *per Christum Dominum nostrum*."

If the actors suffered from the wild frenzy of the thirties, of living at the time of the turmoil of gang wars, dust bowls, depression blues, Ku Klux Klan ridings, unions battling industry in bloody reality, trouble beginning to boil in Spain, and soon to set off the evil match to the German concentration camp furnaces of millions of men, women and children, the movies we made reflected this world as melodrama and story. Long before the congressional committees collared some hoodlum and asked him questions about the interrelated crime syndicate that was the second government in America, we were exploiting, exposing the whole rat nest of gang-hard Caesars, crooked police, tainted judges and shyster lawyers. Warners' was a great mill, a kind of transmission belt between the headlines and the studio cutting rooms.

With Cagney, Eddie Robinson and Bogey, I learned to handle a machine gun, a gat, a getaway car with the best of them. I broke into love nests, exposed sellouts in high places, conned juries, traveled from Sing Sing to the Loop, down to the banana republics that were to prove the prey of Castroism years later. I knew the international mobs, spies, murderers and all the gamy or lordly headline makers, all on film. That I played a football coach, a priest now and then, a cop or just a simple man in a simple life, did not offset the violence I helped translate into entertaining motion pictures, and today these same pictures, on television, are documentaries of what we as a nation were like in our most violent moments.

Warners' in fact was so well supplied with an arsenal of deadly weapons that it had its own gun and explosive experts. I remember the story of high army brass coming out as guests of Jack Warner to watch the shooting of a gangster chase scene, machine guns firing in all directions.

An army officer asked, "How do you keep the machine guns from jamming? Ours jam all the time."

Jack Warner shrugged. "We can't have machine guns jamming. It costs time and money because it ruins a take. So I just ordered our machine shop to see our machine guns don't ever jam."

"I'd like to see that invention," said the army officer.

And the device was later used to keep the army's machine guns from jamming!

15

My Only Hollywood Première

In the old days in New York after a return trip from Coney Island with Eloise, we'd play a game, standing in the door of Eloise's Eighty-first Street apartment . . .

"Can I come in for a little while, dear?"

"All right, but not for more than fifteen minutes."

"Honey, you're *not* going to clock me?"

"You know I don't own a watch."

Returning to our Hollywood apartment I said, "How about coming in for fifteen minutes?"

"I have a watch, but come in anyway!"

What did the fabulous Mr. Hughes have in mind for me?

"A loan-out again, Mr. O'Brien, to RKO—*Consolation Marriage.*"

"Thank Mr. Hughes."

The leading lady was Irene Dunne. Myrna Loy, graduating from playing tilt-nosed Chinese maidens, was the other girl. Matt Moore and John Halliday were also in the cast. It is one of my favorite pictures, shown frequently on TV on "The Late Show," and I enjoy watching the Pat O'Brien of those days, if only to envy him his head of hair and his speed running upstairs.

Irene and I went on location in San Francisco with a full crew of technicians and all the necessary sound and camera paraphernalia. We were the only actors in the troupe to go on the trip to a city that for me bears a close resemblance to New York. It was Hollywood's golden years, and we traveled all those five hundred miles on the train, and back, just to play *one* scene.

"It's in the aquarium," said the director, "because this particular episode evolves around two sea-horse fish."

I said, "Couldn't they have built a replica of the aquarium right on the RKO stage?"

"We don't know how difficult it may have been to get sea horses. What's the matter with San Francisco?"

"Nothing. I love it."

Eloise and I were getting our first glimpse of San Francisco and the Golden Gate, and all the corny tourist fun: Chinatown, Fisherman's Wharf, boat rides on the bay, the cable cars. I remember Wilson Mizner's line, "Los Angeles is a blonde floozy —Frisco is a real lady wearing a hat only a week behind the fashion in New York."

When the picture was finished, the première of *Consolation Marriage* was held at the Carthay Circle Theater, a fake Spanish pile of moth-eaten rugs, and gold-plated flush plumbing, with all the fanfare and hocus-pocus that accompanies one of these strange native rites of showing a movie. It was thrilling and exciting for Eloise and myself. It hurt a little that the great majority of the sun-shocked onlookers, as we walked down that red carpet, didn't know who the hell I was. However, Eloise and I were walking on our own personal rainbow trail. An actor's dream had become a reality, a real première. Ken Murray was the master of ceremonies inside, and he announced, "I would like to present the various members of the fine cast to take a bow."

Each actor or actress rose from his or her seat, walked up to the rostrum, crossed to center stage, bowed and exited numb as a clam.

When I got to center stage, I grabbed the mike, like a live neck, and turned to Ken.

"I may never get this chance again. *I'm* going to talk!"

"I can't stop you."

I wish I remember what I did say. I know it wasn't the usual bit about, "I'm taking the bow not just for *me*, but for *all* those fine people behind the cameras—"

Somehow I've never had a Hollywood red-carpet première since, complete with old ladies in tennis shoes, people who come to tear your shirt, and the M.C. who doesn't remember your name and calls you "You dear *dear* people." (There was one held later out of town in South Bend, Indiana, and the picture was *The Life of Knute Rockne*, and another one in New York for *The Fighting 69th*.) It's a good thing I enjoyed that night—the gods were playing a little game with me—or just Howard Hughes. For the roof fell in. Mr. Hughes didn't pick up my option.

Eloise, however, had looked after our money. We had lived frugally, saved some, even if we had sent a hundred dollars a week back home to my parents.

Loaded with bad news, I returned to our little apartment at 1620 Franklin Avenue. "Let's get to packing, honey. We're going back to New York. Mr. Hughes dropped us."

She looked at me as if I had let a smaller boy beat me up. "Talk it over first with Frank and Myron, the agents."

"Why?"

"At that crap game, didn't Myron say: 'I don't want a quarter from you until I better your deal?'"

"He was excited. Rolling a lot of sevens."

"An agent is always working."

"If you think it's worth a try."

"It is, Pat."

I wasn't too sure myself. Hollywood promises are printed on snowflakes. I walked into the glamorous bar, rest room, poker parlor and storage vault that was Myron Selznick's office.

He looked up from a hangover. "Looks like you're going to start paying commission to me, kid."

"I hope so."

He laughed like Fu Manchu and mixed a Bromo. "Frank will take you over to MGM to meet Irving Thalberg. Submitted you for the second lead in *Flying High*. Bert Lahr's the star and this is his first picture."

Outside I clambered into Frank Joyce's Rolls-Royce. En route, Frank said, "Now, no matter what happens during the Thalberg interview, don't open your mick trap. I'll handle everything. I may drop a couple of bombs, but just stand pat! No pun."

There was no waiting in the outer office with the haggard people who looked as if they rented space there. We were ushered in immediately. I met Mr. Thalberg, and he was all that I had read about and heard about from other people—a very pale "genius" with brains, and an idea he knew what the public liked. He didn't look healthy and was too thin, but he reacted like a polo pony, whose one idea was that what it did was the only important thing in the world.

"Frank," he said, "we're definitely interested in him for the part. What's your asking price?"

Without any hesitation, Frank replied, "Seventeen-fifty a week with a three-week guarantee."

Thalberg looked at us as if we were stripping him of his diamond cuff links. "Frank! We know what Pat's contract was with Howard Hughes—seven-fifty per week. Personally, I wouldn't have been shocked if you had asked for a thousand—and might even have gone for twelve-fifty."

"No thanks."

"But you have me with a seventeen-fifty demand. This is no contest."

All I did was sit there. I could see those orange groves disappearing in the distance, could feel the heat of the hard Broadway pavements—but, as Frank had ordered, I stood pat. Very pat and sinking fast. (Thalberg inspired F. Scott Fitzgerald to use him as the hero of his unfinished novel *The Last Tycoon*. It hadn't been published at the time of our interview, and I had no idea of the complex character of this pale young man who wanted to swallow Hollywood, its stars, and as some said, most of its money.)

As we rose to make our exit, I felt sad. I shook hands with Thalberg, thanking him for his time and with a heart as heavy as Joyce's Rolls-Royce, made my way up the ornate corridor, with the man who had asked $1750 a week for me without losing any of his cigar ash.

We hadn't gone twenty-five feet along a rug at least three inches deep, when an office door opened, and a man whose Gaelic features was so obvious he could just have been coming out of the Dublin Post Office, stopped us.

He didn't address Frank, but me. "You're out of your mind, my boy. Passing up a chance like this to work for the biggest studio in the business—and Irving Thalberg. We will give you twelve-fifty a week."

I pumped up some false courage. "Talk to Mr. Joyce—my agent."

Frank said, "Why waste time? Jack Warner is waiting for us. The food's better there, too."

"All right," replied the Gaelic warrior—the studio trouble shooter, Eddie Mannix. "I tried—come on back in, the boss wants to talk to you!"

I signed for $1750 per week, with a three-week guarantee contract. The picture went over of course, to eleven weeks. Chuck Reisner, a tough nut with a shaggy laugh, directed it. He was not a college man, but said he was "right from the school of hard knocks. No degrees, just bumps." Guy Kibbee was in the picture, a pink-faced scene stealer. And a woman who played an important role in the picture plays an even fancier role today as one of the most widely read gossip columnists in the world, Hedda Hopper. Hedda had class and her success as a gossip could be her firm idea no one in town is worthy of her praise. Often, in times of scandal, I think she's right.

It was my first meeting with Bert Lahr, the best of the burlesque clowns. He became a member of our group—loosely built around Cagney, Tracy, McHugh, Allen Jenkins, Frank Morgan, Jimmy Gleason, Bob Armstrong, Lynn Overman—all of whom had a common Broadway background to cement the camaraderie that kept us together.

The gags behind the camera on the Lahr picture were often funnier than those we put on film, sad to say.

One of the character actors was to be the recipient, in the script, of a pail of oil dumped over his head. The oil was actually warm pale chocolate. They shot the scene three times. The wretched performer had to clean up after each take. With the final take, gooey chocolate streaming down his face, the actor turned to Chuck Reisner, "Just be my luck to go home tonight and find my wife has chocolate pudding for dessert!"

Bert Lahr, like most comics, was a grim worrier when not on stage. He would moan, brood, relapse, become ill, ask for medical aid, sure his scene would flop, then go on and kill us with laughter.

Comics are the saddest men I know. They never find anyone as amusing as themselves to laugh at . . . The picture had no sooner been completed than Myron had two more offers for me —from RKO and from Columbia. In our newly expanding world, we moved to Beverly Hills, and rented a home on La Peer Drive, on the "wrong" side of Santa Monica Boulevard, as I later found out. In Beverly Hills, living south of Santa Monica was like living in the slums near the slaughterhouse when I was a kid.

During the California ritual of rental negotiations, Myron received another offer from Universal.

I warned Eloise, "There's no positive assurance it will last. After all, this is all free-lance work—no long-term contract."

"You'd hate diamonds, Pat, because you can't crack them like nuts with your teeth."

"Mommy, we really don't know how long all this is going to

last. So let's have some real fun with this loot and share it with those who deserve it more than we do."

Eloise looked at me quizzically, "What?"

"Let's bring your mother and dad out from Iowa and my mother and dad out from Milwaukee. We'll arrange to have them meet in Kansas City. I'll get them a drawing room on the train and have them come out."

"The Irish sure do things in a big way."

"We've rented that big Beverly house. There's plenty of room. We'll phone them tonight."

"*If* the phone is connected."

We phoned our respective, rather amazed parents. It took them a little while to adjust to what was being offered. They said yes and we made all the arrangements. I'll never know how they recognized each other in Kansas City. They did. The two Methodists and the two Catholics got together, as if to face the West in Indian country, and came across the prairies to visit their crazy kids in Hollywood, which everyone knew was a town of pure sin, set to sporting house jazz.

We had turned in our little yellow Ford on a larger car (still a Ford). When the folks arrived, we bought another Ford. The six of us, on weekends, would go to Caliente, Arrowhead, Palm Springs, everywhere. There were no freeways, superhighways in those days, no luxury motels—and no heartbreaking traffic, or smog either.

We visited all the studios like wide-eyed tourists, met lots of the stars. We had a cook now at home and a good one, a colored girl named Bertha, who whipped up fried chicken better than the morsels I remembered eating in those old days of one-night stands in the South, when I was a mobile young actor. "*These*," I had to admit, as I looked around the crowded dining room table, "are the good old days."

During their stay, I did a picture with Carole Lombard, called *Virtue*, in which Carole played a waitress and I played a taxi driver. She was a remarkable girl, beautiful, down-to-earth and with a ready wit, and was to marry Clark Gable.

Years later, Carole and I were on a bond tour and stopped off at Albuquerque. She decided to go on to New York by plane. I chose to remain on the train. Fate plays strange tricks. Her plane crashed with the beautiful Carole aboard—dead at the height of a glorious career.

Pictures were wilder than usual at this time. Moral values were slipping down with the girls' sweaters in film scripts as the studios tried to recover from the great depression with raw sensation. Some of the films those days would still sizzle the screen today. Yet in their way they were merely earthy without being perverted, frankly violent, but in the American tradition of good clean killings, and only rats shot anybody in the back. Abnormality, dope addicts, incest, all the themes so fashionable today, were not pictured. It was shaking dance steps, sex, Charlestoning knees, bare over rolled stocking, necking in the family jalopy while sipping hooch from a flask, and the use of fists to settle most any argument. We did, in some ways, make heroes of gangsters, but the underdog always got the break among Americans, who hate regulations. And if Jimmy Cagney, George Raft or Eddie Robinson seemed to have the customers on their side, they always got killed in the end. Crime never paid in the Hays Office codes. Will Hays, the film Czar, had issued Twelve Commandments for clean film making. Frank Fay said, "Just like Hollywood, two more than even God felt the world needed."

Actually I soon found out that a few well-publicized scandals among the mink-farm set gave the whole industry a bad name it didn't deserve. Making films is very hard work, leaving little time for the leisure of seduction, or the extra energy for rape. The actor or actress has to be up at dawn, get to a studio usually miles from home, and get made up. The girls have their hair washed and set every day. The males are groomed, and if balding, get a toupee from the dry cleaner. (I always, in films, used what hair I owned except for rare character parts when I wore straggly dome-moss.)

Pictures were shot quickly, and while costs were low then, compared to today's studio-breaking blockbusters—an average feature cost two or three hundred thousand, many less. It was real money and worth about eight times what the sick dollar buys today. After ten or twelve nerve-bending takes a day—complete scenes—waiting under tension, getting rewritten lines down, and often shooting till after dark, an actor just wanted to get home from work, have a highball, some dinner, listen to Amos and Andy on the radio, and sleep.

Those few well-press-agented fools who went in for night life as a diet didn't last long. The camera shows up those hidden wrinkles, those poached-egg bags under the eyes; a thick tongue blows takes. The truth is Hollywood was, and is, a dull night town. It has never had any real original theater, no night club has survived for any long period of time. And its glamorous eating places, but for such really fine ones as Dave Chasen's, Perino's, Brown Derby, Scandia (and only one or two others) are second- and third-rate no matter what the final addition on the bill. As for the much-touted private wine cellars, I was told only the cobwebs are real. A producer, suspected of going to college, who claimed to go in for wine tasting, once introduced a bottle at his table: "A nice amusing little wine." He was nearly laughed out of town. The English given to green tea and scones played polo weekends, and held whist evenings and polished their cricket bats, but they didn't dance around Maypoles. Mostly the studio workers went home and to bed, legally.

Hollywood has always had a bad press. It encouraged the outrageous lies about itself with the idea it helped make super-gods of their stars and characters. But it all ended up leaving the impression it was inhabited by madmen, degenerates, fools, sex maniacs, and was only a short boat ride from Catalina and Sodom and Gomorrah. The impression that the "Last Night in Pompeii" was enacted at almost any swimming pool so impressed gullible tourists that they climbed private garden walls only to see their favorite star, ungirdled, unwigged, among his kids having a weiner roast bake-out, instead of cavorting with vine leaves in his hair, acting out a Babylonian orgy to the shriek of virgins and concubines bathing in pure champagne. One glamorous male symbol only leaves his house once a week, to go to Ah Fong's for a paper bag of hot Chinese goodies.

Like all actors, I was often approached with a wink and a happy leer, and asked to tell the truth, and *where* was the action and how could one get into it. They were shocked when I said Hollywood and its various outlying districts were usually a nine o'clock town.

Peyton Place, the book, if it proved more than that a badly written book about sex would sell to a certain sticky layer of our culture, also showed that *any* American small town can dredge up moral filth. Actually, there are figures to prove that the divorce rate in the picture colony is no higher than the national average. It's just that our dissolving couples get more publicity. In fact, the record for divorces and marriages, I'm ashamed to say, is not held by anyone in the film studios, but by a marrying trolley car conductor in San Francisco, known as "The Ding Dong Daddy of the K Line," who admitted to eighteen visits to the bridal suite.

For all their wise chatter and dancing steps, the natives out here were often more innocent than they would care to have anyone know. A priest once told me a story making the rounds, of the young local matron going into a church for some advice. She was asked, "Were you ever confirmed?"

"Only once, and the baby died."

16

The Police Appear

The Irish kings of old were seafaring kings, and as everyone knows *all* Irishmen are descended from kings. Using this as an excuse, and my affection for the sea, we did not renew our Beverly Hills lease. We forthwith rented a shore-moored home at Malibu Beach. It was a wild hooligan of a salty year. Every Sunday, guests, like pirate hordes in sports gear, would swarm in from all parts of the coast. They were always welcome.

"Liberty Hall."

It was a Sunday ritual at Malibu to have a huge smoky pot of beans simmering in white pork for all. Then we would grill meats, and the sound of popcorn was heard all through the day and evening. I never minded the long trip to the studio, no matter where I would be working. The trip along the great strand of Pacific Ocean front was invigorating every morning. At dusk it was a joy to return to the seaside beach house, to watch the over-dramatic sunset die a ham's death on that pearl-colored horizon.

"It brings back, Paddy, those Coney Island nights."

"Only now I am home. Not just leaving."

I worked in a picture at Paramount, *The Strange Case of Clara Deane*. There was a child actress, age four, who was a fantastic performer. Eloise and I took her under our wing. Her mother was an independent woman who sold stockings door to door, to advance her daughter's career. The kid became a star in her own right—Cora Sue Collins. Movie fans in their prime or just past will remember Cora Sue. She was the starry-eyed brat who always saved Mama's and Daddy's marriage by batting her eyelashes and weeping. Child actors are hard to work with. Their cute tricks can steal every scene. W. C. Fields, while working with Baby LeRoy, coined the classic: "People who hate dogs and children can't be all bad."

One day at Malibu we had visitors. Two uniformed police officers called on us. I was at home, not shooting a picture.

One officer said, "Mr. O'Brien, I would like you to come with us to the Santa Monica police station."

"Why?"

"A charge has been brought against you. Some felony, committed by you in the past."

Eloise burst into tears.

I said, "There's nothing for me to do but abide by the order, honey. Everything will be okay."

"But *what* have you done?"

"I've no idea what it is all about."

I arrived with my escort at the Santa Monica bastille in a damned quandary as to what the charges could possibly be. I was also infuriated at the abrupt firmness of both the officers. A desk sergeant ruffled some papers.

"Our books, Mr. O'Brien, show that in 1928 you were involved in an automobile accident in North Hollywood, in which you were the driver of a car that had struck another one on a bridge."

"This is crazy—real crazy! You say the charge is that I was in an accident in North Hollywood in 1928—right?"

The sergeant wet a finger and pointed to some paper. "Here it is—right on the books."

"That's damned interesting, Sergeant, because I didn't arrive in California until 1931. In 1928 I was either in Baltimore or Cleveland."

A cop said, "They all say that."

I said, "I didn't know how to *drive* a car at that time. Now listen, you've not only spoiled a beautiful day at the beach for me, leaving my wife in tears, but you have dishonored my family pride. Go find yourself another Pat O'Brien."

The police looked at each other, and at me, and the sergeant said, "We will try. Me mother's aunt, you know, was an O'Brien."

I congratulated him and went home, and assured Eloise I wasn't going into a chain gang.

We never heard anything more on the crime subject, but for years we would receive bills that had been run up by the other Pat O'Brien.

He might have been a Pat O'Brien who sued me in 1931 for usurping his name, and also Jimmie Fiddler and Louella Parsons for having mentioned the false Pat O'Brien in their columns, as being the untrue bearer of my birthright.

It was a ridiculous suit, and the judge threw it out of court, saying, "If I admit O'Brien is a rare Celtic name, I'd have to protect the rare Cohen or Smith or Jones from common usage."

My lawyer said, "To get even you could go suing a Pat O'Brien in New Orleans who has a bistro of the same name."

"No, they might have an honest judge down there too."

There was joy in our Malibu beach house during the 1932 Olympic Games staged in Los Angeles. My alma mater, Marquette University, sent one of the outstanding competitors, the colored boy, Ralph Metcalfe. We had him spend a day with us at the beach. In those days one didn't ask for publicity for the deed—in fact, we didn't know we were pioneering racial history. It was an

175

exciting Olympic. We didn't miss one event, day or night. The fights and wrestling were usually held in the Olympic Stadium at night. The famous Dr. O'Callaghan was representing Ireland and threw the hammer an incredible distance. One of the judges— rumor said he was from *North* Ireland—was looking the wrong way and even though the doctor's throw was the best distance, he was forced to throw again because of the wayward judge.

I shouted, "Give it a toss again, O'Callaghan."

O'Callaghan returned to the circle and in fury, spit on his hands and threw that hammer damned near out of the stadium, breaking all existing world's records.

I shouted, "Judge, did you see *that* one?"

Eloise pulled on my jacket. "You're cheering for the Americans, remember."

"Just a little side bet."

The best thing about sport, as you grow older; you don't have to take part. But I'm a grand watcher to make up for it. Today I exercise by swimming in our pool, and cutting the ends off my cigars myself.

Myron Selznick called me. "Universal is making a picture called *Airmail*, and the director, John Ford, wants you to test for one of the top roles."

"Why the hell, Myron, should I make a test? He knows my work. He's seen some of the pictures I've made."

Myron hissed softly, "You're not *that* big yet, you crazy harp! I can count all the pictures you've made to date on my two hands."

"An actor has his pride."

"Don't give me that. This director happens to be one guy that people in this business would be happy just to shake his hand."

"If you say so, Myron."

"Go on out there and make that test, and don't give me any more of that actor's pride crap. There is no market for it. I sell meat on the hoof—not pride."

"Okay, Myron, I said I'm on my way."

I made the test and got the part. John Ford told me later, "Pat, I just did the test to try your reaction. I figured you'd protest just the way Myron said you did."

One incident that occurred during the filming appeared in Ripley's "Believe It or Not" column.

The locale was the arid Alhambra Airport. In the story I was supposed to steal a plane, taking it off the ground to go in search of a character, played by Ralph Bellamy, who was reported lost in a mountain area. An actor, playing a searcher, was speaking over the radio before a crowd of spectators. "It's utterly impossible to make a landing for a possible rescue." At the conclusion of this speech, I walked to the microphone and made a most obscene raspberry into the mike (a popular form of dialogue in movies then—later it was barred by the Breen Office as indecent, as was a married couple in one bed). I then turned and jumped into a plane. In a film situation such as this, the camera would cut away as soon as I jumped into the plane. Then when the plane was airborne with a real pilot, cut back and photograph it in flight. Later in the studio, I would do the cockpit interior scenes.

Paul Mantz, a stunt flier of great daring, was doing all the trick flying. Before we started the scene, John Ford was chewing at his handkerchief (a very characteristic gesture of his) he sort of mumbled: "Pat, it would be great if you took the plane off the ground yourself."

I snorted. "Jack are you out of your Gaelic mind? I've never even *been* in a plane—let alone flown one of those flying coffins."

Mantz said quietly, "There is an easy solution, Mr. Ford. It's a two-cockpit plane, fore and aft. Let Pat take it off the ground."

"What!"

"I'll be hidden face down on the floor. Pat can give it the gun."

"No!"

"Once off the ground, I'll take over the controls."

Ford looked at me. "And Mantz isn't even Irish."

A great silence. A crowd of spectators, extras and crew, were all within hearing distance. With a too casual tone I said, "If Paul says it can be done, I'll *do* it."

We went into action. The cameras rolled. The scene progressed. I jumped into the plane as Paul had instructed me. I gave it the gun. We actually took off!

I've had a lot of scares in my life, but this one topped them all. Once aloft, I sighed and looked around. It was pretty exciting. But what if Paul Mantz had had a stroke while lying on his face on the floor?

It was a cheerful thought. I remembered the corny line that became popular in the two film versions of the World War I flying picture, *Dawn Patrol*. "You can't send up boys in planes like that. It's murder!" How true.

Cruising around, I decided once a hero was just enough. We landed in the camera area to applause. I was rather proud of myself, and still scared. Jack Ford, still chewing on his handkerchief came over. "Pat, we'd better do it again, a protection shot."

I said, stiff upper lip, "If you say so, sir."

I had seen the *Dawn Patrol* myself a few times. So away we went.

Paul did some amazing crazy flying in that picture. On location in Bishop, California, he flew a plane right through a hangar, one of the most daring feats I've ever seen. (I admitted, when the picture was released, "Jack Ford wouldn't let *me* fly that shot.")

I love Jack Ford. Most critics think he's the tops of all American directors. I had the good fortune to work for him a few years later in *The Last Hurrah*, and also the first stage production he ever directed, *What Price Glory?* Often I see *Airmail* on the "Late Late Show" on television, and I say to myself when I see that takeoff, "You were a crazy kid."

There was an amusing sidelight to my first "solo." The young colored boy working for us saw me jump into that plane and soar aloft. He said he kept his eyes skyward and murmured, "Oh, oh! There goes my job!"

He couldn't wait to tell Eloise when we arrived home that

evening. Eloise's only remark was, "You don't change—you're still a crazy Irishman. I think we both owe a couple of novenas to the good Lord."

"I've been thinking the same thing."

I went into a film at Columbia, *American Madness*, with Walter Huston and Constance Cummings. Frank Capra directed. Unlike Ford, he left the scene after great success.

John Ford was an amazing personality, and it has grown with the years. He has a good Irish name, O'Fiernan, but he picked John Ford because it had nothing special about it. He first excited the film world when a little picture he directed—the front office wasn't expecting much—done on the back lot at RKO caused a sensation. *The Informer* made him famous overnight. He had been directing low-budget pictures when he got together with Dudley Nichols, the writer, and they began to scheme about this story of the Irish Trouble. The cast was then practically unknown. Wally Ford, my old pal, working his way up from the flip-fast program pictures, and Victor McLaglen, a big buster of a boyo, who had a wild life all over the world, but was not then rated as much of an actor.

Ford made a masterpiece of *The Informer* and won Victor an Academy Oscar. There was a great deal of gossip that Jack got Victor drunk to play his big confession scene in utter believable confusion.

Jack's pictures were all action pictures, beautifully mounted and photographed, and composed of vital living material. *Lost Patrol*, *Long Voyage Home*, *How Green Was my Valley*, *Stage Coach* (the best Western ever made, it pushed John Wayne to stardom), all are film classics.

His pictures always had taste, reality, a feeling for the common man, for the sad plight of those who live by their muscles, and face a world hostile and tragic. Jack fought to make his pictures his own way.

In his later years he remained a fine picture maker, not given to much use of dialogue on the screen. The great themes he needed were hard to find, the powerful sagas he could do best didn't come along. Dudley Nichols died, the writer he worked with best. But Ford has gone on, still making films, resting a bit on his reputation, but always, to me, the master. His staying power is remarkable. He has outlived so-called younger geniuses. A John Ford picture reveals in every scene his vision and skill.

At Columbia studios, to do *American Madness,* my agent took me aside.

Myron said, "Harry Cohn is boss, and he's a roughneck. Was a trolley car conductor in Denver. Started his studio on shaved nickels."

"He really that mean?"

"A monster—and he's proud of it."

I was warned about the big tycoon who ran the studio like a slave camp. My first meeting with Harry Cohn went off well. As the head of Columbia Studios he was disliked by actors and producers alike. He was more than okay with me. I suppose I spoke his mug's language when I had to. I never took any of his verbal guff, and he, in turn, apparently admired the fact that I never figured him as any sainted tin god of a tycoon. I made many pictures for Harry Cohn and our relationship was always the same; wary but friendly. His language was not usually the most elevating. He was a hard taskmaster. And to weaklings he was a sadist.

I used to remind him of the times when he was a song plugger. He seemed to enjoy talking about those old days. I think he was lonely, bored and indifferent to his wealth.

Years later, during the filming of *The Last Hurrah,* Harry Cohn died. I felt sad at his passing. In charity I can only quote some lines: "The evil that men do lives after them—the good is oft interred with their bones."

I've long observed the hard, usually illiterate men who made the Hollywood film industry. For over three decades, I've been on the scene. The opinions I've formed of them is that of a group of men, mostly from slum backgrounds, and dismal sweated trades who saw an opening in a despised new entertainment form (actors refused to use their own names in the early flickers), men who began to see its possibilities, and who were the first. They hung on with tooth and nail once they had brought it to a kind of strange growth. They were Jews, Greeks, Irish, Swedes, and here and there a Dixiecrat.

They were almost all uneducated, with a kind of splendid cunning and a feeling that every means could justify every end. They had great skill in weaving together simple stories, pretty faces, passions, popular ideas, glamorous clothes, legendary daring deeds, into the great dreams that the world wanted. Images as things to take people away from their everyday dismal and dull lives. Americans know how to put the product on the assembly line.

The men who owned or controlled the studios, who hired the talent who sold the pictures, were kings by right of conquest and salesmanship, kings by right of ownership. The greatest stars were often slaves to unfair contracts. The less pleasant details of the private lives of these celluloid czars, who had come from ped-dlers' pack to Rolls-Royces in one generation, made often un-savory reading.

Yet their often directionless energies kept the studios open for fifty years.

I admired them for their drive, their ability to make any pictures at all. Studios were so madly involved in private feuds, politics, stock fights, bank credits, sons-in-laws and cousins, temperaments, and the whims of imported hams and sneering directors from UFA, that only the manager of an insane asylum could have brought anything at all to a finish as a salable product. If millions were wasted, if men and women and great talents were destroyed, there were great films made; actors performed for good pay; the world shouted for more and more of the dream drug as made in Hollywood. It was pleasant, and fairly harmless.

They had little taste, but for that which they could buy. They showed no mercy when their power was threatened. They ruled like a Khan of Asia, and had their slave girls and concubines, as was only to be expected. It did not decrease their loneliness, their unhappiness, their tics and ulcers.

They were not, with only one or two exceptions, pure monsters. They had power, and as the historian had said, "All power corrupts, absolute power corrupts absolutely." The end result was a stone-hard, coagulated, rigid series of values and procedures that merged into what was known as Hollywood. (Hollywood doesn't exist—never did—there is no such post office address.) It lost touch with reality, with the world and became, as Milt Gross said: "Instant Pompeii."

When time came for change, picture makers could not bend, could not move with the times. The Warner brothers saved the industry once with talking films. Cinerama, wide-screen, color were only shots in the arm of a failing corpse. There was no new vitality that could break the system, the stranglehold of old men and their relatives on the industry. They failed to see the challenge of television, the deadly power of the agents; new wolves in the fold. They ignored the fact that in an atomic, often godless world, the old pat formulas of boy meets girl, dogs with IQs, could not compete with the motion pictures made abroad that used the new realism, the new shocks, a more direct approach to men and women, to the problems and laments of the expanding jet-age world.

The colors of their world died, but they did not retreat. They still paid themselves their over bloated salaries, bonuses, expense accounts; they went on hurling millions upon millions of stockholders money into films called blockbusters, few of which brought back any of their costs. There was no removing the old men in command. Only death could clear them from their solid gold caves, only the grave would make way for the waiting young, the talented, the believers in life, and the job of creation.

Many think the time of a new age on film is at hand. So, with some respect to some of the old men of the tribe who made and destroyed a great industry, I pass on to my own story again; they were human as I saw them—perhaps too, too human and given to guile. Their motto was, "What's in it for me?" Their flower was the six-petaled ulcer in full glowing colors.

Myron scoured the free-lance field for me with a frenzy. I did a strange independent production opposite Bette Davis. Neither Bette nor myself make reference to this epic with any great affection. I made a new friend in Bette. She was vital, high-strung, biting, so alive, so able to eat her way into a part. Soon after my first picture under the Warner Brothers banner, I would be playing opposite Bette Davis in *The Bureau of Missing Persons*.

Myron had gotten me the Warner contract. He was at the height of his power as a talent agent. He almost singlehanded had made the talent agent the most powerful figure in the film industry. Before Myron there were few agents; mostly high-nosed outfits whose members wore spats, or were hole-in-the-wall hungry types more deadly than a sting from a rattlesnake. The studios liked to find their own stars, and sign them to contracts that, while rewarding, were as undemocratic as a slave on the block in the Old South.

Myron first saw the value of controlling box office names, and the fact that the star usually had more drawing power than the picture. He began to collect actors, directors, writers; began to put on the screws with the studios for bigger wages, better terms. They screamed, but he had the names that brought in the customers by the millions to the box office, that never stopped, in those days, laying the golden egg.

In time, combines of agents—MCA, the Morris office, and others, more stable but not as human or as brilliant as Myron, took over. The decline in creative quality, in part, has been blamed on the big agents, the flesh peddlers. They became the other side of the shield of the old studio bosses, bearing the same features— as powerful, as chilling as the forces they sold the talent to. Some like MCA had combined the function of being agents with being studio owners, TV-series makers, bankers, backers and spinners of the wheels that turn Hollywood. Power and more power fell into their hands.

Myron, whose days were numbered, but in bright colors, had only a glimpse of the strange things he as a Frankenstein had spawned.

17

Man and God in Filmland

A friend of Lewis Milestone was the tramp author, then very famous, Jim Tully. His fame was fleeting but the man was real. A hard Irish potato of a little man, with a rough carved weather-beaten face, curly uncut red hair, he knew he was a kind of folk hero. He drank everything, he read everything. He used to visit the set, and once said to me, "Some day, Paddy, I'm going to write a story for you, and it will be part of my own limping, shouting life."

After I finished the picture with Bette Davis, Tully submitted a script to the Selznick office and said: "Let Paddy read it." Universal bought the story and I played it—*Laughter in Hell*, a story of the dispossessed, the discarded. Jim was a great little guy and spent a lot of time with us on the set during the shooting of his story.

He met Mom and Dad on one of their later visits to California, and wrote an article using my mother as the main character in the story. He called her his "Irish Dream Girl" and Mom, who knew the right answer said, "He was a dear broth of a boy." I am the happy possessor of many of Jim Tully's works, most of them autographed. He was an intriguing writer, self-educated, and perhaps he played his one note too long, but he played it well. Some writers, like some actors for no known reason fade too quickly and are forgotten. Jim was one of them—the hobo who went a little mad with love of words.

Soon another turning point in my celluloid career appeared. Hal Wallis had succeeded Darryl Zanuck as the head man at Warner Brothers. He negotiated a term deal through Myron for me to work at the studio. Myron, as always, drove a hard bargain. My first production there, as I have said, was the *Bureau of Missing Persons* with Bette Davis.

She was not yet a star—young, slim, blond, but already very sure of herself and just developing that strutting pop-eyed drive that made her more than a great star—she was an actress.

For me began an exciting era—new friends, new directors, the eventual teaming up of Jimmy Cagney and myself as co-stars in a lot of hard-paced, punch-packed pictures.

One had to be young in those days—the stories usually came right off the front pages, and were violent and action-packed. "The gat and gag epics," Jimmy called them.

With the Warners' deal signed, and a guarantee of three years work, life was really expanding for us. Now we could have the folks visit us twice a year. Mother and Dad had an apartment where they lived whenever they came to the Coast. They seemed happier by themselves, visiting us whenever they wanted, and spending weekends with us. The trips became so regular that I finally said to Dad, "Talk to Mother to see if you can't come out to California and make it your permanent home. You seem to love it very much out here."

"Oh we do, Pat—but it's *so* sunny all the time."

In Milwaukee, when Mom would get lonely, she would call the

local Warner Brothers office downtown. They would arrange for her to be picked up and driven down to the Warner projection room. She would sit and view one of my pictures and this she would constitute as "a great visit with my boy."

Dad passed on to Mom my desire they come to California to make it their home.

"It's a difficult decision for me to make," she said, "to take up and leave the place where you spent all those memorable years. Leave all of those wonderful old friends of ours, leave sisters and brothers—well, now. It takes a bit of thinking out."

Soon Mom thought it out and they left Milwaukee for good. It was no easy departure—loud and weepy farewells with all their old friends and Mom's kinfolk.

Dad said, "We move because the years are crowding us, and we want to spend the last of them with our boy and his wife in California."

Eloise and I met them at the Santa Fe station.

They asked, "Where will we stay? The same little apartment we loved?"

"We'll work out something."

Eloise said, "First we want you to meet some new friends of ours. We think you'll love them."

We stopped at a little cottage on Cherokee Boulevard, just a block from the Blessed Sacrament Church. Inside, the house had been beautifully decorated, and there were flowers everywhere.

Mom said, "*Where* are the people we are to meet?"

"Look in the mirror, Mom."

Reaching into my pocket, I handed Dad the deed. "This is *your* home. Remember when I was a little kid? I promised you that one day I would buy you your own home. Here it is."

Naturally we all sat on the porch and had a good old Irish cry. In a few minutes, Mom recovered, and was off to church a block away, "to give thanks."

I can still see the expression on their faces as they were staring at the deed, trying hard to realize, after all the years, they had a home of their own, "in all that sunlight."

Warner Brothers was a busy place. The world of films was enjoying great success; picture houses were crowded as never before or since. I was getting a fat check each week from the Brothers Warner. There was only one thing to do. We did it. We brought out Eloise's mother and dad from Des Moines. They arrived and after some scouting around, Mother and Dad Taylor decided they loved the country, and we bought them a home in San Bernardino up the coast.

I record these events to please myself—they have no drama for the reader, who didn't know these people.

Dad was still a roaring sports fan, and we went to all the events—fights, baseball, and football games. He was also still a shark at playing billiards, at the Masquers Club. He was as adept with the stick as any of the younger so-called champions of the art. It kept him in good cigars—"and keeps the old eye in trim."

One of the football seasons, I sat on the dais at the U.S.C. banquet, the night before the Notre Dame game. There was much talk, loud speeches, wild rantings of the alumni, exaggerated predictions of the results of the forthcoming game. After the banquet, Dr. Rufus von Kleinsmid, president of the California college, who looked like a Dutch pixy turned Santa's helper, said to me, "You're attending the game tomorrow, Patrick?"

"Doctor, I imagine I am."

"Who will be attending with you?" He had a formal prose style.

"My wife, Mom and Dad."

"Would you all be guests in my box tomorrow?"

He had me there. A brief silence—certainly he knew where my heart—Irish and Catholic—was as far as the contestants were concerned. But I answered that of course, we would be honored. The next day we all sat numbly polite, with the doctor and his wife. Dad, Eloise and I were seated in the three front chairs, and the doctor and his wife and Mom, directly in back of us. There were 102,000 people in the Coliseum that day, and it was anybody's ball game. There were not too many Notre Dame rooters on our side of the field. The kickoff, two or three plays, Notre

Dame scored! Screaming pandemonium broke out on the opposite side of the field. I sat blandly with the president of U.S.C., trying to subdue my elation over the first touchdown by Notre Dame. There was a brief pause, a tap on my shoulder, and the doctor whispered in my ear, "It's quite all right, my boy. You may cheer if you like."

"Thank you, sir."

I let out a banshee of a cry in victory and pride.

The Irish failed to convert. The score stood 6–0 in favor of Notre Dame. Again the kickoff, and in less than three plays, U.S.C. scored and the home team side of the field threw their show cards into the air, forgetting all about their arduous rehearsals of the week before and what the cards were to have spelled out during the half. The score was now 6–6. A grim silence fell over the sunny Coliseum. The S.C. kicker dropped back to convert the extra point. Another tap on my shoulder and Dr. von Kleinsmid whispered, "And now, Patrick, say an Ave for me, please."

I refrained, and U.S.C. also failed to convert, and the score still stood 6–6. The final score was 13–13.

Mom said on the way home, "U.S.C. plays fine ball, for Protestants."

On one night previous to a Notre Dame game, Archbishop Cantwell of Southern California was introduced from the dais at the U.S.C. banquet. His acknowledgment of the introduction was crisp: "Gentlemen, this will probably sound like heresy to many of my Catholic fold, but I am a Californian and tomorrow I am rooting for U.S.C. to beat Notre Dame!" They cheered him for at least ten minutes.

When I rose to say a few words they were, "The last time U.S.C. beat Notre Dame, I'm sure there was a definite reason. My theory is the Notre Dame boys couldn't hear the signals due to the pious rattling of the beads in the stands." My closing was, "Of course, the most graphic definition of an atheist is one who goes to see Southern Methodist play Notre Dame, and doesn't give a damn which side wins."

I suppose the tolerance of Hollywood is best expressed by the burial of Mark Hellinger, the producer, one of the brightest of men who first filmed Hemingway (*The Killers*). A drinker, hard liver, always in dark blue shirts, a white tie, a bullet-proof Caddy, he wore out before fifty. A Jew, he was buried as a Protestant, with a Catholic medal around his neck.

There was an itch in me every time I saw a pretty house set in a green salad of its own lawn, or I passed a FOR SALE sign. I knew the fearful moment was coming on me, the most dangerous to a man next to romantic passion. I wanted to become a house owner. Put down roots where the Spanish, the Indians, the mission fathers, the land grabbers, town boosters had walked. Few of us escape this disease.

Living took on strange shapes in California. Up the coast a poet, Robinson Jeffers, had built himself a house on the Pacific out of huge crude boulders, ugly, drab, but strong. Several medieval castles stood unfinished among the palms in the Hollywood hills, with dry moats and dungeons filled with old coke bottles left by courting couples. Death Valley Scottie, an eccentric desert rat, but a rich rat, had built himself a French palace on Sunset Boulevard, and rumors were he cooked campfire beans in the imported Italian marble fireplace. On Wilshire Boulevard an Indian chief, who had become a millionaire from his Oklahoma tribal lands sprouting oil, lived with his blond wife in a huge oversized Cape Cod Colonial. The only odd thing about the chief was he liked to direct traffic an hour or so a day, standing regal, dark-skinned, white-gloved, moving the traffic north or south east or west. No one seemed to mind. Pickfair (English Tudor mostly) was the Buckingham Palace of Hollywood, where Mary Pickford and Douglas Fairbanks had ruled the town. And Falcon's Lair, built by Valentino, in style labeled Wedding-Cake Arabian, was on the market. But I didn't buy it. I wasn't *that* showy.

The prevailing style of the period was Christopher-Columbus

Opera-Carmen Spanish, with rough smallpoxed finished stucco sides, three-foot-thick walls, red clay tile roofs, and much rusting iron grill work and exposed rafters. No more solid houses were ever built in California; later as they slipped out of fashion, the grill work was cut away, the rafters whitewashed, and they were breathlessly retitled by real estate agents as Italian Villa. Modern piano box stuff was rare. Josef Von Sternberg (said to have been born Joe Stein in Brooklyn), discoverer of Marlene Dietrich, had a modern bookend of a house, shaped like a truss. And Frank Lloyd Wright had done a few of his strange best for the disturbed rich. One lady called him during a rainstorm to say she was sitting in her chair under a leak in the new roof: "What shall I do?" Mr. Wright said, "Move your chair."

"Eloise," I said one morning, "it's about time we found and bought a house of our own."

"What do you have in mind. A Dublin castle?"

"Going with our love of the sea, darling, we want to live as close to the Pacific as possible.

"Not easy. The best Malibu homes are only leased, and the price sky high. We can't take a chance at those prices."

By casual accident (or call it luck) we discovered a little place in Brentwood. Two sun-tanned spinster gals, the owners, were desirous of selling, wanting as they said "to make a cash deal."

We bought the place—it was on Marlboro, a Spanish grandee-styled home with a small pool—basically very cozy for us. I enjoyed hanging the pictures we had gathered through the years on the walls of the den. With each nail I drove, I said, "This place belongs to *us!*"

At the studio I was assigned to a picture, *Personality Kid*. I played the title role, a prize fighter. Jack Warner said, "I give you three weeks (with pay) in which to get into condition for the role of the ring warrior."

"I can *act* like a boxer Mr. Warner."

Mushy Callahan, the studio trainer, and Jackie Fields, the ex-welterweight champion, said I had to "*fight* like one." They accompanied Eloise and myself to Arrowhead high in the mountains. I went through the road work and various athletic ideas that Jackie gave me. The really tough part was at night. They and Eloise dined like epicures. I was on a diet of boiled eggs and toast.

"I'm hungry."

"Now, champ, that goes along with the fighter's prescribed training."

"Look, the picture is no Academy Award contender."

Eloise said, "Stop talking. It makes you hungrier."

The Personality Kid was sort of Cassius Clay character who would enter the ring wearing a derby hat and do a few gay dance steps around the squared circle. He was a complete extrovert, and had never been a winner in the Golden Gloves. My conditioning was necessary for the part because I had to look the role when I stepped into the ring.

Back at the studio I felt too weak from hunger to climb into the ring. "Mushy, I need a steak."

"Only if you get hit in the eye. Steak is great for a black eye."

My stomach protested, loud and clear.

Mushy Callahan had been the junior lightweight champion of the world, and as I've said, Jackie Fields, the welterweight champion. I fought them *both* in the picture. Actually everything worked out very creditably and looked great on the screen. Of course, they didn't open up on me. Another fighter in the picture had never been a champion and I think he resented it and felt my fights were fixed. When the time came for us to play the big scene, we entered the ring and were given our instructions by the referee. Both Mushy and Jackie had rehearsed this block of scar tissue, and taught him how to pull punches so he wouldn't actually hit me. We went over and over the scene before the cameras turned. Then the bell rang and the director called "This is it!" At the sound of the gong, my punchy opponent bounced out of his corner like a fire horse smelling smoke. I knew instantly, as I saw him prance around the ring, sniff and beat his gloves together, that *this* was to be a fight for survival. I got on my bicycle and kept moving—that glint in his punch-crazy eye was for real. The cameras kept grinding and I knew the only way I could stop this guy would be to shoot him—and this wasn't a Western.

I managed in the clinches to whisper, "Take it easy, fella, you're fighting in a *movie*—not Madison Square Garden."

"Huh? Huh?"

His reply was that crazed look in those glazed eyes. I backed away on the bicycle as fast as I could back pedal. Then I went into another clinch.

"Look fella, it's a game, see? A game."

The action in the scene called for me to see a good-looking girl sitting at ringside, turn to her, wink at her and in lip signals give her my phone number.

I did it just as we had rehearsed. I turned, winked at her—but Old Punchy didn't adhere to the rehearsal. He began to throw a punch clear from the floor—it hit, and for me the sky caved in! He hung one on my chin and I thought the studio had fallen on me. They could have counted to one hundred over me. Somewhere, far away, I vaguely heard the director yell, "Cut. It's great—print it." I returned from out of space. They were throwing water in my face and massaging my jaw.

"Beautiful," said the director. "We don't have to do that one over again."

"Good," I whispered.

Old Punchy stood over me and said, "Did I hoit much? Huh?"

I replied weakly, "I'm not sure. I think you only broke my jaw!"

"Hell, I used to hit dames harder than that."

"*Some* dames," I said, and fell back.

People seeing the picture would comment to me: "Gee that was a great fake fall you took, Pat."

Mushy said, after X rays, "See your jaw wasn't broken. You only have a *slight* fracture."

"Would you like one?"

I ate my meals through a straw for days after the incident.

Because of the violent stories we filmed, this was only one of many fights that used to occur during the making of films at Warner Brothers. There were few pictures that I did not have some hard brawls—not always played in the prize ring. Jimmy Cagney and I battled our way through a raft of film epics, and never got a scratch in any of the encounters.

Not all the Warners' Stock Company actors in those days were fighters. Under contract were Bogart, Joan Blondell, Glenda Farrell, Frank McHugh, Allen Jenkins, Guy Kibbee, Kay Francis, Dick Powell, Joe E. Brown, Errol Flynn, John Garfield, George Brent, Wayne Morris, Edward G. Robinson, Paul Muni, Ann Sheridan. We worked hard. The pictures were entertaining, even if not world-shaking. They served no cause but Jack and Harry Warner.

It was Harry Warner who had first said: "No message in my pictures, please. If I want to send a message, I use Western Union."

Most people have the idea that seeing a motion picture being shot should be very exciting. Actually the filming of a movie is rather dull to watch. Time passes on leaden feet. Most of the time is spent waiting for an actual scene to be shot. What you see in your theater (as you munch your popcorn) as a moving dramatic bit of action, is really made up of very short strips of film that take about twenty seconds, and rarely more than a minute or so to photograph. A film editor pastes together all these short ends; your eye and mind fool you into thinking that you are seeing a continued action.

So, on set, the actor waits, sits, reads, picks a horse to bet on, gossips, scratches *and* waits. Lionel Barrymore used to knit; Red Skelton painted clowns. Each scene to go on a strip of film has to be lit, composed and photographed as a moving shot, a pan shot, a close shot, tight two shot, long shot, or long *long* shot. Director, cameraman, set designer, lighting expert and film editor stand around and decide. Then the carpenters, prop men, wild wall riggers and light handlers set up for the shot. Each director has his own style. Ernst Lubitsch's was simple. "If the people don't move, the camera does."

I, the actor, having read the script, and been told what will be shot that day—they hope—am ready for the run-through. A picture is never shot in proper order, as it will be shown. The actor may be doing a scene from the end of the picture first. Often he has very little real idea of who he is and what he is doing. Some actors read *only* their own part. The classic story is of George Bernard Shaw writing the play *Pygmalion* for Mrs. Pat Campbell to star as Eliza Doolittle, (you may remember the musical version, *My Fair Lady*). He gave her the script to read overnight, and called her the next morning, very excited, knowing he had written a masterpiece. "Well *how* do you like *my* play?" Mrs. Campbell merely answered, "Where the hell am I between pages 72 and 81?"

When the director yells *"Camera! Action!"* the actor goes through his part. It is called Take One. Some directors have been known to film forty takes before they yell, *"Print it."* By Take Ten an actor has usually given his all to the scene. But he keeps trying. When a take has hundreds of extras and the action is very involved, the director tries to keep it down to one master take, with several cameras working at once.

The best story of a master snafu on such a big take I ever heard happened when Cecil B. DeMille was making his final *Ten Commandments*. He was shooting the climax of the Jews escaping the Egyptian army, crossing the Red Sea. Thousands of extras, brought to the burning desert, were on hand; costumed stunt men, chariots, horses, were set in place across miles of raw desert. The master cameraman, on top of a mountain, controlled the battery of focused cameras. DeMille, using a loudspeaker system ordered the scene to begin, and gave the cue to the cameras to start—over the loud outcry of actors moving into action. Nearly a million dollars worth of people, animals, location trip costumes and placement agony were soon in action. Horses reared, fugitives ran, Egyptians roared, and a great dust cloud arose. DeMille danced with delight at the success of the thing. Pleased, he rushed toward the master cameraman, shouting: "Well?" The master cameraman, who had heard no command to start the cameras over the roar of the mob, made a circle of thumb and first finger and shouted back, "Any time you're ready, Mr. DeMille."

Yet a motion picture is only part reality, part craft, part of the scientific marvel of lens, and sound on the edge of film, the deceptive art of cutting and editing, of adding music, or performing miracles by back-projection of a living London or Tokyo behind actors in a Hollywood studio. What a picture becomes is something they cannot write into it. It comes from an extra dimension, deep inside the people who make it: Cagney's dancing in *Yankee Doodle Dandy*, Spencer Tracy simply smiling and shaking his head, yet making every thought in his mind clear to us; Mae West's first hip wiggle, W. C. Field's undelivered billiard shot as he explains why he is called Honest John; Garbo's pout; Liz Taylor's eyes; Mickey Rooney at any age; all bringing personal voltage into a scene.

So the actor sits waiting, on a canvas chair (with his name spelled wrong on it if he's lucky enough to have a chair) knowing the machines and the lights are the smallest part of it. Aware that a man called a director can inspire him, or let him alone, can help him, or spoil his best work.

One outdoor roughneck of a director, as a favor, once used a society woman as a nurse in a film. When she asked what she had to do, he said, "Honey, just screw around with the bottles."

John Ford, the old master, is the orderly type. Working for him is like being part of a ballet. He hardly ever moves the camera, but composes his shots like a master painter, a Rembrandt or Degas. The actor becomes part of the scene. Ford lets the action swirl past his lens. But the reality of his seamen, miners, dust-bowlers, horse soldiers, or Western heroes, when he is at his best, is a literature that the screen rarely gets. Working for him one feels a special pride. Lewis Milestone is a bouncing camera mover. For him the seeing eye is all. He stands the camera on its head, rolls it, rushes it, brings it in on the run. The actors are part of the scenery, and they must fight to survive, come alive while he catches them on the run. Neither men are static directors. They don't care for too much talk in their scripts; or stage business over meaningless chatter.

Women's pictures (so-called) are talky pictures. Their use of the cigarette and the telephone break the talk, talk, talk of soap-opera storytelling. John Barrymore once said, "Have you ever thought what the stage and the movies would be like without the telephone and cigarette to break the monotony? Why, I can light a cigarette in twenty different ways, and smoke it in sixteen positions. Frankly, for me, it has saved many a lousy picture; where the tobacco was better than the dialogue."

As a picture actor I worked hard, for even waiting is wearing on the nerves. Take after take, a moving of props and lights, repeats of the scene from other angles. Shooting goes on often into a late hour and night scenes and weather scenes and rain scenes have killed many an actor who neglected a little cold or a pain in the chest. I don't say we should get medals, but I can understand that yen that comes over a picture actor when he thinks of the stage and playing a scene right through for all it's worth, being in a part for two full hours with no cuts, light changes, and no one signaling to schmaltz it up. I know—for this year I did four plays in summer theater . . .

18

Masks of a Troubled World

The trek West of actors continued as old time silent movie stars
—in many cases, could not cure the falsetto tones of their voices.

Jimmy Gleason, who had given me my first job with the stock
company in Milwaukee, became firmly established in Hollywood,
as did my pal, Bob Armstrong. Jimmy had tried out a play of
his own in the Milwaukee stock company days, called *Thursday
Night*. After it closed he tried to peddle his play to every producer
on Broadway. There were no takers. None had confidence in
Jimmy and his talents as a playwright. So he had it printed. Jim
didn't care too much for the title *Thursday Night*.

"Sounds like a Turkish bath ad."

The printer agreed. "Why don't you call your play by that line
what runs throughout the dialogue—*Is Zat So?*—huh?"

"*Is Zat So?* Sure."

Under its new title the play was produced with Jimmy and

Bob, along with Lucille, Jim's wife, and Marjorie Crosland. It was a smash hit on Broadway, and as I said earlier had a lengthy run, went to London, where it repeated its success. Frank Mc-Hugh was the stage manager.

Two years after the phenomenal success of *Is Zat So?* Jimmy was having lunch with Al Woods at the Players Club in New York. There was a legend around Broadway: "When Al Woods arrives at his office in the morning, his desk is piled high with manuscripts and plays submitted to him by playwrights of all sizes, young and old—maybe the potential greats of tomorrow. Woods, so they said, would gather up all the scripts in his arms, toss them into the air, and only those that hit the desk would he read."

On this particular day when Gleason and Woods were lunching, Woods speared an olive. "Jimmy, your play *Is Zat So?* is a smash on two continents and you're a cinch to make a mint on this great comedy—how come, you dog, you didn't let *me*, an old pal, read the script?"

Gleason grinned. "Al, I guess mine must have been one of those that fell on the floor."

In Hollywood Jim and Bob were in great demand, and both signed contracts at Pathé.

Legends were easy to make in California, for example, people, fully sober, frequently said to me, "I saw you when I was only *so* high!"

Just the other day a maturing male approached, proffering his hand: "Pat O'Brien! I used to watch you on the screen when I was in knee pants!"

"Why?"

"Why *what*?"

"Why in knee pants? Were you a butler?"

I took a good look at this fellow. He was anything *but* juvenile in appearance. He looked like he might even be in my age bracket. "How old are you?" I asked, not smiling. I was tired of middle-aged frumps who claimed to never get out of knee pants.

He seemed rather surprised at my effrontery. "Well—why—er—I'm in my late fifties."

"Or early sixties. Now listen. I'm your age. I was thirty-one when I made my first picture. You must have been a living doll in those short pants then."

Maybe it was a little cruel. I'm often of the opinion some people think I have been in pictures for a hundred years. I was never in silent pictures, yet the porter on that train that got my twenty-buck tip must have thought so when he figured I was Chief Dan O'Brien of San Francisco's son, George.

I never got over my love of returning to New York whenever we had the time to spare. I'd sit around the Lambs just listening to new anecdotes made old—and old ones made new. One night, everyone was full of baseball recollections. Spencer Tracy brought up the episode of Mr. Frazee, who was then the owner of the Boston Red Sox. "One evening, friend Frazee was giving a drinking party at the Ritz-Carlton in Boston. Along about four A.M. there were only four men virile enough, including the host, anxious to continue. Unfortunately we had run out of drink. Frazee said to the surviving guests (three to be exact), 'Come on, let's get a cab and go out to the ball park.' It was midwinter. Snow covered the glum Boston Common. The temperature was well below freezing. They had brought in the brass monkeys—it was *that* cold. We seekers were fortunate in getting a late cruising cab. The red-nosed driver turned to Frazee. 'Where to?'

"Frazee waved, 'The Red Sox ball park.'

"The cabbie scowled, 'What are you—a comic or something this time of the morning and this kind of weather? What the hell d'you mean, the ball park?'

"Frazee, an impressive type, summoning all the dignity at his command, 'This is on the level. We ran out of booze at the party—we're going to open up the clubhouse. We're going to continue toasting next season's World Series. By the way, I am Frazee, owner of the Red Sox.'

"The driver turned turkey red. He jumped out of the cab and

said with a great shout of pain, 'So *you're* the bum who sold Babe Ruth to the Yankees?'

" 'Yes.'

"The cabbie swung at Frazee and we never made it to the ball park."

At the Lambs, talking pictures were still not taken seriously. Frank McHugh and I were once sitting at a table among scoffers. Most of the successful actors around Broadway were the unbelievers. One said:

"Talking pictures will never supplant the stage."

Frank said, "You remind me of a guy who had made a film test at the Fox studios in New York. He and another actor were standing in front of Warners' Theater in New York. A huge figure, of gigantic height was on display over the marquee. It was a blown-up cutout of the old wrinkled features of George Arliss, the most famous character actor in the world. After gazing for a long time at the face of the English star, the young juvenile turned to his companion, 'Look at the kisser on that bum—and they told me *my* test was lousy!' "

Frank McHugh came of a long line of McHughs, and in his early days in show business the entire McHugh family played together. There was Cutie McHugh (his father), Mother McHugh, Kitty McHugh, and his brothers—Jim, Eddie and Matt. Frank's dad played in *Of Human Hearts* longer than any other actor in any production and that includes Eugene O'Neill's father in *Count Of Monte Cristo*, and Frank Bacon in *Lightnin'*.

"Old actors never died," Frank said in those days, "they just got lost looking for a friendly saloon and were never heard of again."

The only thing that made leaving New York bearable on these visits was the fact that jobs were still hard to find on Broadway, and that I always had work in Hollywood.

Studios had a flavor in those days. At the completion of a picture at Warners', we would stage a cast party at our Brentwood home—have a barbecue and swimming party. We didn't throw the first fully dressed guest into a swimming pool, but we hold the record for the distance flung. Since the time I was ten, I was a great handball fanatic. In California at the old Butler Club, atop the Equitable Building, we had tournaments. There were some great handball competitors in those days—Allen Jenkins, Jack Haley, Howard Henshey (my attorney for thirty years), Bill Gargan, Buster Collier, Gene Delmar (his wife Viña wrote *Bad Girl* which brought film fame to James Dunn). The director, Dave Butler, large, chubby, was one of the most adept at this sport; George Meeker, another outstanding player. I decided to make handball more convenient and home-grown. I built a four-wall court on our grounds. It was equipped with a powerful lighting system so we could play at night. Strangers seeing lights, hearing thuds, were once told by Milt Gross, "The O'Briens are holding their monthly bat-catching hunt. Naturally it's only a night sport. It's not cruel—they catch them by crushing them between two hands clapped very fast."

In 1934, the Masquers Club gave a testimonial dinner to John McGraw, famed manager of the New York Giants. When the banquet was over, several of us went out to the house to play handball and do some barbershop quartet singing. Bob Armstrong, Frank McHugh, Lynn Overman and Bill Frawley usually constituted the warbling troubadours. That was the night the neighbors thought we had given up bat-catching for crow-trapping.

One had to exercise; Warner Brothers actors appeared in so many action pictures, one had to keep in trim.

James Cagney and I were teamed in our first picture, *Here Comes the Navy.* The picture was almost entirely shot aboard the *Arizona,* that ship that was to meet its doom that fateful December day at Pearl Harbor. The *coup de grâce* from the enemy bomb came right through the funnel, and it sank, taking with it many of the men who had appeared in the picture we filmed in San Diego.

The *Arizona* was docked in San Diego Harbor for film making. On one of its cruises it struck a Japanese fishing boat which resulted in fatalities (an ironic and grim omen before Pearl Harbor).

Lloyd Bacon was the director, the son of the Frank Bacon who created the top role in *Lightnin'* that broke all long-run records on Broadway.

Many people think all I ever appeared in were service pictures, except those who think I only played priests, or those who have the impression I only acted football coaches or prison wardens. Actually, while I did play these parts, most of my roles had nothing to do with the above, not that they weren't great parts.

I became aware that like many movie people, I was living in a bubble. There was another *real* world out there and things were not going well. To Spain soon would come a civil war of brother against brother, and both sides would commit fearful things. The outside world would take sides and kill more and more Spaniards. Mussolini was growling in the direction of Africa; Hitler swore the *Anschluss* was just around the corner. Munich would come, and Peace in Our Time. And F.D.R. told us we had nothing to fear but fear itself. I remember it all as a wild film montage, only it was for real.

Orson Welles (in those days down to only one chin) was the bright-eyed boy wonder of radio, and I knew we were all jumpy when he scared the nation with a "news report" of an invasion from Mars, based on H. G. Wells' *War of the Worlds.*

I tried to think the flowers looked better in the morning, the sunsets more glowing as the fear grew in us all that things could not ever be again as they had been. We had grown up and fearful changes were indicated.

The nearly hopeless work for peace in the world went on. Pope Pius XI had delivered the first Papal benediction heard simultaneously all over the world at the inauguration of the Vatican's own radio station. Father Coughlin, the radio priest, had also found radio, and the Church admitted it had a problem on its hands. It kept its dignity and waited, and in time Father Coughlin was banned from radio, as many of his talks began to parrot Nazi propaganda. Most Catholics approved his silence.

The depression we had come through had sobered most of us.

In one year Hollywood reported only sixty divorces, but this was counterbalanced by the appearance of a new monster I ran into one day—the juke box—a flashing, too vocal creature of mean color and loud sounds, to which I found the young people jitterbugging. Nearly half a million were to appear—mostly, it seemed to me, in the wrong places.

We built a nursery on the home we had purchased—two large sunny rooms a bath, and a little kitchen. What a dream house, all pink and white and fluffy. All of our dreams fairly seeped out of the nursery walls, and this angel's cloister reeked in feminine décor. Yes, the first one had to be a girl—and she was. When she arrived the world revolved only around her—her tiny Dresden hands reaching out and her eyes dancing like blue animated diamonds—her baby talk was a language we definitely understood. Her ever-present sunshine peeking at us was a daily reminder that here was a girl of our dreams.

Margaret Mavourneen, Gaelic for my darling. For us began a new kind of life. The joy in the first-born can never adequately be put into words, at least not by me. Perhaps love of a child is the greatest love. It is a visible growing thing, one of God's greatest miracles, and no evolutionary theory or biology test gives anything like the real wonder of a tiny human bud unfolding.

Eloise and I were emotionally moved when the Prince of Wales, after he became Edward VIII, gave up the throne to "marry the woman I love."

"Good for him," said Eloise.

"What if he finds out he doesn't like her cooking?"

"You ever eat English cooking, Pat? After that he'd never know the difference."

Yes the world was changing, I had to admit—even I was changing as I knew when I looked into the mirror. Show business had gotten out of the depression. But slowly, as was the nation. Not only the Okies of Steinbeck's *Grapes of Wrath* were in trouble. In the early thirties, there had been thirty-seven burlesque theaters working in New York City. But depression and bluenoses soon tamed it, killed it. And the great comics had gone elsewhere;

Jimmy Durante, Bert Lahr, Abbott and Costello, many others came out, pale and wondering, into the strong California sunshine. Gypsy Rose Lee graduated to the Follies, talked like an intellectual, and stripped as if Doctors Freud and Kinsey were in the front row taking notes.

Wherever we went we felt the influence of Fred Astaire's and Ginger Rogers' pictures. Their rumbas, cariocas, continentals were popular and set old spines shaking. The Hays Office, that became the Breen Office, fought a losing fight to keep certain dismal or exotic facets of real life off the screen.

In 1934 the Catholic Church organized the Legion of Decency to express in concrete form its repugnance to the objectionable films so prevalent at the time. The impression has been that the Legion was trying to force its opinions on all Americans. Actually, it provided for Catholics a moral evaluation of the pictures being offered to the movie-going public. Soon the Breen Office would only certify pictures that were 99-44/100 per cent pure. In New York, the Dunnigan bill was passed. It provided that one man should have the power to decide what New Yorkers should see, or not see. Pressure on the governor from Catholics, Protestants and Jews on the grounds that the bill went too far caused it to be vetoed.

The Breen Office tried hard to regulate moral behavior in movies, but some of its rulings, in the light of today's "anything goes, *but* anything," seem oddly funny. Married couples could not be seen in films resting or asleep in the same bed. Twin beds seemed to take over American marriage. If two people were shown in one bed—married or sporting—the rules called for one of them, usually the considerate gentleman, to keep at least one toe touching the floor. Kissing had to be done with a dry, closed mouth, and could not run more than four seconds. No one could be shown actually killing another person. What the public thought of as killings were cleverly made film cuts. Showing a gun going off, then a picture of a body falling, was forbidden. Knife killings were frowned upon. Americans, it was felt, killed in a good clean outdoor way. The fastest draw in the West was for a Colt .45.

Only certain foreigners were permitted to use a knife in the back. Villains were a problem, I remember. I used to wait on the set for hours while it was decided to change the Republican banker to a Mexican bandit. (Later the Mexican had to be changed to a Russian. Today the Russian is changed to a Chinese, or something green and gooey from outer space.)

Dialect humor, the most enjoyable simple folk art, was no longer acceptable as Hitler rose to power. First, Jewish accents went out of scripts, then Italian, as Mussolini frowned, and soon even the innocent Dutch burlesque classic, "Dis muss be de place" was barred.

Oddly enough, as an actor, I saw that the rise of Hitler and Nazism gave a great deal of work to German accents, and anyone who could shout "Achtung" "Schweinhund" with vigor worked in anti-German films. Most of these evil-looking fellows with the shaved heads and fat necks were actually German Jews. One of the meanest of the crew was Otto Preminger, whose Nazi roles were so mean that people began to hate him personally when they met him in the street. Today he is a top director.

I became aware that men, even actors, grow older. As a young actor, death to me was something that happened to other people in other countries. But now as the years pass, I know people close to me will be touched by it some day. Irving Thalberg died at thirty-seven; the man who had given in to my agent's price at Metro. He had driven himself with a megalomania of responsibility to the end, in that fatal, agonizing desire for power that is the dismal goal in the upper reaches of big studios. Will Rogers died in an Alaska plane crash; George Gershwin died young, too young, while we were still humming his catchy tunes.

The dominating figure in America was the President (in his way a pretty good actor himself). It's hard to explain Franklin Delano Roosevelt only by the history books. To have been alive when he was in his prime made a difference. The wars, the issues, the great moments are all somewhat dusty now. But to have come through the depression as I did, to go from the tune of "Brother,

Can you Spare a Dime?" to "Happy Days Are Here Again" was more to us than something on the "Hit Parade." F.D.R. had kept his promise about repeal and one could be neatly overcharged in bars, legally. Radio showed F.D.R. was a true showman; the Crosley rating system gave his Fireside Chats a grade of 38.7, nearly as high as Bing Crosby's show. Even Philadelphia changed. (Fred Allen said, "I went to Phillie last Sunday, but it was closed.") There was talk of permitting Sunday dancing in Philadelphia, but no Sunday drinking.

If I was feeling a respectable citizen of the world, who was set in Hollywood, and my head got a bit swelled with the progress of my career, I could always be cooled down by Eloise showing me what *other* actors were earning. Claudette Colbert—$302,000 a year; Warner Baxter (who remembers him?)—$280,000; Jack Benny (thirty-nine years of age even then)—$250,000.

And this was before the big tax bite, the deflated modern buck, and Parkinson's Law was in effect. "No matter how much wealth a company or a nation earns or collects in taxes, it will always find ways to spend it." Oh brother, and how.

If the New Deal brought hope, it also brought headaches to the motion picture studios, which had operated like pirate captains. We all knew of the interlocking control of the industry of all production, distribution and theaters. Block booking sold pictures a year ahead, when only a title existed. European films were frozen out, relatives were spawned in high places like fleas in a tramp's vest. Now the New Deal trust busters were demanding that the studios break up the combines, stop forced block selling of unmade pictures and get rid of the theaters. The relatives? No one ever found out anything to do with them. Someone suggested a short Indian massacre.

I said, "If this closes the studios, I'll tour with *Jiggs and Maggie.* Where can I get a woman to play Maggie?"

Eloise said, "Not me."

19

Among the Better Horses

The nearest I ever came to being a millionaire was when Bing Crosby, myself and others organized the Del Mar race track. The stock became fabulous, but by that time I had long since sold mine. Those were fine times—gay, wonderful, sunny days at Del Mar, the baby Saratoga of the West.

Those happy years at Del Mar gave a small inkling why some men destroyed their lives to follow the horses, why it became a way of feast-or-famine living for many. It wasn't just the gambling —the idea of hitting a daily double or a long shot coming in at 30 to 1. It was the crystal atmosphere warm with life. Long golden days with the deep blue shadows coming in over the grandstand; the color of the holiday-held crowd milling around, the slight salty breeze on the banners, and the tang of the best horses and the pungent whiffs of stable life. The jocks and their agents were drama; the high-paced legs of the overbred horses. It had a smoky taste, an outdoor vitality, all color and movement; a series of contests between heart, muscle, greed and past showings.

It absorbed the feel of the blood-charging moment when they broke in a good field from the barrier, the jocks moving for position on the rail, the whirl of legs and the pound of hoofs, and the packed people standing as if one person, to let out their breath as the entries took the far turn; the favorites still waiting, holding back, then at the half pole, the three-quarter pole, the turn, the whips beginning to lift and fall, and way out on the outside some dog of an outsider moving; stepping fast and around for the last desperate rush, jocks high on horses necks, no mercy shown in the drive across the finish. Three noses *all* in line and the sign: PHOTO FINISH; PLEASE HOLD TICKETS FOR FINAL RESULTS. Then would come a sharp breaking out of talk. The wait and the final results posted, to be greeted in a hoot and holler, a groan or a cheer. The happy winners starting for the payoff windows; the losers going back to form sheets, grimy notes and chewed-up programs. In the winner's circle, the steaming animal was unsaddled.

Del Mar was also a new kind of morning on the workouts—the stop watches held up, eyes meeting as a two-year-old maiden came in fast, the cap-topped colored horse handler smiling, and the panting beautiful creature being rubbed down, and the hot walker moving the colt in a circle to cool her. The old stable hands remembering Man o' War, and telling great lies; track killings, fixed boat rides, ringers in far places, and wonder horses that killed jockies and were backed for mysterious millions. All in the smell of sun on wood and grass—and horse liniment, hamburgers cooking and a sharp scent of mustard, stable litter, hay; a cockeyed hound dog asleep at a stall door, and the touts preparing for a day of mooching in the healthy out of doors. It was exciting.

But always back to the studios and work.

During the making of *San Quentin*, the director, Lloyd Bacon, asked me: "Pat, any of your gangster or con men race track pals who might want a job as technical director on this picture?"

I replied indignantly, "What do you mean—*my* con pals?"

"You know a few—I'm not intimating they've been your house guests—I was just wondering whether one of them might have just been sprung."

"Just who do you think my friends are?"

"If it would be okay with the parole board, I could give a man a good job as technical advisor."

"I do happen to know just such a character. . . . Doc Stone. He's just been released from prison, served time on a bad check score."

"He a real criminal, Pat?"

"Has spent some fifty years in and out of jail."

"Good."

"He's been a bindlestiff, gold brick man, pickpocket, dealer in frauds of any and all variety—but he is endowed with a certain vagrant charm."

"Get him!"

I went to the Brown Derby and saw Bob Cobb.

"Doc Stone? A likable chap."

I told Bob of the situation. He said Doc could certainly use the scratch, "and he can't steal a studio—can he?"

Doc Stone got the job; $300 a week. All he had to do was answer any questions about prison and prisoners that might arise. Doc was a charmer, could remove the spots off a leopard with the leopard never knowing it. He could also talk without moving his lips. We had been shooting two weeks, and one day Doc hadn't returned from lunch. Bacon asked me, "Where's your stir pal?"

"Don't worry—he'll be here. He never misses lockup time."

Hours passed and at four o'clock Doc walked in obviously on his fourth or fifth reefer. He was on cloud 712 and practically jumping over matches. I walked over to him and said, "You're letting me down—where've you been?"

"What's the matter, Paddy, is there a beef?"

"Bacon's on the verge of firing you."

"To hell with him. If he says anything I'll go over the wall."

When I told the director what Doc had said, he replied: "That kind of dialogue deserves a fifty-dollar raise."

Doc continued to be in demand. Prison pictures were very popular in the late thirties, as they had been almost since the movies started. Americans I sensed, had such a strong feeling for the underdog, that they even made heroes of depraved, evil and desperate men under lock and key. The lawlessness of the bootleg era had not completely evaporated from national life, and men like Dillinger, who broke jail with a soap pistol, after giving the lady sheriff a big hug, gave the movie viewer, the humdrum, bored, hard-working American, an easy thrill.

Doc Stone said: "Looking at his own wife at his side, and then at them glamorous gun molls played by everybody from Sylvia Sidney to Jean Harlow, puts some itchy feeling in the square American guy that the jailed big shot certainly had it great; a loyal and fascinating silk-underwear moll who would love, cheat, lie and arrange for his escape. Prison pictures—they're just kick entertainment. It may seem nuts, but a head-feeler in Beverly Hills I sold some oil stock to once told me lots of his patients came to him with dreams of breaking out of some stir with machine guns blasting the screws."

Doc didn't take much stock in the glamor of crime. "At the best, Pat, it's a living; the real hustling money is made by the legit boys who live off us time servers: The bail-bond boys, the fancy law shysters, taking cops, judges; parole-board fixers, and the political fat cats who know somebody. Pat, if you want to be a thief, be an honest one; get an official elected title and never steal anything small."

What time I could get free of making movies, I spent down at Del Mar in the seaside cottage.

I still remember those beautiful tranquil nights when Eloise and I would sit on the porch overlooking the Pacific. The indifferent surf, beauty and glory in a visible planet; over all the huge golden harvest moon. We'd remember our early nights at Coney Island with its own moon hanging like a watch on a fob over Steeple-chase.

I said, "Same moon, all right, but when you are down to your last couple of bucks and wondering what the future holds, that old Coney Island moon didn't pay the rent."

"It looks low enough to bite, *and* time for the grunion run."

Among our guests, one weekend, we had the Ed Kellys—mayor of Chicago and his wife Margaret. His honor had never heard of grunion.

"Pat, my boy, put me wise. What's a grunion? A Republican?"

"Who told you? About grunion?"

"They talk of hunting it on the beach."

"We don't like to talk about it, your honor."

"Is it dangerous? Tell me."

"A lot of people think grunions are a myth—an old wives' tale. I was one of them once, your honor—but they are an actuality, when it *happens* to be grunion time."

"What is this damn grunion?"

"A tiny fish of the smelt family; they come up onto the beach by the millions, and in the light of the full moon they stand on their tails and spawn; then they go back on the next wave to the sea. California law forbids their capture with any tool or device."

"The devil you say. *How* do you nab them?"

"You use your hands."

It's an exciting adventure and the beach at Del Mar would be lined with hundreds of people—adults and kids alike, all bare-legged, shouting and laughing, armed with flashlights and all with the same idea—catch as many as you can.

Tiny as a grunion is, they make a marvelous, wonderful breakfast, rolled in corn meal and fried.

The mayor joined in the damp dark trek along the Del Mar beach and his enthusiasm was as great as any campaigning for office. We garnered over 350 grunion that night. I had, however, neglected to warn the mayor to remove the beach tar, from passing ships, from the soles of his feet before entering the house.

Eloise shouted, "The rugs!"

The mayor said, "They've caught smallpox."

"It's tar. Beach tar."

Margaret Kelly, on her hands and knees, took to cleaning tar off the rug.

The mayor said, "What a picture for posterity and the next election—we'd be sure of the charwomen's vote!"

The following day at the track another Irish mayor, from the eastern seaboard, was in plain sight—Mayor Hague of Jersey City; a hero to some, a rogue to others—certainly a powerhouse who owned his city, lock, stock and city hall. There was a horse running called Hizzoner. Before the full word got around at the Turf Club that Kelly *and* Hague were among the throng, the majority of omen-seeking bettors completely overlooked betting on this horse.

"It can't fail," I said to Eloise.

We placed a small wager on the nag's nose. The horse won and paid 35 to 1. Had the bettors known of the presence of the two vote-collecting civic leaders, they would have bet on Hizzoner themselves, and automatically brought the price down.

Eloise said, "It was selfish not to spread the news."

One day, Eloise bet on a horse—I don't recall his name, but the jockey was Chinjacki. She bet $2.00 across the board—six bucks.

I said, "That's right, show them no mercy."

The horse won and paid 60 to 1.

I said, "Honey, how could you possibly bet on that horse when you saw what price it would pay?"

"I saw that little jockey at Mass Sunday, so I just figured I'd encourage him with six dollars."

"Next Sunday, if he goes to Communion, *double* your bet."

We had a theme song that is still played at Del Mar after the national anthem, and it's always played just before the opening race.

The tune has been ascribed to Johnny Burke, Van Heusen, Johnny Mercer, but the lyrics came from Mrs. Herb Polesie—Midge, as she is better known by all who love her, and wonder at her wild betting.

"Where the turf meets the surf
Down at old Del Mar
Take a plane—take a train
Take a car.
There's a smile on every face,
And a winner in each race,
Where the turf meets the surf
At old Del Mar."

Eloise asked, "Could Cole Porter or Ira Gershwin do it?"

I said no—and it's true.

As I've said, I sold my stock to avoid being a millionaire. At the time Bing Crosby made his exit from the venture. It made sense to me: he's out, I'm out. Actually, he was forced to make this move because the law was, and is, you can't own a race track and be the owner of a baseball club at the same time. So Bing's affiliation with the Pittsburgh Pirates automatically forced his disinheriting himself from the Del Mar race track. But I didn't know that, and denuded myself of the stock and lost a fortune.

We kept our home on the beach and it was always a grand vacation spot for the children and ourselves.

One Christmas, a beautiful sunny day (when, the novelist William Faulkner, writing on the lot, said, "A leaf falls in one of those canyons and they tell you it's winter") at Warner Brothers, we were engaged in the filming of a picture called *I've Got Your Number.* Joan Blondell played the lead and Allen Jenkins played my fellow worker. We were telephone repairmen. The day before Christmas was always a short day in the industry—as it's called— but because we were a few days behind schedule, the director said: "We work the full day, December twenty-fourth."

Jenkins flipped. He grabbed the set phone and called Bill Koenig, general manager of the studio. In a loud, heated tone, punctuated with a few overripe epithets, he spoke of holiday, holly berries, "Silent Night," concluding by shouting ". . . and you can take my contract and *tear it up!*" (or words to that effect). "Tear it up," he added in a voice that could be heard in Pasadena, "and that goes for my dear old buddy pal, Pat O'Brien, too!"

I grabbed the phone from Allen's grip, and said shakily, "Look, I make my own decisions. Just tear up his."

Allen screamed, "What are you—a Moslem!"

Fortunately, nothing ever came of defending Christmas. Allen was one of the best mugging comics in the business, but I didn't particularly appreciate his sense of humor that Christmas Eve, even if the tree and turkey were paid for.

20

I Meet Mr. Hearst

The only picture I did with Marion Davies was *Page Miss Glory*.

It's no secret she was Hearst the press lord's great love. He was once asked if "there is money in movies?" He said, thinking of his floundering film company, "There should be—I've put twenty million in it."

Few know the good Marion did during her active Hollywood days. Her many charitable acts were never publicized (at her request).

The Madame Pompadour of Yellow Journalism was a small, well-built honey blonde, who when under stress stuttered a bit. She was a marvelous comic, and had a great skill, somewhat like Lucille Ball, for slapstick grace in funny situations. But William Randolph Hearst kept her mostly in romantic little-girl parts, and that bored Marion, and usually the movie audience.

Hearst was a portly man, large, heavy, a perfect Edwardian.

He never entered the post-World War I world. He had a shrill high piping voice, like a choir boy, when it got away from him. He was often on the movie set, playing a long-distance Svengali to his love. The thing about him that was clearest to me was his sense of absolute power. He naturally didn't conform to what others accepted as the social pattern, but did things his own ducal way. That he bought entire castles, tore them apart and crated them, and brought them over here is well known. His art collection was, an expert told me, good, but not great, and he was the victim of odd dealers ("Are there any others?") and the bad habit of rich Americans of saying, "I'll take *that* and *that*, all of anything like that you have." So they loaded him with a vast collection of historic debris and sacred wormholes.

San Simeon, the palace of sudden whims and millions, which we visited, was a vast pile still building. It looked like new-made clean ruins, decorated by a twelfth-century monk who liked cracked marble and high ceilings. The drive up to the main house was as if into a new Kingdom of Oz. There was even a well-stocked private zoo, and once when Hearst ran an ad in his San Francisco paper that he wanted a giraffe keeper, and would pay $40 a week, six of his reporters (who were getting only $33 a week salary) applied for the job.

The palace, when Eloise and I saw it after making the picture, was not in bad taste. As Milt Gross told us: "It's vulgar without being laughable." Lunch and dinner, we found out, were served to us on a huge plank table free of tablecloths, and the ketchup bottle was passed from hand to hand, as the food was often hamburgers on Louis XIV plates. From time to time the guests' baggage was searched so that Marion would not find any hard drink available (Hearst in *some* ways was a Puritan). Friendly guests would hide their gift booze for her in the flush tanks of the bathroom plumbing.

Hearst was getting old and creaky, but was still very active. He ran his publishing empire, noisy newspapers and magazines from an ornate office at San Simeon. He was a great firer-and-hirer man; I felt right at home; he was a kind of gentile Jack

Warner when it came to making the help dance to his tune. No one dared question his whim or will, and the newspapers and magazines were not doing well. But Hearst continued to live like a Medici prince, and he died like one, in his barber chair, in which he slept the last few months of his life, feeling that by lying down, one would carelessly set oneself up to getting buried. He felt the same way about San Simeon; he never finished adding wings to it; having been told by some teacup sage he would be dead when it was complete.

Orsen Welles, in the film *Citizen Kane*, did a cruel, unkind cartoon of Hearst and Marion. Actually, they achieved a long-lasting love, and Marion was neither numb nor stupid. She had a flashing Irish sense of fun, a gay wit, and among friends could be bright and charming.

I saw Hearst as the last of his kind, Henry Luce is only a pale echo of the absolute monarch of the glen that Hearst was. Hearst's taste in journalism I leave to the professors to fight over, but his zest for living was real, and one had to admit *he* wasn't going to miss anything in life. He belonged, of course, to a larger, wider, more civilized era, when the millionaire playboy, the trampling great man could say, "After me the deluge." (Old J. P. Morgan, I remember, built a lying-in hospital, and didn't care when they said, "He'll try and fill it too." Hearst was above showing kindnesses, and he was not taken in by the guests at San Simeon—a strange society of partygoers, free loaders, and yea-sayers milling around him. If there was a sense of the chill of power in my few contacts with him, it was an experience I wouldn't have wanted to miss. I remember Milt Gross, who worked for Hearst many years, saying, "It wasn't that his journalism was so bad. Today's is no better; only we don't use as many red headlines and the reporters don't write as well and with as much skill." Hearst, in his prime, was a better taker of the public pulse than our news weeklies, and super-newspapers. But he didn't really care for money. He wouldn't go count every penny in the till. He was a great man, a very great man, and unlovable.

A lot of the cast of *Page Miss Glory* went up to San Simeon to spend a few days. I still see William Randolph Hearst, in his seventies, playing a furious game of tennis and swimming in that huge pool like a whale-spouting Weismuller. We were assigned the "Cardinal Richelieu" suite.

Eloise said, "The Cardinal sure had a hard bed."

"Mr. Hearst has transported this suite in its entirety from France."

"I hope he didn't keep up the payments. Good night, Pat."

Marion always presented every member of the cast, technicians, and every member of the crew with some lavish gift at the close of a picture. I received an amazing wrist watch; every number on the face of the watch was a baguette diamond.

"It's a little too dainty for me to wear."

The inscription read, *"With love to Pat from Marion."*

I asked Marion, "Would you object if I had this piece made into a lapel watch for my daughter Mavourneen?"

"Of course not. You're lucky you didn't get a gold nose ring. I don't know *where* W.R.H. gets these jewelers."

Another Hearst type of man, mean to tangle with, was E. F. Albee, head and czar of the Keith-Albee vaudeville circuit. He was not the most popular of the show business tycoons of that day; a barking martinet. Workmen were once excavating near his Palace Theater. The depth of the operation went deep into the bowels of Manhattan. Joe Frisco, as usual unemployed, was watching the tremendous activity, when I asked him, "What's going on Joe?"

Frisco replied, "Mr. Al-bee's kid lost his b-ball."

As a sample of my prose style of the thirties, here are a few pages of my diary of a trip we took by boat to the islands; to Honolulu:

Wilmington, Cal., s.s. MARIPOSA: *April 7.*
    Wanted to go to New York. Bride wanted to go to Honolulu; had a moral victory. Sailed for Hawaii. Grand ship which goes all the way to Australia. Our first boat ride since the Old

219

Mill at Coney Island. Shove-off time at 10 P.M. Everybody celebrating the return of BEER. Al Jolson and Ruby Keeler, Bert Wheeler and Bob Woolsey on boat with us. Tough spot for billing for an O'Brien. Be lucky to get a laugh in my mirror.

Phone rings. Bill and Mary Gargan to wish us bon voyage. Phone again. Party in Bert Wheeler's stateroom. We join the gang. *Everybody* in Hollywood there. Some seasick. Boat still tied to California. Last chance to flee. Don't take it.

Shove off at 3 A.M. And so to an uphill bed.

April 8.
Relaxing in stateroom. Not sick. "Just tired." Eloise O'Brien laughs. Admit I'm seasick—and homesick for land. Pacific belies its name. Humps like a mad camel. Ignore first call for breakfast, lunch, dinner.

Lose the ship's pool. My enthusiasm still sea green. One consolation. All pals sick too. Woolsey without the inevitable cigar. When we get back to Hollywood will be looking for guy who told him to drink brandy as sure preventative for seasickness. Walls still moving in. Rough paved sea.

April 9.
Only good sailor in gang, Mrs. Frank Borzage; Mrs. Jack Ford with her. Claim out to beat the Hawaiian travel records held by Dorothy MacKail and Janet Gaynor. Am well enough to win the ship's pool and enjoy it.

April 10.
Sea legs now. Going in for the deck sports. No flying fish. Swimming pool built originally for midgets. And not more than two of those. Horse races in miniature. But no chance for an inside tip *or* fix.

Play the slot machines instead. The robbers. Al Jolson wins ship's pool today. Night comes. Whole Hollywood crowd reports at the dinner table to go for the groceries for first time in big way. Pray it isn't mistake. It *is*. Sea full of moving green rocks. No flying fish today either.

April 11.
More sports today. Deck tennis. Great game if you like deck tennis. Don't. Shot clay pigeons. Uneatable. Wheeler

wins ship's pool today. Bribed pool clerk with cigars is rumor. Denies this with tears at dinner.

April 12.

Acting profession have so far split the ship's pool like a fixed blackjack game. I top the billing, winning two. Five days at sea. Five pools, five actors! How's that? Much talk. Not about flying fish. *Still* invisible.

Arrive in tropical waters. Molokai in the distance, pencil-scribble of land, geeking of birds. Feel like Melville, Stevenson, London, but most like Pat O'Brien. Planes roaring overhead . . . For me? Steam into the harbor, surrounded by yachts, sampans, fishing boats, diving natives, just like travel pictures, Royal Hawaiian orchestra. Fragrance of *leis* tell us this is the place; Honolulu. Royal Hawaiian Hotel looks like the Taj Mahal. Met man claims has movie shots of flying fish. Not too sober. Hope to enjoy rest soon as crowd settles down.

April 17.

Beautiful wedding today. Patsy Parker's sister, dainty little blonde, marries stalwart young army aviator.

Site of the ceremony, old Hawaiian church doing its best to keep alive the breath of rapidly native dying race. The old symbols, but no red flowers used in decorating the church. "Red flowers bring bad luck." Military wedding. Bride daughter of army officer from San Antonio, Texas.

Bert Wheeler gives bride away; does a comic hurdle over the bridal veil, rather than a casual walk around the bride's train. Woolsey says, "Church or no church, I knew that guy would louse it up." Bride and husband leave church, under canopy of swords held aloft by the white clad officers. Hear swords used to spear pig for native luau. Could be.

Girls crying. Woolsey and Wheeler and Jolson, big sissies; mugs wiping a tear or two. Me? A Gael always sheds a tear at a wedding. Part of our code.

April 19.

Waikiki is Asbury Park with coconuts—now the Malibu of this troupe of actors. Live on the beach. Tough Bill, Joe Miner and Panama; all Hawaiian beach boys, help us in surf.

Runners-up for surfboard championship. We outrig in outrigger canoes. Learn how an octopus is killed. *Ugh;* say much tasty. Passed it up. Sucker for the Pacific, cinch to become a *Kaamaina.* (One who returns to Hawaii.) Old swimming champion, Duke Kahanomoku, still in vivid prominence. Test him on rum drinks. He tests me. Test each other. Pass.

April 23.

Boxing in Honolulu just like the Olympic and the Legion in Hollywood. Like the fighters. No one can pronounce their names. A surprise referee. "Introducing the world's greatest entertainer and the world's lousiest referee,—Al Jolson." Al will go on anyplace. Does. Great.

April 25.

Ate Hawaiian and Japanese feasts. *Ah-so.* First, Japanese. Groceries tabu until the shoes come off . . . don kimonos . . . Ah-so. Food? Seems like herring scale soup, sea weed salad, moss omelette, raw flounder, green tea. Yes? Ah-so.

Real thrill, native *luau.* Hawaiian for big stuffing. Whole pig, filled with red-hot stones (kill the pig *first*) placed in the *Emu,* underground oven. Pig surrounded by loving bananas, sweet potatoes, fish, other delicacies wrapped in *Ti* leaves, baked several hours. Large bowls of *Poi* (close approach to wallpaper mucilage), squid . . . Eat and enjoy till enlightened to its being "juvenile octopus." Countless other tid-bits not to be found in Sardis. To eat native lie full length on *opus* (stomachs) complications of Luau etiquette demand eating with fingers exclusively. Rumor pig is lost. Pit empty. Rumor wrong—pig found. Too bad.

Gorgeous stage moon comes up over Hawaiian bay. No night club floor show nor orchestral din, just expensive exposed primitive beauty. Plaintive twang of guitars, soft swish of *Ti* leaf skirts of stacked hula girls; crooning of the natives just like in Jack London, as *Malahinis* (newcomers) admit that Hawaii "mus be de place."

April 27.

Girl, sixteen, more than her share of adolescent charm, cursed with a heart ailment so grave to cause finest doctors to wonder. We troupers decide to give her a little life. Suite in the Royal Hawaiian Hotel—girl guest of honor. Music by our beach boys—entertainers, Jolson, Keeler, Wheeler, Woolsey, Mona Rico, Winona Love and O'Brien. O'Brien attempts imitations. Ruby shuffles Off to Buffalo in inimitable Keeler style . . . Jolson? Al sings *Yacka Hackey Hickey Doola, California, Here I Come, Mammy*, and finally that *Sonny Boy*. Tears of pleasure of doomed little guest. Always reminded in life—we are in the midst of death. Lesson here someplace, too tired to unknot it.

April 29.

Holiday nearing end. Put Wheeler and the Woolseys on big Japanese liner pointed for Yokohama. After three shots of serums to guard against diseases, they look green—cigars look greener. All get sadder and sadder as the Osama Maru pulls out leaving us to prepare own leavetakings.

May 1.

Today bid farewell to Hawaii. Adieu will linger we hope forever in hearts. Again, as upon arrival, strains of the Royal Hawaiian orchestra echo melodies across Pacific. Prepare to cast off, Tough Bill crying—so is O'Brien. Everyone shouting "Aloha, Pat." Have new hat—place cigar in the band of chapeau to weight it down. Fling it over the side to pal, Tough Bill. Catches it—tosses his own into the sea—music is still *alohaing* . . . Pull out . . . Round Diamond Head. Fling *leis* into Pacific. If they float ashore we are sure to return. Just before going down to dinner saw a flying fish. Saw several. *Amazing!*

I am only a moderate joiner. I don't even stand in line to have a package wrapped in a store. I don't rush into every organization available to me. Even when the exclusive Jewish club—the Hillcrest—opened its doors for two token Christians, I did not rush my application. But there are two organizations, the Lambs and the Players, without whom my life would be leaner and more lonely.

Hollywood joiners were a little different than the New York City ones. There was always a rushing to follow the fashionable glad-handers, glamor pusses and phony titles at overrated eating places. To be seen, greeted and overcharged (and stained by careless waiters). Once to be put in the back room by the self-anointed "Prince" Mike Romanoff (born Harry Gergusson) was like being caught stealing chickens. Many actors joined the Academy mob for awards that have been press-agented and advertised for; and plotted for with a zeal (as if they were getting immortality, at least the Nobel prize).

Are the Oscar Awards fair? Sure. It's how you look at it. Certainly the Academy doesn't represent the full industry. It's controlled and paid for by the major studios. Nor does it have among its members the majority of the really creative people. It praises those of a small self-interested minority. Besides which, the selection of nominations by small committees inside the body is so securely controlled that most pictures made outside of Hollywood (and their stars) are usually swept under the rug. The major studios, because of their hired hands who are in the Academy, can usually pile up a lot of votes in the right place.

The only true reward an actor gets is that voice inside: "You were pretty good."

Awards of all sorts, sizes, colors and races are given in Hollywood at the wink of a press agent's eye. And they usually mean nothing and need constant dusting. Every social organization and club group give awards they buy and give by the dozen just to get free speakers. Few take these awards as seriously as one producer did (he's since left to assault Broadway). He has a hunger for them, and has a special room set aside just for his scrolls, battered brass lettering, and plated cups of praise. He would join almost anything, go any place to deliver a Model-T speech fit for any event, with blanks left in for the name of the organization making the award. Some prankster one night called this producer at three in the morning, and told him in an earnest hurried voice to dress

224

and hurry down to some Santa Monica address. By oversight he said the producer hadn't been notified he was getting the main award at a dedication of a new modern comfort station built by the city. He was dressed and half way to the garage before it dawned on him it was a practical joke. . . .

There is an irony to fame. One morning I picked up the newspaper to read that this producer had had a mild heart attack while cruising on his yacht and, in the same paper, that Preston Sturges, one of Hollywood's true creative writing and directing geniuses, neglected, forgotten, had died in a back hotel room, unable to pay his bill, his shoes worn out from trying to find somebody in the film business to back him in a film he was trying to make. Preston left no room full of awards, just some of the best films ever made, from *The Great McGinty* to *The Miracle of Morgan's Creek*, and the hundreds of friends with whom he drank his own brandy when he was endowing the town with its only cosmopolitan eating place: the Players. When Preston was told he had just lost two million dollars running the place, he poured a fresh brandy. "Good, I'm going to order them to build a hundred-thousand-dollar theater out back of the Players, to give *live* plays in Hollywood with *live* actors. I've got to use up that tax loss as a write-off."

The Players is now a Japanese tourist-tortured eatery, with chopsticks.

The Players I was asked to join in the early thirties was the famous actors' club in New York City. No prouder ham walked the rug when I got the telegram that I had been voted a member. The fact that I was in California when that happened, and the club in New York City, didn't bother me. It would give me an excuse to visit the East. I was accepted by my fellow actors into a club where membership was, to the theater, something as sacred as the College of Cardinals.

And a fine and wonderful place it was on my many visits. As Edwin Booth said, on the evening of December 31, 1888: "Gentlemen: Although our vocations are various, I greet you all

225

as brother Players. At this supreme moment of my life, it is my happy privilege to assume the character of host, to welcome you to the house wherein I hope that we for many years, and our legitimate successors for at least a thousand generations, may assemble for friendly intercourse and intellectual recreation."

With his own money Mr. Booth had bought the property at 16 Gramercy Park, had the building remodeled by Stanford White (a charter member, who gained odd fame later by being shot by a jealous husband, Harry Thaw, on a roof garden).

In the club, adjacent to the pool tables, are hung cues of deceased members who have spent many hours at the table. Among them is the cue used by Mark Twain, above a portrait of him done by a fellow member, Gordon Stevenson.

One rainy afternoon Mark Twain put up his cue and started to leave the club. He met with bad news. The doorman said, "Mr. Twain, your umbrella has been appropriated by Chauncey Olcott, who asked me to explain that he had to go to a funeral." Mark Twain turned back to the pool table growling, "I hope the funeral is a failure."

At the time of its establishment a rule was made that ladies were not to be allowed in the club except on April 23, Shakespeare's birthday, when a Ladies' Day, is given to feminine friends and relatives of the members. A few exceptions were made for such special guests as Sarah Bernhardt, Madame Modjeska, Lady Forbes-Robertson, Mary Garden, Cornelia Otis Skinner.

Later another concession was made to the ladies. "During winter months, one Sunday night each month known as Open House, will serve a buffet dinner to members of the Club and of the opposite sex."

The Players makes for a real bond between the actor, the writer, the painter, the musician, the journalist; based on common experiences and a sympathetic and tolerant understanding, *and* the skilled use of a pool cue on the table.

I always get a sentimental Irish rush to the heart when I reread Don Marquis' lines hung on my wall.

A Certain Club

I have seen ghosts of men I never knew—
Great gracious souls, the golden hearts of earth—
Look from the shadows in those rooms we love,
Living a wistful instant in our mirth:
I have seen Jefferson smile down at Drew,
And Booth pause, musing, on the stair above ...

21

A Guy Named Toots

To record a big event in our lives; again we were blessed with a child, this time a brother for Mavourneen. He weighed close to nine pounds and measured twenty-one inches in length. Father George Gallagher, who had baptized Mavourneen, christened the boy Patrick Sean (Sean, the bullock). Mrs. Joe E. Brown and Walter Catlett were the godparents, and neither played it for laughs—and another new life was joy to the O'Brien ménage.

He was destined to be a tall lad. He is now six feet two inches and making the Air Force his career. How we watched his progress as a baby—wondering—would he speak his first word as quickly as his sister—and—when would he take his first step, the way Mavourneen did? And what a boy he was. As I look at the man he now is, it's hard to realize that this was the tiny lad I used to toss into the air and pray that God would make him, first of all, a godly man, a family man and a great live American.

He came of age on all three and took unto himself a bride, a French girl, Monique by name, whom he met while he was stationed in Dreux, France, in his early years in the Air Force. They, too, have three wonderful children and it is a delightful little bilingual family.

I shall never forget my first meeting with my grandson, Patrick, Jr. I stopped off to visit Sean and Monique at the air base at Langley Field. Upon my arrival the boy I had never seen raced toward me, leaped into my arms and shouted "Grandpère." Shades of my Irish ancestors! Grandpère O'Brien!

I spend a lot of time at home, but sometimes I couldn't avoid the occupational disease of show business—testimonial dinners. At the Masquers one night it was for Douglas Fairbanks, Sr. Later, as was the usual custom, several of the guests embarked for the Hotel O'Brien to add a few additional toasts to our friends and taper off the evening. A young man sat down at our piano. He idly fingered the keys and said with a slight German accent, "I don't know whether Hollywood is the place for me—I think I'd better go back to New York."

"My daughter should play half as well."

He smiled. "Ah, for her I adlib a gay little tune, and I dedicate *this* to the little fraülein."

I would have remembered this, in spite of what happened in the following years, because the despairing young man at the Steinway was Fritz Loewe. His return to New York was obviously the proper move because there he wrote the music for *The Day before Spring, Brigadoon, Paint Your Wagon* and that incomparable smash, *My Fair Lady*.

We all missed New York. It had a livelier beat, and the characters were most refreshing. On all of our visits to New York, my first stop off, even before registering at the hotel, was to go see a walking bear called Toots Shor. Maybe too much has been written about Toots, but there he is, an Irish-looking Jew, twice life-size, built like a bulldozer, and features to match.

229

"I'm unique," Toots will modestly tell you, as he puts a ham-sized paw on your shoulder and gives you that craggy smile of friendship. "I'm a bum's bum."

What is it that made Toots' old saloon, and his new saloon, such a delightful madhouse, rally point and escape hatch from the piled-up cares of the day? Maybe, for all the beautiful chicks, Toots' world is a male one, built on the idea that men can like each other, drink together and not be slaves to some chi-chi philosophy, or the fashionable hobos, or passing excitements of the moment. It is this naturalness at Toots' place, this mug's eye of the basic world, its exclusive setting for guys who made it, that makes Toots' the last hangout of the men who got it the hard way. And want a little fun and a few insulting words from a friend.

Through Toots' doors, one enters the memory of joints, brawls of one's youth, the good sound of men laughing and wits roaring. Theirs is a feeling of reality, even if it is only presented as a big drink and the friendly stare of a willing barman with a strong back. It's more than a club, less than a gang, and wider than just a man who has set up a high-rent trap to hustle a buck from the fancy trade among actors, sportsmen, sharp guys, word sling-ers, and good judges of a woman's legs, batting averages, fast horses, and the proper way to make a martini so dry you see desert mirages as you sip it.

Toots is what the longhairs call a natural. He exists purely by a hard instinct that there are only right guys and wrong guys. "And I don't want the wrong guys in my joint." No matter how much rare wood paneling and crisp linen and fancy bottles, Toots keeps his saloon a joint, in spite of what it costs you to eat, drink and exchange words.

"The way I see it," Toots will tell me, eyeing some white-tie trade that is being turned away by his headwaiter because the signal has gone out—*not them*. "The way I figure percentages, Paddy, is, I don't have to like everybody, only my friends. And nobody dares call me an enemy. Know what I mean?" And he'll try and knock me down by slapping me in affection, on the back, with a blow that would have jarred John L. Sullivan himself (who Toots thinks a better man than Plato, or the best days Max Schmeling ever had).

It is a friendship that has endured over thirty years. Almost as old as Toots' best brandy and worst waiter's term of service.

One night he and I had closed the joint.

"Paddy, know what?"

"What?"

"You ride behind a horse lately?"

"Only on a ten-dollar ticket at Hollywood Park."

"So we commandeer a hansom cab."

"It's pouring rain."

So we found a hansom cab at the Fifty-ninth Street exit of Central Park. We insisted the cabbie get inside and be *our* passenger, and after a great deal of uncertainty on his part, he did.

"The horse is jumpy, gents."

Toots and I drove majestically up Fifth Avenue.

"Paddy, let's pay a call on our pal, Bill Corum, and his dear old mother."

"Why not? They like horses."

Toots instructed the cabbie to wait in the barouche. Our visit completed (Mama didn't even smell our breath), Toots and I again mounted our seat and drove on to Toots' apartment. The torrential rain continued.

"Musta bust a cloud someplace."

It was four A.M. We damply alighted from the hansom. Toots bade our weird companion, "Join us, fella." The bizarre little man we had adopted for the evening resembled a character out of Dickens, crossed with a fugitive from some drab Bowery mission. "Tonight you are our buddy."

"If you say so, sir."

"Yep."

The three of us strode into the apartment, Toots with whip in hand, our buddy between us, smelling of tired horse. Toots woke Baby, his wife, by shouting, "Hey Baby, guess what?"

"Not now—no guessing games, Toots."

"Just take a gander."

She came down. She took one look at us and in horror-stricken tones shouted, "*All* of you get out."

We started for the door. Toots mumbled, "How do you like that? That girl's narrow-minded. She wouldn't even buy us a drink."

"The horse is lonely," said the cabby. "I better go."

Toots slipped him a twenty. "Go buy oats."

Baby glared, sighed, shook her head and forgave us, but refused to join us in a night cap.

"Why didn't you bring up the horse?"

Toots snapped his fingers. "Gee, Paddy, why didn't *we* think of *that*."

"Too late," I said. "He's gone."

Baby said, "And don't think Toots wouldn't have brought the nag upstairs."

During the war years, when notice was served on all restaurants, bars and night clubs that there was to be no serving of liquor after midnight, many of the hostelries played the cheat and would serve you drinks after the midnight hour. Not Toots Shor. "You don't get a drink in my place after the stroke of twelve, whether you are a star or a lettuce king. Anyone who can't get loaded by midnight just *ain't* trying."

On all of our trips back East, Eloise and I frequented the mad Club 18. There's never been anything to equal this off beat insult-tossing bistro. Jack White was the host, so-called. Pat Harrington, Sr., and Frankie Hyers worked there, and a fat young unknown comedian who did a pantomime bit at a pinball machine—Jackie Gleason, who already had plans for a rich life.

"Everything I can't afford, that's *all* I want."

All the entertainers on the floor of the club were ad lib and mean and fast. One had to have a lot of courage to face the jibes and barbs fired at you during the evening. One night, Eloise was wearing a hat with a tall red feather reaching skyward. Jack White glimpsed her, stopped the band and said in a voice that could be heard on Times Square, "Pipe the skimmer with the feather on Pat O'Brien's wife—Drums Along the Mohawk!" (You had to be there—the humor didn't travel well.)

The girls always hesitated to go to the powder room, because invariably, White would rush up to the door yelling and rapping sharply with his cane (a permanent and dangerous prop), "You've been in there long enough to read *Anthony Adverse!*" It got so the girls would rush across the street to 21 to go to the little girls' room.

The waiter would lean over some nice innocent, bewildered gal, looking her straight in the face and leer, "You still getting plastered on gin?"

Oddly enough, being insulted in the club became famous and its greatest draw. The so-called slummers from Park Avenue would make an entrance, and they would be touted to the purchase of the vile house champagne. It didn't take much to encourage them, they were usually on the extrovert exhibitionist side. Soon the corks would pop. At the sound, the band would jump up in unison and sing, "We're going to get paid tonight! We're going to get paid tonight!"

The cruder the better; the suckers liked it.

One night, one of the longhaired major European producers, one of the high moguls of Hollywood was sitting at the table next to the Shors and us. Pat Harrington left the band stand and, walking over to the tycoon, shouted, "This guy, pat him on the back and without turning around he'll say, 'There will be a check in the mail in the morning.'"

Newcomers were always given the special treatment. Jack would welcome them with great flowery aplomb. Then present them with a rancid stale cake with one candle, bowing low. "Welcome to Club 18—make a wish and blow out the candle."

As the sucker, cheeks full of air, leaned over to blow, a long string would yank the cake back to the kitchen. The laughter was enough to greet one of Oscar Wilde's best bon mots.

Often, right in the midst of dinner, Pat Harrington would leave

233

the band stand, enter the kitchen and rush back out yelling: "Hey, Jack, the chef caught that rat!"

Naturally people paid a lot for food they didn't eat. TV could use some of the club's earthy humor, *if* it is humor.

It was there that the late Leon Errol, the rubber-legged comic, told me of an incident that had happened to him. A famous cartoonist (who was pretty far out too), a pal of Errol's, used to hang out at the Club 18. He was continually boasting of the wonderful doughnuts his wife made.

"No matter where you might be, Pat," he would always say, "my wife makes the greatest doughnuts in the world."

"After months of listening to this expansive endorsement of his wife's damn great doughnuts, I asked him, 'If those doughnuts are so damn great, why don't you ever bring any to the Club?'

" 'I'll do more than that! Come on home with me to Great Neck right now and we'll sit down and have a platter of them tasty babies.'

" 'Great Neck?'

" 'Just around the corner.'

"I said, 'Let's go!'

"It was the middle of winter, Pat, freezing cold and plenty of snow coming down and all over the ground. The storm grew worse and by the time we arrived at Great Neck and alighted from the train, there were no taxis to be found.

"He telephoned his house, but because of the storm, the wires were down. We had wisely procured a jug at the Club before our departure and we proceeded to warm ourselves, utilizing it for medicinal protection against the cold. We valiantly set forth to walk in the snow. After all, there was a platter of those famous doughnuts waiting. I had heard too much about them the last months. I'm mad about doughnuts.

"So it's four A.M. when we finally arrived at the house. The cartoonist had forgotten or lost his keys. He knocked at the door, he rang the bell—no answer. He called softly, he called loudly, he called plaintively. No answer. Turning to me he said, 'You wait here, Leon, I'll climb through the window.'

"He managed to crawl into the house without breaking his neck. There was a long, long wait as I paced up and down, trying to keep warm, because we had consumed all of the medicine before we reached the house. Finally, after a half-hour, a window opened on the second floor and the damn cartoonist poked his head out. 'Sorry, Leon, you can't come in. I can't come out.'

"'But here's a doughnut!'—and he throws me down *one* lousy doughnut!"

Back in California, one of the few solid old-timers was the former world's champion, Jack Dempsey, who lives only four short blocks from our home. His favorite anecdote, told in his bruised voice, was of the prize fighter who was hauled into court by his wife, who charged he had beaten her up for years.

"Up to then, she had never brought charges against him. The doll was deeply in love with him. But after about the ninth year of his punching her around, but good, she could take it no more and she yelled police. The judge who knew the fighter said, 'Ed, is all this true?' Helen here says you been beating her up for years. Ed said, 'Pay no attention to her, your honor—she's punch-drunk.'"

Dempsey, whom Damon Runyon had given the title "the Manassa Mauler," was not a tiger out of the ring. He was a gentleman and simple and kind. I remember him when our children were young, he would play crazy mind-reading games with them. He was very patient in teaching them the games. He was, he admitted, appreciative of their laughter and love for him. "You can trust a kid. Everybody *else* is a guy betting against you."

Gene Fowler had a deep affection for Jack, and had known him in the old Denver days when Gene was a young and raunchy newspaper man. Jack himself was a very devoted father to his own two daughters, and when his children were babies, it was a study in proud fatherhood to see Jack Dempsey wheeling a pink, lace-filled baby carriage in Central Park. "And nobody laughed either."

Eloise said, "I wonder why not?"

I was lucky in my success in Hollywood, for talent, skill, even genius didn't always make the grade in that daffy kingdom of make believe.

Hugh O'Connell, my sponsor in the Players Club, came to Hollywood after successfully starring on Broadway in many productions. He made a vivid impression in the play, *Whistling in the Dark*, and was given a screen test. By accident, I was in the projection room at MGM waiting to view the rushes of *Flying High*, when Irving Thalberg and Eddie Mannix (Mr. Big and Mr. Middle Big of Metro) ran the screen test of Hugh. It was magnificent. Hugh was truly a great clown, with (let's say it) heart. The scene he made for the test was brilliant; his nuances, his underplaying were fabulous, creating monumental laughs from all of us. In the middle of the test, Mr. Thalberg bounced up like a rubber ball, and exclaimed in fevered excitement, "Look at that!"

"You bet, I.T. I sure did," said Eddie.

"That raised eyebrow—that voice intonation—look at that."

"Solid, I.T., real solid."

"Quick—*who* does he remind you of?"

Mannix replied, "Edward Everett Horton."

Thalberg slapped his own head hard. "That's right! Get *him!* Sign Horton for the part."

"You're a genius, I.T."

Thalberg wiped his face, with a shrug, as if to signify, who was he to disagree with Mannix's verdict.

That was the end of Hugh O'Connell's motion picture career— a career that ended before it began because Thalberg was a genius.

Jack Warner gave me the loan-out treatment again and I went over to do a picture for Walter Wanger. At one time Walter was the only producer in town who admitted he had been to college— he had a narrow broad A and eastern tailoring. Later he was the harassed producer of the Liz Taylor *Cleopatra*.

The picture, with Broderick Crawford, was *Slightly Honorable*. During the filming, Brod, a big broth of a lad, and I had a fight scene that was topped only by Wayne and McLaglen in *The Quiet Man*, but not by much. No doubles—for us they just cleared the set. No holds barred and we went at it. Fortunately, Brod knows every trick of pulling punches, and I had learned a few from Cagney. There were no serious injuries, just a few bruises and aches, discolorations, but the scene was worth it, Walter said. If you ever happen to be watching it on TV, remember—*no doubles*.

That year, 1939, my dad died at sixty-seven. It was sudden and strange. In the afternoon, Eloise, Mom, Dad and I had driven out to the Valley to visit Edward Everett Horton and his mother. It was one of those especially beautiful all gold-and-umber California Sundays, and we had a delightful day with Eddie and his charming mother. We drove Mom and Dad back to Hollywood to their cottage on Cherokee Drive.

"We're going to the Derby for dinner. Join us."

Dad said, "No. We're going over to Frank Shannon's and play some cards, and make it an early evening."

"I think we'll do the same."

"Good night, Pat."

After dinner, Eloise and I returned home and were asleep by eleven-thirty. The phone rang. Eloise answered it and looked wide-eyed at me.

"Honey, it's Mollie Shannon."

I don't know much about extrasensory perception, but there it was that night.

As I took the phone from Eloise, I said, "Honey—my dad is gone."

Why did I say it? The Shannons often called this late to say they were having fun and to report just who was winning the card game.

Mollie Shannon's voice was in my ear. "Pat, come to your folks house quickly—it's your dad."

We rushed down, and my mother met us on the porch, her arms flung up in despair.

"Oh, Pat. We had come from the Shannons' after finishing the card game. Frank drove us home and after a few blocks, Dad turned to me and said, 'Maybe I'd better put this robe over your

237

knees, it's getting chilly.' He did just that, laid his head on my shoulder, and died."

I was in shock. "Mom, Mom! He was my father—my best friend."

"Oh, darling," said Eloise grabbing my hand.

"He always joined in all the games when I was a kid—was a sports lover, played in some of them himself. Billiards, bowling. He was with me at all the sports dinners, baseball and football games—the fights."

"Yes, dear. Stop talking—you're rambling."

"Dad's gone."

Mom turned away, her shoulders shaking.

Only the knowledge that in death, too, there is life sustained us. I never thought Mom could survive the loss, but she was equipped with the fortitude of a Jacqueline Kennedy. She insisted I go to the studio the next day.

"Your father would have wanted you to."

And I remembered just a few days before, Dad had been resting on the sofa, and he had opened his eyes and looked at me. "I know something terrible about you, Pat boy. I kept it secret. You were *once* a chorus boy."

I did my scenes on the movie set. They were not good. They never even printed them. The picture was *Night of Nights*, and Lewis Milestone, the director, said I was only a moving shadow and credulity was completely destroyed. I was a clown in the picture—naturally a sad one. The only time I played a clown in make-up.

22

Knute Rockne

Soon after this, Mark Hellinger, Broadway columnist turned producer, wearer of blue shirts and white ties, owner of a gangster's bulletproof car, approached me on the lot.

"Pat, got a great idea for a picture. If I have my way, *you* are the guy to play the role."

"Get your way."

"I'll try—I'll really try."

A day later Jack Warner called me into his office. "Pat, we are going to do the life of Knute Rockne, the football coach. Mark Hellinger has had this idea for a long time and suggested you for the title role."

"A good suggestion, I think."

"We'll go into production as soon as we have legal clearances from Mrs. Rockne and the family, Father Cavanaugh and the Four Horsemen."

"You haven't said I've got the part."

"You are the actor to play Rockne. Mark swears it."

"Don't you agree, Jack?"

"Sure—I *always* cast Irishmen to play Swedes or Norwegians."

When the rumor spread around the lot that Warner Brothers were going to film the Rockne story, a young man, one of their contract players, approached me. He had been a Midwest sports announcer from radio named Ronald Reagan—turned actor, not too successfully.

"Mr. O'Brien, have they anyone in mind to play George Gipp?"

"I don't really know, Ronnie. Haven't given it much thought."

"I have."

"It's one of the pivotal roles in the picture."

"Mr. O'Brien, if you haven't anyone else in mind, would you put in a word for me to Mr. Warner and Hal Wallis? I've been a great fan of Gipp's throughout his career, and I've read just about everything that's been written on him and Rockne."

"They may want a name actor."

"I can play the part. I won't let you down if I get the assignment."

I had seen Ronnie work in very small roles in various pictures. I liked his excitement. I spoke to Hal Wallis, head of production. He remembered signing the boy.

"Yeah, Pat, a hick radio announcer back in the Middle West."

"Hal, I've watched this kid around the lot. He not only resembles Gipp, but his knowledge of Gipp and of football should help the picture."

Ronnie got the part. His characterization of the immortal George Gipp made Ronald Reagan a star overnight.

To start the film, I was told, the first thing Warners had to do was to get Mrs. Rockne's approval as to who was to play her beloved husband. They brought Bonnie Rockne and her daughter Jean, escorted by the president of Notre Dame, Father Cavanaugh, to California. I sweated out a series of tests that were all subject to her approval. Still shots were made of me with about ten different sets of wigs. I spent painful hours in the make-up room in the company of Perc Westmore and Gordon Bau having my Irish map transformed into Norwegian features. All of this consumed days and days, and prayers. Eloise claimed I even had non-Catholics saying novenas, and agnostics saying Hail Mary for me. I waited, hoping I'd meet all the demanding qualifications. Eloise and I were with Bonnie when she carefully went through all the still pictures of me as her husband. She said softly, "I have no reservations whatsoever."

"None?" Eloise asked.

"None."

The first week of shooting, Bill Howard directing, was mostly exteriors, to be done before we entrained for South Bend. Bill was trying for a comeback—a once fine director come on hard times, given this one more chance.

Bob Fellows, the producer assigned to the film, came to my home on a Sunday morning. He looked like a mother cat who'd just seen her kittens drowned. He was in bad shape.

I said, "What's up, Bob?"

"Pat, you'll have to come with me—I can't do it alone."

"I've no idea what you're talking about."

"They're taking Bill Howard off the picture and replacing him with Lloyd Bacon."

"This will *kill* Bill."

"I know. Front-office orders."

"He's a great director—they know it—even though he's been on the toboggan so long. This is his great chance for a comeback."

"Bill only lives a short distance from here, doesn't he, Pat?"

"Yeah."

We walked over. It was like going to a wake—the "Dead March" from the opera *Saul*. Bill greeted us enthusiastically, with the script in front of him.

"Making changes for the better."

Bob Fellows looked at me. I looked away.

Bob said softly, "I don't know how to tell you this, Bill, the easy way. They're taking you off the picture."

Bill stared his disbelief at us, rose and walked to the end of the room and beat his fists together.

"Boys, this will destroy me."

I said, "It's not that bad, Bill."

"It is—a fade-out."

It was. Shortly after, Bill Howard died.

There is no mercy in Hollywood studios. Perhaps there can't be. A mistake can cost millions. Stockholders expect profits. Maybe Bill was finished as a director—he certainly wasn't as a human being.

Lloyd Bacon took over with not too much initial joy. "Hell, I'm a great friend of Howard's. His chair is still warm." After a few days, we got down to cases and plunged into our work with a vengeance, wondering if any more sacrifices would occur.

I was facing a crucial test. Bonnie Rockne came on the set for the first interior shot to view a scene being played. The setting was the president's office at the university. Rockne, as a young man, was explaining to Donald Crisp, portraying the president, that he has made his decision not to stay on and teach chemistry. (Knute Rockne was considered an expert on synthetic rubber.) He was terribly in love, he said, and planned to work during the summer and get married, and that he wanted to become a coach. He spoke fervently of Bonnie in a warm, earnest voice. The scene ended.

I started off the set. Mrs. Rockne was seated a short distance away and had been watching the scene closely. I couldn't wait for any delayed action. I went over and knelt beside her chair, not saying a word, just looking at her. She placed both her hands on my face.

"Paddy, I watched and I listened. I could have closed my eyes and thought you were making love to me."

At first I didn't say anything. I just knelt and felt thankful. Then I found my voice.

"You think I can really play Rockne?"

"Not play. You *are* Rockne."

The public is unaware how rarely an actor, in his entire career, gets a great role. The public remembers his favorite in two or three parts, and accepts him in minor productions, because of the memory of the great image-creating part. I've been lucky, had many juicy parts, *and* three great ones—Hildy Johnson of *The Front Page*, Father Duffy of *The Fighting 69th* and Rockne. Many great actors have told me of the agony of looking for that one shiny perfect part, and spending their life getting old and shopworn still hunting. John Barrymore, a gushing, wasted talent, did a remarkable, still remembered Hamlet, a lot of historic swordplay and bedroom gestures, but never really had the roles he could have done in his prime. Were Bette Davis' pictures ever worthy of her? And my friend Spencer Tracy, how many of his fine roles were those of an actor making something fair look very good. Cagney too; how many George M. Cohan parts could he find?

I was lucky and I knew it in playing Rockne, *if* I could sustain it, and make it alive and true—make it something different than what I had been doing for rent, bread and a beach house.

Playing Rockne, I began to understand what Lon Chaney went through.

I had to be at the studio every morning at six A.M. to prepare for a three-hour make-up job. Playing Rockne in his later years, naturally, was not nearly as difficult for me as the characterizing of him as a very young man. The combined efforts of Perc Westmore and Gordon Bau on my face, with rubber, paint and the proper wigs, created the youthful personality. It was an agonizing, monumental make-up task each morning—three hours, but I would have gladly sat for five hours in the torture chair, I was so gloriously happy to be Knute Rockne before the cameras. I tried to find the core of the man, the solid center of a creator of *what*? Fleeing moments on a dark afternoon playing field? the hard play of young muscles? Rock's mother had insisted that the name be "pronounced K-nute and *not* Knute." That problem was easily solved because the name reference in the film was usually "Coach" or "Rock." But could I find the man inside the role?

Some of our exteriors were done at the Loyola University campus. Eloise would bring Mavourneen and Sean to pick me up at the end of the day's shooting. On one of these occasions, Sean, aged four, was gazing with horror at the assistant make-up man as he peeled the rubber features from my face. It didn't hurt, but the procedure looked like the Inquisition processing a heretic —he would pull and pull at the rubber skin, nose, chin to get them off. Sean couldn't stand it. He cried out, his eyes wet, sobbing, "Please! Please stop tearing my daddy's face!"

It took us quite a while to assure him that nothing injurious was happening to his dad, and they weren't peeling me like a banana.

We entrained for South Bend, Indiana, to work on the Notre Dame campus, mingling elbow to elbow with the student body and black-robed faculty. Rockne, as I've said, was a difficult assignment to me, as he had been alive so recently. He was killed in an air crash in 1931, and in 1939 most people still remembered him from newsreels and radio interviews. There were hundreds and hundreds of thousands of people who had their own vivid image of Rockne. I was uncomfortable with the thought that many would be quick to say, "*That* isn't Knute Rockne—he wouldn't talk like that—he never made that kind of gesture. It's just some Hollywood ham."

My fears were allayed with Bonnie Rockne at my side, with her aid and counsel. I was nearly satisfied that I was on the right track. I played Rockne not just as a sports figure, but as a man dedicating his life to the cause of youth—a great humanitarian. I had his recording of a locker-room speech. I played it over and over again, trying desperately to absorb his voice intonation, his unusual delivery and vocal attack. In some scary moments I *was* Rockne, and not Pat O'Brien.

A vital sidelight in the life of Knute Rockne was not included in the picture. It was his decision (after winning one of the national championships) to become a Catholic. Bonnie had never asked him to, any more than I had asked Eloise.

Bonnie Rockne told me a story concerning a football player called Moon Mullins. Last heard of, he was coaching at St. Ambrose. On one of the team's train trips to California, coming out to play U.S.C., Moon came into Bonnie's drawing room.

"Mrs. Rockne, could I speak to you a moment?"

"Sure, Moon, sit down."

"Mrs. Rockne, I incurred a rather bad injury during scrimmage. You know how Rock feels about his boys getting further injuries. I'm positive he's not going to let me play against U.S.C."

"Lots of other games, Moon."

"This is an awful blow, Mrs. Rockne. My home is in Pasadena, and this is the first time my folks would be seeing me in action— I've got to play in that game."

Bonnie stopped her story and went on slowly. "I thought awhile Pat, and then reached for my purse and took out a little medallion and gave it to Moon. 'Take this medal, and pray—pray real hard.'

"I don't say, Pat, the medal did it or didn't, but Rock sent Moon in for one play and the Fighting Irish won that game.

"When we returned to South Bend, Moon went to Rock and told him what had happened in that drawing room en route to California. 'Coach, would you return this medallion to Mrs. Rockne and thank her for me?' Rock took the medal and slipped it into his pocket."

Bonnie looked up at me. "Paddy, when they found Dad on that hillside in Kansas, in the wreckage of the plane, he had in his hand the medallion he had forgotten to give back to me."

I related this story to Bill Stern, the sportscaster, at my home one Sunday afternoon, just previous to a Rose Bowl game. He asked, "Could I use it on the air?"

"Bill, that decision isn't up to me—that would be up to Bonnie Rockne. Call her."

We had a phone call put through to the Rockne home in South Bend, and Bill got permission to use the story on one of his programs.

The research and stories I heard about Rock helped me see the man clearer and closer, and I tried to evolve the full figure. It was not easy in a fast-moving, action-packed picture. The actor in any Hollywood film is up against the problem of telling a story that brings in and holds the customers. The director, cutters, editors, producers are all at work trying to move the picture faster, cutting, trimming, pacing it so that the actor is often aware that if every inch of film isn't vital, it is going to end up on the cutting-room floor. And some very marvelous footage has ended up in the discard cans that went out to the refineries, which burned them to recover the metal in the silver nitrate the films were coated with.

Rockne was a film in which I never relaxed, on or off the set. I continued to be on my toes as the picture progressed.

Gale Page played Bonnie Rockne and she fairly radiated charm; an excellent actress and, strangely enough, she bore a remarkable resemblance to Bonnie in the days when Rockne was courting her.

Nick Lukats, once a great halfback and punter in his day at Notre Dame, was technical director on the film. His picture hangs in my little Hall of Fame in my den, along with those of other celebrities I've met. Eloise and I and Father Cavanaugh, former president of Notre Dame, were once looking at the various photographs in my Trophy Room. Seeing Nick's photograph on the wall, he turned to me, "You know, Nick's father was a priest."

I nearly had a stroke. Father grinned and clarified his remark: "Oh, Lukats' dad was a member of the Greek Orthodox Church, and Byzantine law allows married priests."

"Obviously, Father, you said that to try to shock me."

"Try? Pat—your chin touched your chest."

Another technical advisor on the picture was Jim Thorpe the man the King of Sweden called, at the 1912 Olympics, "the greatest athlete in the world!"

Jim was a full-blooded Cherokee Indian, and looked it. He also had the manners of a tepee dweller. He had won both the decathlon and pentathlon events. A few years later, Thorpe's medals were taken away from him, because he had engaged in a professional baseball game. When the officials reversed their decision, years later, and voted for the restoration of his medals, they could not be found. The rumor was Jim had traded them away years before for the white man's fire water. By 1932, Jim Thorpe had a difficult time getting into the Olympic Games in Los Angeles. No one recognized him, the once great hero. Vice-president Curtis, of Indian stock himself, hearing about it, got the greatest athlete of all times in to see the entire Olympics.

The rumor was Curtis said to Jim, "What this country needs is a good two-day Indian massacre against these whites."

I remember asking Jim one day during production of the picture, "Jim, just how far did you ever kick the ball?"

He looked at me with that impassive Indian mien. "Paddy, I used to kick it the length of the field."

"No!"

"Yes. To do it the hard way, I'd do it *without* shoes."

Rockne and Jim had their run-in in the old days. It was back when Jim was playing pro ball with the Canton Bulldogs. Rock was one of his adversaries playing against him on the Massillon, Ohio, team. Every time the big Indian would carry the ball around Rock's end, Rock would stop him cold as an iceberg. Time and time again, Jim would carry the ball and try to get around Knute, but the Norwegian tackled him hard every trip. After several of these bone-jolting encounters, Jim got up and dusted his pants. "Rock—lotsa folks pay hard-earned money to get in to see old Jim play."

"So, Big Chief?"

"So next time Old Jim comes around end, Rock, you let Old Jim go through."

"Not a chance, Jim. Every time you come around my end, I'm stopping you!"

Thorpe shook his head sadly, "Rock. Folks pay lotsa money to see Old Jim run. Next time, let Old Jim go through?"

"Let 'em send you around as much as they want, Jim. I'll be waiting for you!"

"All right, Rock, you let Old Jim run."

The next play Jim went like a bolt of lightning and knocked Rockne as cold as deep freeze mutton and ran 70 yards for a touchdown. He went trotting back and lifted the prostrate Rockne off the ground.

"That's right, Rock, you let Old Jim go through."

The Life of Knute Rockne is often on TV's "Late Show." Watch for the big fellow in the picture who opens the dressing-room door and says, "Three minutes, Rock." That's Jim Thorpe. He had asked Bacon, the director, "Let Old Jim speak one line in the picture."

Bacon had granted the request. "Sure, I don't want any end run from you *if* I don't."

As I studied records, letters, newspapers, I saw Knute Rockne was probably one of the great psychologists in football. There was the time that Rockne did not accompany his team to the Carnegie Tech game. He stayed on in Chicago to scout Army, which N.D. was to play later that season. His absence may have prompted a little lighthearted relaxation in the boys, or Carnegie had one of its better teams. No one will ever know. Without Rockne the Fighting Irish weren't themselves. It was a humiliating defeat. When the dragtail team returned to South Bend, Rockne never mentioned their defeat. Every member of the squad was sure that sooner or later he would open up with a tirade. Nothing. During the following week of scrimmage, he never mentioned the disaster. Nor the week following. The boys began to think he had decided it was just one of those things.

The team entrained for California to meet their toughest rivals, the University of Southern California. Rock made no changes in the traveling squad. Everyone boarded the train, relieved the coach had refrained from any disciplinary action, or one of those talks that turn a locker room into a Black Hole of Calcutta. That night as each member of the squad opened his bag to prepare to retire for the night, everyone found in his valise the program from the old game with the added big letters: *"Carnegie Tech 20—Notre Dame 0!"* Needless to say, the team emerged victorious over U.S.C.

All during the filming of the picture I never used a double. I was forty years old but I blocked and tackled and was on the receiving end of all the passes in every one of the scrimmage plays. In the long shots, we used clips from actual Notre Dame games, but all of the close shots I did myself. I kept in fairly good shape, swimming, and particularly playing handball.

Knute Rockne stands out as one of the truly memorable experiences in my long and often rocky picture career.

At last it was done and in the can—I could do no more than wait, hope, and pray. The première of the picture was held in South Bend, for Notre Dame. Newspapermen and sports writers poured in from all over the country. Warner Brothers beat the drums. Bob Hope was toastmaster and F.D.R.'s son, Franklin, Jr., was one of the people at the banquet. He read a fine letter from the President. Truly it was a Roman (Catholic) holiday. There were the actors on the dais—Ronald Reagan, Jane Wyman, Ricardo Cortez, Gale Page, Donald Crisp, Gail Patrick, Kate Smith and others. The most interesting guest of them all for me was a little lady who received the ovation of the evening. My mother!

23

Of Many Roles

Interviewers frequently ask me: "Of all your roles, which did you find was your favorite?"

My answer is invariably, "I call it a dead heat. There are so many roles I have enjoyed, it's difficult to say which is my favorite."

The interrogator then asks, "I suppose it's Rockne?"

The reason for this may be that for many years my identity has often been matched with athletes'. To paraphrase Will Rogers' words, "I never met a man I didn't like," I could say, "I never made a picture I didn't like while making it." Of course, later seeing the finished production and suffering the film in its entirety, I might hold a different, even painful viewpoint, as the ghost of a hopelessly feeble idea unreels. But when it's good—it's very damn good.

Actually, taking my entire career on the screen I have been fortunate to have played many biographies. I think, probably more than any other actor, even Paul Muni, but I leave it open for challenge. *Oil for the Lamps of China* was actually the life of Alice Tisdale Hobart's husband, whom I played. Also, I was Father Duffy in *The Fighting 69th*; Major Cavanaugh in *The Iron Major*; another priest in *Fighting Father Dunne*; Colonel Paddy Ryan (founder of the Bombadier School in New Mexico) in *Bombadier*; Gorman in *The Last Hurrah*; and—best, to some—*Knute Rockne*.

Rock's life was the toughest to do because I made the picture in 1939 and 1940, and he had died in 1931. Many of his contemporaries, I found out, watched with critical eyes every movement, every gesture, every vocal intonation I made.

"Is that or is that not Rockne?" I'd ask myself. It wasn't easy playing a man still so vividly remembered.

Oil for the Lamps of China was one of my favorite pictures. The girl who played my wife was Josephine Hutchinson. I had played opposite her on Broadway at the Forty-ninth Street Theater some fifteen years before, in *A Man's Man*. Later at Warners, gentle, soft-voiced, intense Jo and I played man and wife again in *Main Street*, Sinclair Lewis' famous exposé of small-town bigotry, and the problems of a country doctor. The title was changed to *I Married a Doctor*, on the theory, I suppose, that a world-famous novel that rocked around the world might confuse non-readers; a book that helped get Lewis the Nobel prize.

Once, shooting a picture at Coronado, California, for Warner Brothers, called *Submarine D–1*, I began to suspect a sailor's life was not all fun. There was a sequence in the film in which members of the crew of the submarine were trapped on the bottom of the ocean and a submarine bell was to be used to aid their escape. The steel bell weighed several tons. It was to be lowered to the depths of the wrecked tin fish in the ocean, to make escape possible for those trapped within. For pictorial purposes, all that would have been necessary would have been to show me and some men entering the submarine bell and close the lid upon us. Then a fast cut to show the bell emerging from the sea. Then another cut to us occupants of the bell as we came ashore. I didn't like the idea of scraping against real sea bottom.

I said to the director, Lloyd Bacon, "Why in hell do we have to go down with it to the bottom of the sea? You sure can't photograph us down there!"

"Stark realism, Paddy. Shall we get started?"

To avoid argument, and being called chicken, and to keep the cameras rolling, Wayne Morris, George Brent and I entered the dank cold bell. The cameras rolled, the signal was given, the bell was lowered—and that was all that could be photographed. They lacked the tools to photograph us underwater. A sailor accompanied us and we went on descending, four foolish men in the grip of the ocean depths. I was scared, I mean *scared*, but actor enough not to show it. Let one of *them* show how they felt first. I felt doomed.

Minutes passed like hours. The air smelled of stale rubber and was heavy as a wet dog. I asked the navy man, "How deep are we now?"

There was a drawn-out silence. He looked at Morris, Brent and myself and shook his head.

"Don't look now, but this gauge is busted."

I wondered how my fellow passengers felt. (The only time I was ever more frightened was when I flew over the Hump from India to China in 1944.) We all looked bug-eyed at the dead gauge; instead of the arrow moving clockwise, it was absolutely as stationary as an Egyptian tomb painting.

"Oh boy," said one of us. "Who knows a prayer?"

I saw us in a rusting ball, resting for thousands of years on ancient clam shells, forgotten and encrusted with coral.

"We're moving," said the sailor.

"Up?"

"We'll soon know."

In the rushes (which were run later in San Diego) we all saw this huge cylindrical bell emerge, sway in a crazy dance, and crash back to float. The hatch opened and four panicky guys, including the sailor, came out to blink in the sunlight.

Brent, overeducated, said calmly to the grinning director, "My point is, we should never had had to descend. Realism frequently becomes synonymous with sadism."

The director asked the cameraman, "Do we need to do it *again?*"

It's my fault for being an outdoor action type. Mike Curtiz was shooting *Angels with Dirty Faces* in the railroad yards of downtown Los Angeles. He failed to tell the engineer of a moving train what the full action of the scene was to be. The two boys who were playing the roles Cagney and I were doing as adults, were supposed to be running away from the police, and were to cross the tracks in front of an onrushing train. Someone forgot to check the train speed. The train barely missed hitting the two boys, who leaped aside like salmon. The shaking engineer clambered down out of his cab; he looked like death at bargain prices.

Mike, a true Hungarian, just smiled at him. "*V*ery good. This was part of the action of our story. I purposely did not tell the two boys before you go so fast."

It was only the quick action of the crew on the picture that prevented this engineer from killing Mike Curtiz.

Mike later shook his head and, in his mangled English, said, "How do you get realism if not take chances?"

Some directors, disappointed actors, also have the reputation of enjoying a performer flirting with real death. Such humor escapes me.

John Ford never asked an actor to do anything he himself wouldn't do. But he would do *anything*. At Fox, in *Up the River*, Spencer Tracy's first picture, a professional knife thrower was to pitch blades all around an actor, missing him by a hair's breadth, if you please. The actor, Warren Hymer, panicked at even the thought of standing up and having knives fired at him.

"Not me, Mr. Ford."

Ford asked him, "If I do it, will you?"

The actor said a feeble yes.

Ford stood and took it. He sucked a cut on his finger. "Easy, see? Now get up there."

The actor did and his knees sounded like a bass drum in a jazz band. But Ford got the shot.

If I didn't like a picture, I didn't do it. An assignment came up at Warner Brothers, *Stage Struck*. I read the script and told Jack Warner, "I don't do it."

He asked, as he lit a cigar, "Why won't you do it, Pat?"

I replied in direct studio terms, "It stinks!"

"I don't smell anything from it. You're under contract, fella—and you are going to do the picture."

"Call my agent, Myron Selznick."

Myron came and said sweetly, "You're absolutely right, Jack—Pat *is* under contract to you. *But* he doesn't have to do the picture—he can take a suspension."

"Some solution," said Mr. Warner.

I took a suspension. Warren Williams was given the role. When the picture was completed, Myron said, "Pat, you're vindicated. You know why? Warren Williams' contract is not renewed, and you return to work."

Jack Warner was a hard man to outtalk, and he was naked studio power. I fought it down the line with him often. His brother Harry was the silent watching type. He wore a public humility like good tailoring. Walking to the studio commissary one day, he came alongside me. We discussed the pictures they were making at that time. He clutched his side often.

"Anything the matter Mr. Warner?"

He looked as though he were in pain. "No. No."

"Anything I can do?"

"No, Pat. This happens every so often. When I was a young fella I was a cobbler, and leaning over a cobbler's bench hour after hour. Years later it still causes this pain in my side."

Jack and Harry were two surviving Warner brothers who ran the studio. There is a brother Albert, not too active, in New York.

There had been a fourth brother, a fireball, Sam, who had pioneered talking and singing pictures, and saved the studio from going under. He died soon after that, worn out, some said, by his efforts.

Jack was the extrovert brother, always smiling through a tan, under thin oiled hair, and a practical joker. Most people thought he was not too seriously interested in film making, and not given to great intellect. They were wrong on both counts. In his seemingly casual way, he ran the studio with a whim of stubborn pride, and it made fortunes. While his education and background were not things to endear him to art lovers, intellectuals and the moaners for better taste or art in films, the studio in those years made the best and most exciting contemporary melodramas—a kind of history of their times.

Jack was a man whose greatest vice was an idea he had a sense of humor, and skill in reckless games of gambling. In later years he was usually away from the studio a great part of the year, on the Riviera, gambling at Monte Carlo and other places. He distrusted writers, didn't dig them—he once told Stephen Longstreet he couldn't understand how "they can remain chained to their typewriters." Actors he revenged himself on, with a sadist's delight, when the mood was on him. He liked long-term contracts at low prices, and no matter how big a money-maker a star became, even Bette Davis, Errol Flynn, James Cagney, Humphrey Bogart, he would think nothing of costing the studio millions in profits by suspending them over some well-merited, well-earned demand.

Harry went along with Jack in these matters. But his job was not studio production so much as the financing end; deals in studio stock, production costs and contracts. Money received Harry's silent and efficient attention. He once had a racing stable that cost millions.

I was often on Jack's carpet. Once he called me into his office and looked at me poker-faced. "Jim Cagney has taken a powder, contractually speaking. He is on suspension."

"I've been there myself."

I didn't know what was on Jack's mind. One thing I was sure of, I knew he wasn't going to give me a raise.

"Pat, you're pretty close to Cagney. I ask you as a favor—I want you to get him to come back."

"Jack, I'm close to Jim, he's my pal and I love him, but . . ."

"But *what*?"

"I'd never make any overture like that to Jim. And Jack, you can't suspend me for *that*."

"You're right—I can't."

James Cagney stayed away two years, at great loss to himself materially, but free in soul and spirit. They brought him back, but it cost them. It *really cost* them.

Bette Davis once ran off to England to break her contract— but Warners, like the Northwest Mounted, got her even there. Maybe she too could have been kept happy with a little kindness.

I was under contract to Warner Brothers for many golden years. It built my home in Brentwood, on the corner of Marlboro and Rockingham Road, a fine modern replica of Mount Vernon. The plumbing is better; we use Mr. Edison's electric, and the plantings are tropical. Also, George Washington didn't have a swimming pool. Eloise and I watched nearly every nail and every board that went into this home where I write these words at this moment. Four lively, wonderful children were raised from infancy into their teens and beyond.

Our housewarming motto was: "This is the house that Jack built."

Frank Borzage was one of my favorite directors at the studio, back in the thirties. He was assigned to direct *Flirtation Walk* with Dick Powell, Ruby Keeler and I playing the leads. I had the role of the hard-hitting sergeant. The entire picture was shot in the green gentle landscape at West Point. Always a sentimental slob, on graduation day I was deeply touched and wept unashamed tears as the cadets marched by on parade—a stirring magnificent sight.

256

During the filming of *Flirtation Walk*, the director told me: "Pat, we have about two weeks of shooting where your services won't be required. Why don't you and your Eloise go to New York for a week or ten days? We can contact you if we need you." The tab was on the studio.

"That's kind of you and the studio."

"We're a long way from the studio."

"They don't know? Good."

Frank grinned. "Max Baer is fighting Primo Carnera for the world's heavyweight title, and you might like to see the bout. I'll arrange for your tickets with the studio's New York office."

"Better and better."

"Be my guest."

Eloise and I took off for New York. We saw the fight and saw Max hit Carnera so hard he broke Carnera's ankle. Max became champion of the world.

And death nearly got me in his grip.

On the second day in New York, I ran into Hal Skelly at the Lambs Club. "How's about coming up to Connecticut for the weekend, you and darlin' Eloise? Actors get a lot of fun breathing that fresh New England air."

"Hal, love to, but I promised Borzage I'd stay on call at the Algonquin. Can we have a rain check for some future date?"

"Make it any time."

I never saw him again—alive.

We stayed on in New York and Hal went on up to Connecticut.

Destiny played a tragic joke on Hal, and nearly on me, if I'd gone up with him. One of the dogs on his New England estate had run away, and Hal went out in a car on the prowl for him. He was driving a car model he hadn't driven before and wasn't too familiar with the shift. He approached a railroad crossing. Hal thought he was in reverse, but actually was in first when the train hit the car and knocked him two hundred feet into eternity. My guardian angel must have been watching over me. Had I gone up to Connecticut, I would of course have been with Hal on that tragic ride. Life at Warners' continued with its stock company that has had no peer before or since, a sterling assemblage of actors and actresses, nuts and hams, who could play or portray any role assigned to them; kook or goddess, hero, heel or just folk.

I was told I was to portray Father Duffy in *The Fighting 69th*. I had met Father Duffy in the Lambs Club years before, but I never expected I would be privileged to relive some of his life through the media of films. My pal Jimmy Cagney was playing the lead in the picture and this made it harder. Jimmy can steal a scene by lifting an eyebrow.

We all worked hard on the picture, and tried to add to its realism and its spiritual content a feeling of the complexity of life in times of turmoil.

The première of the picture was one of the most colorful and exciting (that is to say, in its day). New York City was the place and the thrill of the night of the opening left an indelible joy in me. The cast in *The Fighting 69th* was top-rank: Cagney, Frank McHugh, Alan Hale, Sr., George Brent, Dennis Morgan, Tommy Dugan, William Lundigan, Sammy Cohn. Jeffrey Lynn played the role of Joyce Kilmer, the poet of "Trees" in that fine scene where we trudged through the mud while he recited "Rouge Bouquet."

Just before we left Hollywood for the première, a studio worker approached me on the lot.

"If you're going to New York for the opening, maybe you'll go to Washington for President Roosevelt's birthday ball."

"I hope so."

"You suppose you'll get to see him personally?"

I answered, half kidding, "Jimmy—anything I can do for you?"

He was quiet for a moment. "There sure is—would you give him a message for me? Tell him I'm having a rough time, trying to keep from losing my home."

"That's a pretty tough assignment, but if I do get that close to F.D.R., I'll sure try to deliver your message."

"Thanks. I know you will if you get the chance."

F.D.R. had that effect on people; the simple knowledge that

maybe he cared. The late John Kennedy too had some of that magic—rest his martyred soul.

By shifting timetables we actually got to Washington before the New York première. We, among many others, attended the President's birthday party. To say it was an exciting event is putting it mildly. It was a gay madhouse—two days of being in and out of the White House. The great afternoon we were all given a personally conducted tour of 1600 Pennsylvania Avenue by Eleanor Roosevelt herself, and we were to meet F.D.R. at the end of the tour. The usual protocol we were told was "to stand in line, approach the desk where the President is sitting, stop a moment to greet him and retire so next in line could approach him."

I was in a flop sweat as I neared the desk where the President waited, smile in place, cigarette holder tilted at a jaunty angle, the golden voice booming out in one of his chuckling laughs. I kept thinking about Jimmy, that stagehand back in Hollywood and his too simple poignant request. Mr. Roosevelt held up his hand and called my name.

"How is everything with you, Pat?"

I was speechless. Eloise, behind me, with a gentle push, said, "Go on, dear, tell him what Jimmy asked you to do."

I gulped. "Mr. President, this may seem foolish—there's a worker—I wrote it down here—on our lot who is about to lose his home—his name is Jimmy."

"He gave you a message?"

"Could you make a helpful move in his behalf?"

The President smiled. "You tell Jimmy if he doesn't hear from us in two weeks to wire—not write—the White House, and we'll see if something can be accomplished."

I muttered, "Thank you, sir, for not thinking me nuts." I backed away.

Eloise said as we left, "You read your lines fine."

Returning to the Mayflower Hotel, I sent a wire:

DEAR JIMMY JUST DELIVERED YOUR MESSAGE IN PERSON TO THE PRESIDENT

PAT O'BRIEN

Months later we were working on the picture, *Torrid Zone*, shooting at night. Jimmy, the grip, was a member of the crew high on a camera crane. Mrs. Cagney and Elosie had been attending a Marian Anderson concert at the Philharmonic and stopped by the studio to pick up Cagney and myself after the last shot. Jimmy, the grip, saw the girls from above. He clambered down and I introduced him to Billie and Eloise.

He removed his gloves and said shyly, "Thanks, Mrs. O'Brien, for pushing your husband onstage. The President saved my home for me."

A sentimental, sloppy story—but if I left it out, it would leave out something I never regretted doing, and now that I've put it in here, people can say, how corny can a grown man get? But I don't care. Mom used to say, "People are most ashamed of showing they are human beings, with something to celebrate."

I once knew an atheist who wasn't ashamed to admit he gave up his non-belief. "And you know why, Pat? They don't have enough holidays."

One of the most glamorous leading ladies I played opposite was Kay Francis. Not only was she a big dark beautiful creature, but she was endowed with a wonderful sense of humor. I saw Kay a few years ago when I was playing in Falmouth, Massachusetts. She and Eloise and I dined together and I reminded her how completely uninhibited she was.

"Whenever you played love scenes, you always took off your shoes."

"I was taller than most of the men I played with."

It more than enhanced her grace. She was a statuesque beauty, as was Ann Sheridan, who was my leading lady in five different pictures.

I only made one picture at Warners after *Knute Rockne*, with John Garfield and Frances Farmer, *Flowing Gold*. Jack Warner and myself couldn't come to terms on the renewal of my contract and so we came to the parting of ways.

"You'll be back, Pat."

"Anytime, Jack, you know my terms."

"You an artist or a banker?"

"For you I'm a money-maker."

I felt sad leaving my Alma Mater (which it had come to be). It meant leaving a coterie of pals; Bette Davis, Paul Muni, Cagney, McHugh, Bogart, Dick Powell, Barton MacLane, Allen Jenkins, Joe E. Brown, Joan Blondell, Glenda Farrell, Alan Hale, George Brent and many others.

It didn't take Myron Selznick more than two weeks, and I was a hired hand at Columbia, with my friend, the disliked Harry Cohn. He signed me for two pictures, one of them was the first of Glenn Ford's early ventures, *Flight Lieutenant*; the other, *Two Yanks in Trinidad*, co-starring with Brian Donlevy, and Janet Blair, her first picture. The late borscht-voiced Gregory Ratoff directed *Two Yanks in Trinidad*. Greg claimed to be a royalist White Russian officer and had a picture of the late czar in his dining room. Moss Hart seeing it, said, "Ratoff, what I really know of your relatives, it ought to have a frame made of matzos."

In the story conference preceding the production, I asked Ratoff: "Greg, how do you visualize my character?" With an accent as thick as sour cream, he said, "Poddy, een thees scene, you are how do I say it—the Irish Bugsy Siegel."

I had played handball with Bugsy, an upper-class hoodlum, at the Beverly Club frequently and when I told Bugsy of this graphic description of the character, he laughed: "Give it class, Pat—this picture for me has *got* to be a smash!" Bugsy died with class, machine-gunned to death in a Beverly Hills mansion with a beautiful lady resident.

After Columbia, Myron negotiated a great contract for me at RKO Studios, where I was to become associated with Charlie Koerner. He was endowed with more warmth, charm and generosity than anyone who had ever headed a studio during my time. Irving Thalberg would be in second place; he was a charmer, but he never had any close feeling for the people around him, or warmed so fully into life as did Charlie Koerner. Charlie not only mingled with the artists, but was a pal to the technicians, the back-lot people, as well. If the electricians, grips and gaffers happened to be having a card game during a coffee break, Koerner if he happened by, would always stop a moment, kibitz a little and proceed on his way.

When he died, so did RKO. It's hard to know why a personality could keep a studio afloat—yet often the lack of one destroys it.

My first picture under contract (I was to spend nine years there) was a service story, and made a lot of money for the studio. I began to feel as feisty as I had when I first came to Hollywood for Howard Hughes. The picture was *The Navy Comes Through*, directed by Eddie Sutherland and co-starring Jane Wyatt and George Murphy. Max Baer (father of the present Beverly Hillbilly) and Jackie Cooper were also in the picture. There was a young Cuban in the show, an avid, fanatical card player; so were many of the cast and crew with the exception of myself. We were shooting on location out on the old back lot at Pathé. They had erected a few tents. The Cuban played cards whenever there was an idle moment. He had quite a chili-and-rum accent, and a lot of the boys used to heckle him about it. A game was at its height, and some loser upset the tent and it tumbled down on all of the participants in the game. The Cuban rushed out of the fallen tent and in boiling words interspersed with a few foreign exclamations, shouted, "All right, all right, smart guys! You all be sorry! Some day I buy this studio and show you!" He was sure a prophet in his own land. His name was Desi Arnaz, and eventually he and his then wife, Lucille Ball, did buy RKO with their TV loot.

24

The World Begins to Burn

There was war talk and sounds of war at the end of the thirties. The foul and fearful days of Hitler's madness; the *Bund* in America and Lady Astor's Cliveden set in England happy with Nazis, and Chamberlain and his furled umbrella, with words about "peace in our time." How did we react? We continued, I remember, to go about our affairs; we talked of the fearful thing that a war would bring; and some of us prayed. We prayed for peace, understanding, tolerance, while the first of the millions of Jews were already moving toward their horrible deaths in concentration camps and furnaces. For us born early in the century, it was all so dreadful, unreal—so much over life-size that even in Hollywood, where almost anything was possible to put on film, we too could hardly believe the horror was there and moving toward us.

We went on making the same kind of motion pictures we had been making, only now the villains were mean and snarling Germans with thick comic accents. It was to be the last great age of the motion picture as a king supreme in entertainment. Its power and its strength were as yet unchallenged. Television was little more than science-fiction talk and a few experiments. There was a screen writer named Larry Hazard at MGM, who had a four inch TV tube built into a set as clumsy and large as a baby grand piano. Monday nights there would be a half-hour experimental newsreel broadcast, that's all. So sitting in Larry's living room, and Larry on the floor under the machine adjusting and rewiring, one would wait. When the half-hour of television came on, the set was usually not functioning properly, and one would leave with a feeling of nothing but blurs, and sparks in one's eyes. No, the monster that was to wound, deeply wound the movies, was still a spotty infant of not much range. The war would sustain the movie box offices; people would stand in lines all over the world to get into a warm cheerful movie. But it was the last moment of power, only we didn't know it.

Munich and its cozy betrayal passed; the attack on Poland began, the *Panzers* ground acid into our hearts. The Battle of Britain produced the world's finest performer, Winston Churchill. All the world was his stage, and with the freedom of much of the world at stake he rallied his nation.

Our personal life went on.

In July of 1941, another blessing arrived, another son, seven pounds and some odd ounces and with eyes that twinkled like every star in the firmament with roguish Celtic luster and would continue to do so during the years. Ah, he was the roly-poly one and seemed to laugh the day he was born. We christened him Terence Kevin O'Brien, and what greater initials than that could the Gaels have bestowed upon him? T.K.O.—Technical Knockout O'Brien! And then again those days of watching his progress with all the glow of parental pride, counting the days until he would say his first word and toddle his first step—watching him become an honor student at Loyola, win a scholarship to the University of Madrid in Spain, and then return to enter the

29. Jinx Falkenburg and I entertain the troops in the Burmese jungle in 1944. *U. S. Army*

30. General "Vinegar Joe" Stilwell and myself at Kunming, China. *U. S. Army*

31. Air transport during the war was pretty rough, especially going over the Hump. Here are Mr. and Mrs. Jim Dodd, a sad-looking me, Betty Yeaton, and Jinx Falkenburg on the way to China from India. *U. S. Army*

32. All kinds of weapons were used by the Chinese at Luchow. We were hastily evacuated from here when a battle overran our position. *U. S. Army*

33. A lighter moment during a grim war, Jinx Falkenburg and I visit the Taj Mahal during the brief respite between entertaining the troops.

U. S. Army

34. Eloise and I visit Galway in Ireland in 1946.

35. A glorious occasion indeed when an O'Brien gets a degree with a cardinal. This eminent group gathered at St. Francis College to give Cardinal Spellman, Archbishop of New York, and yours truly a degree in 1946.

36. Eloise and I are presented to Her Majesty, Queen Elizabeth, in 1946. King George is in the background, and Katina Paxinou is facing the camera.

37. Later in the same year we had the unforgettable privilege of an audience with His Holiness, Pope Pius XII. Here Eloise and I pose with two Swiss Guards just before the audience.

G. Felici

38. Terry, with Spencer Tracy and Irene Dunne as godparents, at his christening. Terry is wearing the christening dress in which I was baptized. All the children wore it at their baptisms.

39. Sean O'Brien at the age of three claims the drumstick at the Thanksgiving dinner at the O'Briens'. With him are his maternal grandparents, Mr. and Mrs. Carl Taylor, Eloise, my Mom, and on my left Mavourneen.
Associated Press Photo

40. A happy occasion, Christmas at the O'Brien household in 1948. In the usual order, Mavourneen, Terry, Eloise, Brigid, Pat, and Sean.

41. Another gala event, Brigid's christening in 1946 with Nell and Artur Rubinstein attending. Eloise is holding Brigid.

42. Our pride and joy, Tara, the home of the O'Briens in Brentwood.
© 1940, Warner Bros. Pictures Inc.

43. The children and I discuss a serious problem at poolside. Mavourneen, Terry, Sean, and Brigid.
Pat Robbins

44. The O'Briens assembled in full force. Pat, Eloise, Mavourneen, Sean, Terry, and Brigid, standing in front of Tara.

45. I visit with a dear old friend, Sister Mary Norbert, who had taught me in 1907.

46. A happy gathering at a testimonial for Toots Shor in 1963. General Rosy O'Donnell and Quentin Reynolds are on my right, and Michael DiSalle, Former Governor of Ohio, is on my left. Toots Shor, as the guest of honor, is seated. *Bill Mark*

47. Here I am in my role as Harrigan in the television series *Harrigan and Son*. With me are Roger Perry and Georgine d'Arcy.

48. A guest shot on television that I thoroughly enjoyed—playing the role of an old miner on *The Virginian*, who of course is Lee J. Cobb.

49. Another role I thoroughly enjoyed, Finian in *Finian's Rainbow* which I played in summer stock in 1963.

50. Here are Eloise and Brigid and myself in Indianapolis in 1961. We were doing summer stock under canvas.
George Tilford,
The Indianapolis News

52. The role I like best of all. Eloise and I after more than three decades, still facing the world together.

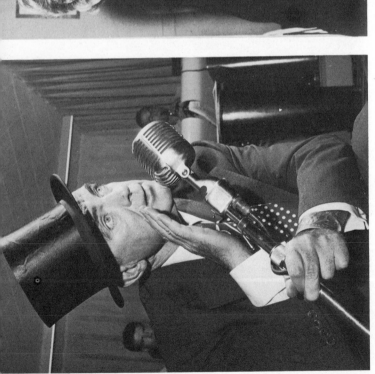

51. Here I don top hat for my night club act.

School of Foreign Service at Georgetown University in Washington, D.C., from which he was graduated in June 1964.

Too soon came the seventh of December—Pearl Harbor—and the nation was in a Second World War. I seriously contemplated re-enlistment in the Navy.

My agent shook his head. "Wake up, Paddy. At your age, forty-one, even though you might receive a commission, there is a hundred per cent chance you'd be relegated to a desk job—probably recruiting in San Diego."

"That's still doing something."

"Offer your services as an entertainer."

"And why not?"

So I signed up, got ready to amuse harassed young men in uniform in impossible places. I traveled through the Caribbean, to China, Burma, India, Persia, Africa and Egypt, and the war went on. Between one of many war assignments I did a fine film, *Bombardier*, under the Koerner regime at RKO. It co-starred Randolph Scott, Anne Shirley, Bob Ryan and myself. This was the biography of Paddy Ryan, the man who started the Bombardier School in Albuquerque, New Mexico, where the greater part of the picture was filmed.

But the real war, not on film, kept calling me back, even if only to entertain with a few stories, a dance step or two. The USO decided to send Will and Gladys Ahern, along with some other entertainers and myself, to the Caribbean with the parting word: "This is supposed to be a *great* place for a pleasure cruise."

It was anything but that during the war. Among death-carrying insects, and wolf packs of hunting German U boats, we entertained in the British and the Dutch Guianas. The American merchant marines were making their valiant voyages, often death runs, night in and night out. Many of them went down to an oil-spread death in their torpedoed ships.

Some of our troops were stationed up the green screaming jungles. There was a small disciplinarian army prison near Devil's Island, a miniature Alcatraz. We went in by river boat. There were actual cannibals in the area, and I reported home: "We were lucky, it was Lent and they weren't eating anyone."

The man-eating Indians would come out to the boat in canoes to greet us. We had been told before we left for the trip that the most prized gift we could give them was straw hats. We brought along about sixty. I'd skim them over the water like flat stones, and the natives would scream and yell with glee as they donned the treasured gifts and paddled back into the jungle for dinner. If the boats stank, the planes we flew in through that area were creaking chicken crates, marked UNSAFE as on these overexciting trips on actual battle fronts.

It was mean and miserable travel, but it was heartwarming to see the reaction of our tired, often depressed battle-weary boys. We journeyed on long trips to give them a few laughs. They appreciated it. Damp and weary on a camp cot, I often thought we were the ones who in some ways profited most. The joy of giving happiness to others is I suppose a selfish one, good for the ego. Yet one does gain from giving.

I shall be haunted all my mortal life by personal memories of dank dawns on crazy horizons, of hard, back-breaking bucket seats in a coughing plane, with the smell of oil leaks and unwashed actors. We waiting, peering through the torn mist, and the pilot wondering if we were on the right flight pattern. The strange noises on the radio, and then from a dirty window, some hint of a cruel brass sea under us, the first sign of wild growths, the shape of an overgrown landmark, the fearful mud and debris under us. Then the rough bump of landing on an airfield, most likely just bulldozed out of coral rock and prehistoric jungle. The first sight of the camp area always was depressing, the battered tents, the unpainted wood, the sight of young faces, unshaved, heat-rashed or insect-tormented, always tired, under burdens of weapons and packs. The hospitals were an ordeal—the seriously wounded dazed with drugs, the surgeons working just beyond a canvas wall.

The show areas usually were some wooden planks laid in the mud, the sound and speaker connections fuzzy or missing, and we entertainers in muddy or dusty shoes, facing a sea of faces, all eyes. All waiting to see somebody from a lost place called home, somebody that was girl with real hips and sleek silk stockings and long soft wavy hair. So I didn't waste too much time with the jokes and stories. I'd get them into the mood and the girls would dance and sing, and there would be cheering. They all looked so young, so earnest, so eager for some answer we didn't carry. All we could give them were a few laughs, and glimpse of something alive and animated kept from them. Then, many of them went out to die in a far place, to give up young life for something a lot of them never knew the meaning of.

Some were believers in God and prayer, some were not. There seemed to be no truth in the old slogan: "There are no atheists in foxholes." Many of the boys found a peace of sorts in God and His words. But I don't know of any hasty dramatic battle conversions. Man is complex and stubborn, and under stress, he often does not change, but rather digs more firmly into those lines of thought he holds proper for himself; holds on to it as if to a lifeline. Nor were they all unthinkingly brave. Fear sat on us all, with the dreadful knowledge that death was often just a flaming second away.

In many ways real life, war, was not at all like the movies showed it. It was more earnest, monotonous and reasonless.

During one visit to the troops, to one of the outposts of New Guinea, just before our show one night, we were told a huge plane bound for Russia had set down for refueling not far from the base. A group of GI's and I commandeered two jeeps and drove over to the plane. The pilot of the giant tin buzzard greeted us. We were welcome to go aboard.

"Maybe you might see someone from home that you knew."

To my great joy I discovered among the passengers, my old burly, shaggy friend, Quentin Reynolds. After solid greetings, Quent said: "Paddy, how about it—can I come over and watch your show? We're here for hours—waiting."

"Quent, not only can you watch it, you're going to be in it!"

"I'll try my buck-and-wing."

I walked out onto the tiny, improvised stage. "Boys, one of our best war correspondents is en route to Russia. That's how *I* keep secrets. He's been forced down here for an undetermined length of time, and this guy has been kind enough to come over and join us. I know you'll want to hear the top man in his field on how to win the war and go home. I give you Quentin Reynolds."

Reynolds was marvelous but he never did do the buck-and-wing. He talked for half an hour and regaled and highlighted his speech with a firm optimism, saying that, "In my opinion, it will not be long now before the war is over."

That started a big cheer.

He asked me, "How was I?"

"Quent, with that curtain line, how could you miss?"

Back at the Hollywood studio, Charlie Koerner had purchased *The Iron Major*, the life of the late Frank Cavanaugh, the famous football coach of Fordham and Dartmouth. Back I went into gridiron togs.

I was told, "This is a beautiful story with an abundance of filial love, of family and country. Cavanaugh had eleven children."

"Just enough for a team."

Ruth Warrick played my wife in this production and Bob Ryan stole some of my usual ecclesiastic glory as the priest, and gave a magnificent performance. The première of *The Iron Major* was held in Boston, there being Irish there. The real Frank Cavanaugh had gone blind, and on his deathbed he said to his family:

"Always remember these three important things. Love of God —love of country—love of family." Those were the Iron Major's last words.

Another war film waited for me, *Marine Raiders*. I insisted that Bob Ryan be co-starred with me.

To switch from so many war pictures, I did a comedy, *Having Wonderful Crime*, co-starring Carole Landis, George Murphy and myself. It was to be made on location in Carmel, up the coast, and Eddie Sutherland and I rented a small cottage for the duration of the filming among the Monterey pines, the dazzling sunsets and the geeking sea birds.

A wild-looking man with six-inch mustaches was pointed out to me as Salvador Dali. We gave a party for the entire cast one night, and the gathering became louder and more raucous as the evening progressed. War nerves and tensions needed a lot of loud byplay. About midnight the phone rang. A man's voice with a very odd accent said, "I live next door. My wife, she is quite ill. The noise is most distressing and could you please be more quiet?"

I said, "Sure, sure, who's calling?"

"Salvador Dali."

"No kidding, Mr. Dali, I'm truly chagrined and completely mortified. I apologize for all of us."

"Oh, Gala is not that *seek*."

"Say, what about you and your wife, if she is well enough, joining us—Eddie Sutherland, Carole Landis, George Murphy and me tomorrow at five for cocktails?"

"The cocktails—but of course!" He accepted graciously with Latin verbosity.

"Good."

"Most happy to join you—so sorry for having had to make this type of phone call to you."

Carole said, "Who was it?"

"A guy named Dali."

"The modern painter?"

"He did say he paints."

"Oh boy, does he paint!"

We all had an early call for the next morning's shooting, and the party broke up. After the departure of the guests, Eddie and I tried to console each other for such thoughtlessness of our neighbor. "Especially," I said, "because of Mrs. Dali's illness. He's a painter."

"Hell, they don't paint the houses more than every ten years here. He'll starve."

The next morning at my light breakfast at a nearby hotel, I

saw the Dalis on the other side of the dining room. I couldn't resist rushing over to offer more apologies in person.

"I'm terribly sorry about last night. If we'd known of your wife's illness, Mr. Dali, we certainly would not have been so boisterous, but we are so happy that you and your lovely lady are joining us for cocktails this afternoon."

Dali stared at me in utter bewilderment, as though I were a monster from another planet. He turned to his wife and said something fast and crackling in Spanish. The voice was *wrong*. Shrugging his shoulders in utter amazement, he again looked at me as though I were completely out of my mind.

Then it *hit* me. It was a rib, that phone call. I had been taken and taken good. There sat the real Mr. and Mrs. Salvador Dali in person, and Mrs. Dali was a lot healthier than I was at that moment.

"Look, folks, forget it. I've made a complete idiot of myself trying to apologize for something you know nothing about."

Dali shrugged and went back to his food. I backed away from the table. I tore out to where the cameras were set up for the day's shooting, to wait for the characters who had concocted this poor joke. I recalled that George Murphy was a good man with a dialect, and I was convinced he was the ribber, and I also had a very strong hunch my dear pal, Sutherland, had had a hand in the plot—he and his talk of Dali as a house painter! But nobody admitted to the rib. I looked too burned up I suppose.

"Cancel the cocktail party!"

"You can't," said Eddie. "Suppose the Dalis do show up?"

Everyone invited came for cocktails, with the exception of Mr. and Mrs. Salvador Dali.

Later someone reported Dali said, "The Americans are so lonely they push themselves on total strangers and try to get them drunk."

I was loaned to Universal to play in *Broadway*, co-starring with George Raft, Broderick Crawford and Janet Blair. In the film I played the same role of Dan McCorn that I had played when I met Eloise years before.

Phil Ryan, an old friend of mine who had once been with the Selznick office, purchased a story from *The Saturday Evening Post*. It was a cloak-and-dagger tale of the FBI, and for marquee value, Phil changed the title to *Secret Command*. He came to me. "Pat how would you like to co-produce this with me?"

"Where?"

"I've approached Harry Cohn."

"That's dangerous, some days, if he's feeling his power."

"This was a good day I picked to see him. He agreed we could produce it at the Columbia lot. Mr. Koerner gave his sanction. It's still a loan-out. You're still under contract."

I became a producer. Phil and I cast the picture. Ruth Warrick was my wife, and Carole Landis played the other lead, along with Chester Morris and Wally Ford. I proceeded to put as many of my pals to work as I could crowd into the production; which is a mistake for a producer, for when the news got around, I never knew I had so many friends. Because all of my buddies didn't all get assignments, I probably made a few enemies.

Phil grinned. "Now you know why Jerry Wald is so fat—to have room for all the knives in his hide."

Terneen Productions was the classy title of our company, a composite of Terry and Mavourneen. Somehow or other the name Sean could not be fitted into the title. In order that my son Sean might not be eliminated entirely, we called one of the main characters in the story Sean. The picture was a success and everybody made a couple of bucks. Then back again to my home base. I loved that RKO lot, as did most who worked there. "It's homey, without being chintzy." It exuded more friendliness and warm camaraderie than any studio in which I ever worked.

The dismal war was still raging. Again came the summons to entertain on the battle fronts. The war was at its worst, and all over the globe our troops were just holding and suffering, engaged in bloody encounters, and in need of entertainment and hope. There weren't actually, to be truthful, too many in the USO who volunteered for dangerous assignments. Joe E. Brown and Bob

Hope were always ready. They covered more mileage than most of us combined. The one edge I have over Bob was that I flew the Hump. He did not.

This assignment was—I later found out—the most precarious of all, flying the Hump over the high, chilled Himalayas, and over jungle Burma. We were sworn to secrecy and not even our immediate families knew fully our destination.

I was forty-four, and said a sad farewell to my wife and three children, setting out like a young cluck, for a far-flung Jap-infested frontier. Our little group had six wondering worried people: Jinx Falkenberg, Jimmy and Ruth Dodd, Betsy Eaton and Harry Brown, pianist extraordinary in any weather or any music box. Harry proved to be the real solid core of the trip, an easy humorist and a friend of mine down through the years. Later, others made the trip over the Hump during the war: Joe E. Brown, Paulette Goddard, Ann Sheridan, Keenan Wynn, Carole Landis, Bill Gargan, Ben Blue, Pat Moran, Lily Pons and husband André and others.

So there I was, on my way to Asia, and the worst place in Asia. Whatever the Chinese-Burma front needed, it wasn't just actors.

25

In the Real War—Not a Movie

We flew to New York for the long way to Asia. Our pilot got off the beam and we were real lost somewhere over a hazy Tennessee and forced down in a heavy fog, to find out where we were. We arrived in New York five hours later. The following day we were given our medical shots. We had to be inoculated for cholera, yellow fever, beriberi and a few more diseases that I am happy to forget. I staggered through it and when we were finished with those shots our arms looked like a chunk of Irish lace.

The doctor said, "This should kill anything in Asia."

"Doc, it's killing me right here."

The following morning we lifted off for Miami, where we began our new flight, stopping en route at Bermuda, the Azores, Casablanca, Tripoli, Cairo, Karachi, New Delhi and Chabua (India) where we were briefed for our trip over the Hump.

"Each of you will be given your own oxygen tank and instructed how to bail out in case of emergency over the Himalayas."

I don't know at which time I was more frightened; the flight over the Hump, *or* that time I was stuck under the sea in the submarine bell I mentioned previously. I was under certain conditions a well-conditioned coward.

A new member had joined our group at Miami and accompanied us as far as China. He was a genial companion, but completely shrouded in mystery, like a character out of a bad mystery book or a B movie. He carried a heavy yellow leather brief case from which he never became separated. At night time it would serve as a pillow, and whenever we would alight from the plane, he would clutch it to his side as though it were crown jewels or the secret of the universe. He said he was Commander James McGinnis.

(Years later when I met him in Chicago, he told me what he was transporting in that brief case.

"Valuable information that was to be delivered at Ceylon."

"What was it?"

"I think an order for tea for Mrs. Roosevelt."

He is now vice-president of a large distillery company and hates tea.)

Asia, from the air, is ruins, sand, dust, jungle, wild rivers and vast mountain ranges and unending space.

Upon arrival in Kunming, China, oxygen and all, we wasted no time relaxing, but gave a show in one of the big hangars. Our audience was huge—they were actually hanging from the rafters. It was quite a sea of lonely far-from-home faces. I met General Chennault, known to his fliers as "The Hawk." He was solid-looking, hard-shelled and had one of those bear-trap mouths that belong to men who get things done. He was a great baseball enthusiast and we played a game one afternoon. He let me choose my team from his fighter flight group. We worked as opposing pitchers. My team emerged victorious and the general, I must admit, was a hard loser.

"O'Brien, were you not a civilian, I might have you court-martialed."

Instead, we became friends.

A few nights later, we entertained for General (Vinegar Joe) Stilwell. He invited all of the troops that could get into the compound to watch our show. Afterward, we went to his quarters and visited with him. It was a sad evening.

He said, "I have just received orders that I am to be relieved and sent back to the States."

Vinegar Joe was a fascinating man, and I wish I had had the opportunity of knowing him longer.

One of the outstanding people I met was a General Randall. He insisted we live in his quarters for the rest of our stay in China. So, if into the interior we flew to entertain, we *always* managed to get back to the general's headquarters late the same night or early the following morning. Hot bath water and real ice were rare in China.

Sometimes, we were a little overeager in our flights because we were anxious to entertain all the areas within the realm of airborne possibility. One night we flew completely off course and landed roughly in a rice paddy within the enemy lines. It didn't take our pilot long to realize the potential disaster.

"Gung ho the hell out of here!"

We clambered back into the plane in a hurry and flew to more friendly a landscape.

It was a rough primitive life, and we entertainers got the best there was of it. But it was a strange, unreal, dangerous world, far from all we knew, valued or understood. On all sides a few miles away, a few yards even, were the enemy, cruel little men with deadly tools of war, and fearful habits of torture and experimenting with death in all its dismal forms. Human life had little value. It seemed an old philosophy to the Chinese: "We come quickly— we go quickly." They were all around us, in rags, barefooted, carrying their heavy loads, doing their wretched tasks, bowing and waiting. With us they were silent, among themselves they chattered and sang and gambled. The Chinese are the world's greatest gamblers. They ate their few grains of rice, and stared at us. We didn't fully understand them and they didn't understand us at all. We were intruders from a world they knew nothing of.

The United States was pouring men and supplies across the Hump, that backbone of evil mountains where the blue above seemed afraid to reach down to us, and flying its gorges and its shark's-tooth peaks was something no one could ever forget. Even the daytime hours seemed nightmares.

We actors were on kind of a leash. Luchow, one of our outposts, was extremely close to enemy territory. No one had been allowed to go there to entertain the troops. General Stilwell had been adamant. "No entertainers go into *that* territory, because of the great risk."

But Stilwell had returned to the States. I asked General Chennault if he would object to our making the trip.

He frowned, "Okay, Pat, *but* just you and the two boys go. This is damn risky. I don't want the girls to go with you."

I relayed this information to Jinx, Betsy and Ruth. All female wrath broke loose. They were vehement in insisting they go with us to Luchow.

"Besides, Pat, if you left us here, and there was some bust-up, we would be on our own."

"Okay, gals—we're on our way, and I'll be shot for taking you against the general's orders."

It was not a good flight; much of the ground below was already in enemy hands. We arrived at Luchow, a raw open battlefield. They had already begun to evacuate all civilians. General Casey Vincent was in command. He was a Texan by birth, the second youngest general in the Air Force. He was extremely grateful and worried at our making "such a precarious trip into battle territory." He warned us of the imminent danger.

I said too boldly: "We are here to give a show tonight."

All lights were out and an eerie insect-ticking stillness filled the entire compound.

General Vincent said, "Go ahead—do the show—but it's a little rough on me to okay it."

"Why, sir?"

"The Japs are moving in. Still, I know how hungry the boys are for some type of entertainment. They haven't had any here."

"Good."

"Just remember the enemy is on the march—no encores."

We six performers, frightened as we were, proceeded to do the show. Because of complete blackout of all power lines, we were forced to improvise. Six soldiers lay on their backs and held candles, acting as human footlights. We played across their bellies—and all the time I could picture the Japs advancing.

There were many patrols out on active duty who could not see the first show.

Like heroes we decided to stay and do another show. By this time we could see the flashes of gunfire on the horizon and the sound of firing real close. I couldn't believe I had really aced myself into an actual battle. In spite of our trembling, we gave another show for the men who came off duty later that night. It was nerve-wracking and I wonder if we really were amusing and entertaining.

It was I saw a real war as I packed for the getaway. Sound and fury were all around us as we prepared to fly out, but there was no plane. The trick was to get out of the area. The demolition squads had been ordered to blow up the airfield installations. The majority of the troops were standing by to evacuate. General Vincent wanted to get us out first. He radioed to General Chennault for a passenger plane. I sat up with Casey all through the fearful night, in his tent. We punished whatever available alcoholic spirits he had, which wasn't enough. We talked of home and whether there was a possibility of this war ever ending.

During the war someone coined the phrase, "There are no atheists in foxholes." I am not an authority on foxholes, but I will tell you this. As I talked to Casey that night, I could not help but think that these were times and events which cried out for a belief in an almighty God. War is a terrible tragedy for all of mankind. This is something that comes about because men don't know how to handle their affairs. I couldn't help thinking many times during that evening of the men I had seen under these terrible conditions. If there were no God to make some sense out of this mess, life would be a pretty sorry thing. It is in times like this that it is brought home to us so forcibly that, try as we will, we mere humans are pretty mortal. The only help that we can get in these times is to turn to God who must have the answers; we certainly don't.

Near dawn, General Chennault came through—a plane had flown in for us, and we said farewell to lousy Luchow and were on our way to Chungking. Chennault sent along for us six beautiful Chinese scarves, with the pilot of the plane, in gratitude for what we had done. I wrote a note saying we didn't feel we had done anything special—this was our job and we had been richly rewarded in the lift we were able to give battle-weary GI's. With Jinx, Ruth, Jimmy, Betsy, Harry Brown, I shared the satisfaction of knowing we played places where no other entertainers in their right minds had ever ventured.

General Randall gave me a birthday party in Kunming. General Curtis LeMay was one of the guests. General Randall presented me with a really rare gift for Eloise, if and when I got back to the States. It was a jade Buddha about an inch and a half tall. (Eloise had it made into a pin and, each time she wears it, tells tall tales of its origin, its donor and my bravery under enemy fire.)

Life at the capital, Chungking, in the heart of China, was at that moment a little remote from the battle fronts. We took rickshaw rides and were living in barracks. Outside, China was too big, too confused to comprehend. General Patrick Hurley sent a note that he and General Wedemeyer would like to entertain us in a small gathering at their quarters. It was a grand party.

We were ordered to go into the interior, and there is a hell of a lot of interior in China; in fact, it seemed millions of miles of interior, to a remote spot where Navy Intelligence was located. It was a real bad movie plot. We were driven to a *certain* site, *somewhere* outside of Chungking. We were blindfolded and led to sedan chairs and carried by human horses into the jungles. I never did know how many kilometers we were carried through secret areas, into a valley, out of a Ming painting. The blindfolds were removed and we blinked, and were taken to a Commodore Myles' headquarters. We were sworn to secrecy.

"You are the only outsiders who have *ever* come to this part of the war area since the beginning of the conflict."

I could see why. Navy Intelligence had been stationed there a long time and gotten very cozy. It was a marked improvement from the other dismal places in which we had appeared. There was a beautiful theater and a huge clean dining room. I have no idea how many of the United States Navy were quartered in this taxpayers' Shangri-la. There were many Chinese servants and their families, and that night the Chinese kids gave a native play for us. This was a tough act to follow. The tiny Oriental tots were talented, and their slant-eyed charm put us on our best efforts. Somehow, in Happy Valley, I didn't believe in the war all around us. The Navy had turned it into Gilbert and Sullivan.

CBI (China, Burma, India), as the war was called, had a different connotation to the war battered GI's. They called it "Confusion Beyond Imagination" and rightly so. The waste, the grandstanding, mixups and red tape were on a huge scale and far from prying official eyes. Yet under it, the GI did his duty and shrugged at the confusion.

We went on to Burma, playing up the Burma Road and the Lido Road. The Burma Road was made mostly by the Chinese with hand hoes and bare hands. One of the outstanding groups we encountered were our army engineers, comprised mostly of large Negro sections of our military. They were the king bucks of the world among the Chinese—they really liked being top man and worked the better for it. "Man, *this* ain't Alabama."

The girls on the tour held up fine. Jinx, Ruth and Betsy made us men look like weaklings. They were tireless, brave and rarely lost their sense of humor or hair waves during all those trying, weary months. Somehow or other, I felt I was up to all the bad times—and went along with the action, I hoped.

I got a bracelet I still wear made by one of the GI's we entertained, fashioned from a Jap Zero motor part—shot down by one of our fliers. The bracelet bears the CBI insignia and the letters: *Pat O'Brien 1944—China, Burma, India*. This was at Myitikyina (phonetically pronounced Mish-i-naw) and the going got rougher.

We met many of Merrill's Marauders back in the bush land— they were bearded men who had the love of battle in their veins. We also met evil-looking smelly head hunters who resembled pygmies. They were mean-eyed and carried sharp knives, and eyed my head till I thought I saw them drool. I used to lie awake at night in the midst of a Burmese jungle and talk to myself: "You are forty-four years old. Have a wife and three kids. What are you doing in this itchy, stinking hell hole?" But next day when we would be doing a show and could see these boys' faces light up, I knew why I was over there. I was trying for one crazy moment to make life worth living for these poor kids who maybe were never going to get back home.

It wasn't all physical torment. I was often thrilled to serve Mass in the jungle. Very pleased too with myself that I had retained the Latin I had learned as a boy years before when I served as an acolyte. Harry Brown and I were the only ones in our group of six who were Catholics. The other four would attend services whenever we were able to have them, which was not too often in those remote regions far from supplies and sanity.

Some parts of the Burma country were reminiscent of Wisconsin and Minnesota; their vast forests and tall trees. But its climate was not that of a summer resort, but of a condemned steam bath.

And just what were we bringing to the boys? They didn't want Shaw or O'Neill, and certainly not lectures on serious subjects. Our best bet was Jinx, who would come onstage in a beautiful evening gown and looking a pin-up vision come to animated life. Some of these boys hadn't seen an American girl in three or four years. Their eyes would bug out on stems. Three beautiful girls were really something! Betsy, an acrobatic dancer, mowed them down. Ruth sang loud and clear, and Jim whipped a mean guitar to match the songs. Harry accompanied me, usually on a portable organ. Only once in a Chinese moon would we find a piano. It was never a Steinway.

After Jinx would make her entrance in her gorgeous gown, she would wait for the applause and wolf calls to die down (that was *some* wait). Then, she would slowly unlatch her shoulder strap and her gown would drop to the floor to reveal Jinx in well-tailored tennis shorts. She would ask: "Would one of you boys volunteer to come on stage and be my assistant in the act?"

"Whoa—whoo!"

Usually the boys were shy, so we would search out, before the act, some bright-eyed young fellow who looked sharp enough to assimilate the directions she would give him for his part of the act. We would plant him in the front row and when Jinx would call for a volunteer from the audience, our boy would bounce right up on the stage.

The dialogue was simple and to the point:

"Hi, fella. Glad to see you. You know I have two brothers in service and it's most gratifying to be over here with all of you wonderful Joes. And now, because we've come such a long way up here on stage, I will do *anything* you ask me. Anything."

"Anything?" the stooge would ask.

"Anything."

"You mean *anything?*"

"That's what I said—*anything!*"

The entire audience was always in an uproar at this point.

"Well, thank you, Jinx. You know what I want? All my life I've wanted to watch you drive a tennis ball . . ."

A roar of regrets at this simple request, and another GI would walk on stage with a basket of tennis balls. They had all been autographed by as many movie stars as we could catch before we left home. Jinx would proceed to serve them directly into the audience.

If someone beside our stooge beat him to the act and jumped onstage ahead of him, the entire routine was destroyed. Obviously the amorous GI who had *not* been coached was not going to simply say, "I've always wanted to watch you hit a tennis ball." Jinx was prepared for such an emergency. She had to take over.

"Hi, fella, would you assist me getting these tennis balls into the audience?"

This act wasn't as keen as the one planned. Frequently there was a wild struggle when some overzealous GI would try to get to the stage ahead of the boy we had picked out. That didn't happen too often. Our boy was usually eager.

I had not, of course, been permitted to tell Eloise just where in Asia I was. And one couldn't write "Burma" in the censored letters home. So I wrote her: "It's a great place where we are, which I can't mention, but it's different. This morning I got up early, but the dawn didn't come up like thunder, the way I expected . . ." I figured Eloise would remember Kipling's "Road to Mandalay" (she did) and its line about where the dawn comes up across the bay. Anybody who didn't guess I was in Burma hadn't been properly educated.

As a boy reading about the Seven Wonders of the World, I never expected a war would make it possible for me to see the Taj Mahal, the Sphinx, the Pyramids and the Nile, and they were all just as they were in books.

Weary but pleased, we returned homeward, played Calcutta, Casablanca, Morocco, Algiers, and other places. Then the magic carpet had nearly exhausted itself and I was pretty tired myself.

We moved westward in jumps. There was still a lot of flying to do. We stopped long enough to visit the Casbah and I recalled Charles Boyer and his memorable line, "Come wiz me to the Casbah!" as I stood in garbage, flies, soiled kids and pregnant goats that was the real Casbah. The entire hill was one big germ culture.

On our stopover in Algiers, there was no place to quarter us, but one of the colonel's staff in Algiers finally came up with an offer, and we found ourselves in a most luxurious apartment, ten beautiful rooms, all in completely modern décor.

"Just move in—don't ask questions."

Upon our departure, the colonel in command took me aside.

"Pat, this place we had you in is actually a house of ill fame."

"No!"

"Oh yes."

"The devil you say."

"So you see, Pat, the proprietess of a bawdy house can be not only patriotic, but hospitable as well."

I didn't tell the girls this until we were back in the States.

Jinx said, "Just keep it off *my* record."

Back in Karachi, India, our hotel had been called "The Killarney." Here we met some of Merrill's Marauders suffering from shock, battle fatigue and fever, and on their way home. Some of the most moving visits we made were to the hospital wards. Hundreds here never made it back home. The gals stood up well during those endless trips through the wards of the hospitals in the CBI. A man on his feet is still human, but flat on a bed, burning up with fever, something seems wrong with the plan of the universe.

Back in Hollywood, Charlie Koerner welcomed us with a grand reception at RKO. The GI's in the CBI had sent him a copy of their newspaper, *The Round Up*. He read an expansive, flowery editorial they had written about our little show troupe. How we had ventured into territory where none of our men had ever expected to receive any entertainment, and how remarkable our acts; which showed me how starved they were for words and sights from home.

I was still on call for duty as an entertainer as the war went on. Whenever I was not engaged in a picture, Harry Brown and myself would go out to the various camps and hospitals. A new member was Eloise. Thousands of soldiers recall her warm charm and graciousness as she went the fearful way from bedside to bedside, comforting and telling funny anecdotes in those dismal Bedpan Alleys of the war's by-products.

There was another picture on shooting schedule: *Riff-Raff*, co-starring Anne Jeffreys, Walter Slezak and myself. The young man who wrote the script, Marty Rackin, had skill as a dramatist, and his comedy writing was superb. I went to Charlie Koerner and asked him to be given a studio contract. The boy had been in the Air Force and the going was not too easy after his discharge from the service. Marty is now one of the top executives at Paramount Studios. Strange I don't hear from him any more.

Phil Ryan had purchased the rights to the life of *Fighting Father Dunne* and so once more I put on a priestly collar to portray the St. Louis priest who did such fine work with newsboys. Darryl Hickman gave a great performance in this picture, as did the late Una O'Connor, a little pin-nosed pixy of a woman who whined her way to picture fame.

After that came *Crackup* with Claire Trevor. It was during the making of this film that Charles Koerner died suddenly. It was a personal shock and the studio was grief-stricken.

With his passing the great days of RKO were over. It did little more than limp along until my Cuban friend, Desi Arnez, gobbled it up for TV.

In 1942, I joined the most illustrious group of stars ever assembled, the Hollywood Victory Caravan, sent out on a tour to raise money for the Navy Relief Fund. Some of the cast, and only a small part of it were: Charles Boyer, James Cagney, Claudette Colbert, Bing Crosby, Cary Grant, Bob Hope, Frank McHugh and Laurel and Hardy.

We carried a full orchestra, Alfred Newman, the conductor. The crew of hairdressers, make-up people, prop men and musicians were part of us.

We opened in Washington, D.C., after a reception at the White House, where F.D.R. with cigarette holder traded gags with us. Bob Hope, Cary Grant and myself were the masters of ceremonies. We played almost every metropolitan city across the country, planning to end the tour in San Francisco where Al Jolson was to join us for one night. Rise Stevens opened the show every night with "The Star-Spangled Banner," one of the few people I ever met who really knew all the words. Jimmy Cagney did the finale —George M. Cohan numbers from *Yankee Doodle Dandy*.

In Boston, a million people viewed our street parade. Each star was assigned to a car. An Irish cop trotted alongside of the car in which Charles Boyer was riding. The parade was proceeding very slowly. The officer jogged alongside Boyer's car. In tones audible to all of us within hearing range, he said: "Mr. Boyer, my wife she up and left me on account of you."

The debonair Frenchman, eyebrow up, answered with all the dignity and *savoir faire* at his command.

"I am so vereee sorree . . ."

"She was nuts for you. Didn't think any other man came up to you."

"I do not know what to say!"

The cop grinned. "Forget it, Mr. Boyer. You did me the greatest favor of my life, getting rid of the shrew."

In St. Paul, Minnesota, Cary Grant and myself missed the cavalcade en route to the theater in Minneapolis. Someone summoned up a police car and a motorcycle escort. We started the mad dash to the *other* Twin City. We had traversed about a mile, when suddenly out of nowhere, a little girl appeared in the street. At the rate of speed we were traveling, I saw it was impossible to avoid hitting her. One motorcycle veered to the left and turned over. The other one slowed down somewhat to a scream of brakes just touching the child. She stumbled. Cary and I leaped from the car; God had His arms about us—fortunately, she was only slightly bruised, but in a state of shock. Imagine, if you can, this little girl as she opened her eyes.

"Cary Grant!"

"You all right?"

"In the arms of Cary Grant!"

I was kneeling beside them in the middle of the street, attempting to comfort her, but she was gazing into the face of Cary Grant. I decided she was *older* than she looked.

With all of the greatest stars on hand, the greatest ovation and reception all across the country were always to Laurel and Hardy! Every time they made their entrance, there were loud bursts of applause and cheers.

"Babe" Hardy was a simple soul, a great clown, reminding one of the line, "In every fat man there is a thin man trying to escape." Laurel was more complex, a deep student of comedy; he had come to America with Chaplin in 1911.

When later Laurel and Hardy made a world tour, they arrived in Cork, Ireland. They thought it was a Holy Day. All the church bells of all denominations were ringing. Suddenly Laurel realized their mistake.

"The bells are ringing our movie theme song!"

Thousands lined the streets and as they entered a car, about fifty enthusiastic Gaels lifted the car bodily off the ground and carried it through the streets.

26

Peace in Dreamland

The war did end. For the living, the dead were past celebrating. The miserable Germans, as always after starting and losing a war, begged for mercy. And the world was made safe at least for the Volkswagen. Unthinking politics and lack of faith caused the dropping of the first atom bomb on Japan, when it was no longer needed. The Japanese were, a journalist told me, desperately looking for a way to make peace. And so the world entered the Atom Age by the senseless use of a total weapon that could end all life on the planet. It was not a happy peace but there was a lifting of pressures that the war years had brought. I was older, but I was not feeling the burden of my years. I had a fine growing family, a cozy home base, and I looked forward to more and more films. I was established, the motion picture studios were never in better shape. But the precious hopes of men and groups —as I should have known—have a way of not following the blue prints of our desires.

Still it was good to know the shooting was over and if it was said the hot war would only become the cold war, at least in the U.S.A. we could settle back with a feeling we had made a good fight of it and the hundreds of thousands of our dead had fought decently for a better world; maybe the United Nations would help build it. Such was our reasoning in the year 1945, and I was again an actor, and not traveling any more to jungles and outer wildernesses in planes already obsolete.

My films were playing around the world, and television, that crazy toy, was still something for electrical nuts who were busy taking apart and putting together a screen so small that nobody paid it much mind. There was loud talk and name calling among actors and directors and writers, and the "Unfriendly Hollywood Ten" were in the news from time to time. Old friends often didn't speak; libeling and character assassination made news headlines. But how could it touch me? I was an old-line Democrat, and no studio or producer could object to my politics, my family life, my habits or my working hours. I had it made. *Was I wrong!*

At the time, though, our rainbow, indeed, seemed to have no end—as God continued to shower his blessings down upon us. But —there just *had* to be another girl. It happened in June 1946!

A lot of drama entered into this happy event. Eloise slipped and fell in the library while carrying this baby. She was rushed to the hospital, while we were all frozen with fear as to the outcome, but again—God was in our corner. This birth was necessarily a Caesarean and when I was summoned by Dr. Irving Ress, he explained this was all a part of necessary procedure and that I must be the one to give my consent for this particular delivery. I guess I was not being very ethical when I said to the doctor, "All right, Doc, but you bring my girl back to me!" His reply is imprinted on my heart for the rest of my years. He said, "Who knows—maybe I'll bring two girls back to you."

I retired to the tiny chapel there at St. John's Hospital and the man who knelt beside me was a friend of many years, David Bender, of the Jewish faith. But that night the prayers in his heart were for the safety of Eloise and the baby who would be the fourth in the O'Brien ménage. It wasn't long before our prayers were interrupted by a little nun who said, "You'd better come upstairs, Mr. O'Brien, you have a baby daughter."

I rushed up to see Mommy and it was difficult to determine who was the more radiant—the mother or the child. The baby fairly glistened in her infantile beauty—her eyes were shiny pools. (People say a baby's eyes are never opened this early, but hers *were*, I'm sure!) She looked so cherubic. Needless to say, she was spoiled rotten by her brothers and sister, to say nothing of her mother and dad. However, it was a nice kind of spoiling and she, too, proved that love and devotion, yes, even the adoration showered upon her by her immediate family would never alter her progress into the world of her childhood and, then, young womanhood. She entered into a circle of love that symbolized all that she was to be a part of. We christened her Kathleen Brigid, but she has always been called "Brigie," and her dad's special nickname for her has always been "Brigie Poo." Brigid was born with a caul, or veil. According to Irish tradition, this indicated she was to be a "child of Destiny." Her beauty knows no end—and she grows more beauteous with the years.

Between my collection of walking canes and children, our house was getting crowded.

A few years previous to Brigie's birth, I had met William O'Dwyer, the prosecuting attorney in Brooklyn, New York. We became firm friends. There is a great physical resemblance, some said, between the two of us. Toots Shor once remarked, "You two look like bookends, back to back."

Later, Bill was elected mayor of New York by one of the largest pluralities in the history of New York, and later still, betrayed by political sheenanigans by so-called pals, left in a hurry for Mexico when politics went sour on him.

When Bill read the news that Eloise was with child, he wired me:

When Brigie arrived, this was a wild joyous household. The three other kids had prayed for a baby sister. I contacted His Honor, the Mayor of New York and advised him when the christening would take place. On the baptismal day, Bill flew out with his full entourage of New York faces, Tammany brand. Kathleen Brigid was baptized in St. Monica's Church by Monsignor Connealy. (Our pal, Father Gallagher, was in Ireland at this time, or it would have been the fourth time he would have worked baptismally for the O'Briens.) Flo O'Connor was godmother. The apprehension on Bill O'Dwyer's face was clear to all when he held the child in his arms at the church.

Late in 1946, I was privileged to do a command performance for the King and Queen of England, at the Empire Theatre in London. It was the first time the American film industry had sent representatives to perform for their Majesties. Among those making the trip were Mr. and Mrs. Ray Milland, Mr. and Mrs. Reggie Gardiner, Mr. and Mrs. Walter Wanger (Joan Bennett), Katina Paxinou, Dorothy Malone, the late Eric Johnston and others.

Eloise said, "How do you greet a king and queen?"

"Just say howdy."

"Do we bow?"

"Not too far. After all, we licked them in 1775."

We had a three day layover in New York, and on the night before we sailed on the *Queen Elizabeth*, Toots Shor gave a bang-up party at his establishment to top even a Roman orgy in my estimation. Herb Palasie wrote some sketches for the event. Bob Hope was present, Jackie Gleason, Bill Corum, Bill Powell, Bill Hearst, Jr., Jimmy Cannon, James Barton, Bob Considine, Frank Coniff, Mark Hellinger, Gene Fowler; people Toots could round up when he sent out word, "This is going to be a doozer."

"Don't kid the King and Queen, Toots," I said.

"Coming from a mick, I like that."

"I'm going to be a guest."

"You always were housebroken."

There was a wild swinging travesty on the command performance, Toots playing the King and Dave Shelly and Jackie Gleason
enacting noblemen—boy, some nobles. The party continued into
the night. Fortunately we were all packed and ready to leave for
the boat right from Toots' place or we would never have made it.

"Don't worry, Paddy, they don't dare leave. I've nailed down
the anchors."

Toots and his wife Baby, and Joe Noonan and his wife Katherine, accompanied us to the boat. The party continued in our
stateroom. Toots took to parading up and down the deck, the little English bellboys following like tiny shadows.

"Grow up and come back and fight."

The warning call, "All ashore who's going ashore," sounded;
Toots looked at Eloise and me, shook free some tears, and with
his hand gripped in mine, said, "Pat, I know you haven't had an
opportunity to get to the bank for ready cash."

"I'll get by."

"Take care of this when you get back to dear old Manhattan."

Then he was gone. I had a thousand dollars in my hand.
Months later, in his apartment he picked up an ash tray. Under-
neath it I had placed a check for one thousand dollars.

"What's this all about, Paddy?"

"It's about a thousand dollars which you gave me when I left
for Europe."

"I forgot."

The sea was calm, the party nerves nearly so. The ship sailed
on—returning by boat an O'Brien to a nation that held down his
forefathers. We met a most engaging soldier aboard who proved
to be a good companion throughout the voyage, General Mark
Clarke. Tall, eagle-beaked, still a little sad-eyed for those murder-
ous deadly attacks he launched on Italian beachheads with such
fearful casualties.

Just before we docked at Liverpool, a little skiff came along the
fat side of the *Queen Elizabeth* and a little Englishman clam-

bered aboard and proceeded to the salon to hold a meeting with all of us who were to perform for the House of Windsor. He brought along proof copies of the program and passed them around. Everyone seemed quite pleased. I made no comment. He turned to me and in clipped British accent, out of Ronald Colman crossed-with-tea, asked, "Do you like it, Mr. O'Brien?"

"*Where* is Mrs. O'Brien's name?"

"Oh, my dear sir, the wives or husbands of the performers are *never* presented."

"Never?"

"No, only the stars themselves. Custom, tradition, you know—it's never been done in the history of the Empire."

"Then, pal—I'll do my part as a performer on the stage, because that's my job. My studio has seen fit to choose me to represent them. But you can bet on it—under no condition will I be presented to Their Majesties unless my wife is included."

"You can't go against protocol."

"The hell I can't."

The little Britisher looked as if someone had poisoned his crumpet. He took Eric Johnston aside. "I'm in a bit of a quandary. The O'Brien chap has *refused* to be presented without his wife!"

Johnston told him (he related it to me later), "If that's what Pat says, that's what Pat means. He's Irish."

"They were always troublemakers."

I was angry, hurt and feeling I needed Wolfe Tone, Parnell and the I.R.A. at my side.

Various members of our group tried to reason with me. My friends Ray Milland and Reggie Gardiner, as British subjects, could not very well refuse to be presented to their monarchs. I remained adamant. Eloise tried to remonstrate with me.

"Who cares, Pat? They lost the colonies—they can afford to lose me."

"Honey, you stay out of this. This is my fight and my decision."

"Stubborn."

We got on the boat train, a mixed-up group, and on to London.

It was a gray dank day. The cabbie said, "Gov, it's the best weather we've had this year." Eloise went directly to the Savoy, where we were registered. Those of us who were to entertain, proceeded to the empty echoing Empire Theatre for rehearsal. At 9:30 that evening, a man from the box office came back stage and said, "Mr. O'Brien, you are wanted on the telephone."

It was Eloise with a high excited voice: "Darling, stop worrying—and forget your stiff-necked pride. The wives are being presented!"

"So we did win Yorktown!"

"I guess you broke down some of that British protocol."

"The order that wives would not be presented did not come from Their Majesties, but from their staff."

The Empire Theatre was bursting with tiaras, family furs and old names that night, a full house. It was what the press always calls a gala night, and thrilling when the orchestra played "God Save the King" and everyone stood up as the royal family made their entrance.

Eloise said, "Why it's 'My Country 'Tis of Thee.'"

Mrs. Gardiner said, "Shh—they may not know that."

My act was a pantomime routine I had seen the late Bert Williams do some years previous, "The Silent Poker Game." When I finished, I looked up at the royal box and made a simple speech of thanks to the owners of the British Empire. I figured that it was a pretty decent speech to royalty from a guy whose background was Galway and Cork, and who was an American.

After the command performance came the formal presentation. We stood in a row smelling of the best tailoring. It came my turn to be presented to Her Majesty. I bowed not too low, and with all of an actor's *savoir faire* I could summon, firmly shook hands with the plump Queen. The studios had sent photographers to shoot the presentation. I had about two hundred fifty copies made of myself and the Queen, and sent them back to the States to all my pals. Later I received a cable that had been sent to me in London and forwarded on to the Gresham Hotel in Dublin.

PAT O'BRIEN
C/O BUCKINGHAM PALACE
LONDON ENGLAND

PICTURE ARRIVED IF YOU HAD LEANED OVER ANY FURTHER EVERY
LEPRECHAUN IN IRELAND WOULD DROPKICK YOU INTO GALWAY
BAY

PAT HARRINGTON

Another cable read:

BRING BACK SCOTCH

JACKIE GLEASON

After spending a few days in the glorious English countryside, and listening to Englishmen laugh—they do have a sense of humor, and a fine one, only you must find just the right spot on the funny bone to press—we took off for Ireland. I wanted to get my first glimpse of the Emerald Isle of my genes and bones, mind and marrow from a boat, rather than from the air.

Our first sight of Eire was breathtaking, a smudge of soft green, a sky hung with loose white clouds, and a wind all odors and grace. My first view of the land sent up memory of the lines from "The Exile's Return."

> Doesn't old Cobb look charmin' there
> Watchin' the wild waves motion,
> Leanin' her back against the hill,
> With the tips of her toes in the ocean.

And voices from the past, old scenes, old songs: old friends again, the vale and the cot I was born in—oh Ireland, up from my heart of hearts, I bid ye the top of the mornin'! Ireland about which Kipling wrote, "For where there are Irish, there's loving and fighting, and when we stop either, it's Ireland no more." Imagine an Englishman catching the spirit of Ireland so perfectly.

But even words fail to express the emotion of being in a land I had never seen before. And odd that the greatest of her brood, Swift, Shaw, Joyce, O'Casey, Moore, Yeats, spent most of their lives away from her. Perhaps she was like a too loving Irish mother —too strong, too protective.

Eloise and I were met at the Dublin boat by Bertie McNally, whose father, Walter McNally, had been a great singer of songs during the twenties. Bertie greeted us by tipping his bowler hat: "I took it upon myself to take you direct to the theater."

"What theater?"

"What other—the Abbey Theater after you get through customs. We daren't be late because it's a religion with them—time—and if you're two seconds late, they won't let you in until the second act."

"Let's hurry."

We were all for dashing immediately to the Abbey Theater. But Dublin taxis don't hurry.

We were a minute and a half late, no more. But that meant nothing to the bejowled, red-nosed old fellow who took tickets at the door. He wore a long green-black coat that reached to his broken shoe tops, a testy old character, out of play no longer performed.

Bertie said, "I was afraid this would happen."

He approached the old fellow with a too casual ease. "These are my guests. They just got off the boat—they're from America."

No answer came from the old pub crawler.

Bertie tried waving his bowler. "*This* gentleman is Pat O'Brien, the famous actor from the theater."

The hard-visaged doorman made a thin line of his toothless mouth.

Bertie tried to catch the blood shot eye. "This is Pat O'Brien, star of the films from Hollywood—*Pat O'Brien!*"

There was a slight pause and the old duffer never even lifted his head.

"I don't care if he's King Jarge. He don't get in!"

This was disheartening.

I said, "About George I agree with you. But a visiting O'Brien deserves better of you."

The old fellow glimpsed the bit of Galway sorrow acting up on my face.

"Well now, O'Brien and your darlin' lady, you be sittin' in the first row—you won't be disturbin' none. Go down the side aisle and easy-foot across to your seats—but mind ye be quiet."

We followed his instructions and got seated. The play was *The Righteous Are Bold*, as translated from Gaelic. It contained great character portraits of skilled perfection by the artists of the theater.

The curtain fell on the first act. I looked around the theater and was amazed to find the audience was predominantly women. I turned my eyes to the left, and there sat Maureen O'Hara and her mother and father, the FitzSimons. The audience spotted her and converged in a body for autographs. I was lucky and got the overflow.

Eloise said, "Art or art theater—the autograph hounds are the same all over."

"No, macushla," I said, "here they don't steal the pencil."

There was a little old man seated on our right, obviously I guessed, a farmer, probably from his dress—my Sherlock Holmes training said—from the interior of Eire, who had come to see the famous Abbey Players. The horde of autograph seekers swarmed down, pushing books and paper in a steady stream, nearly flattening him as they shoved toward us. They elbowed him, clambered over him, with no apologies. The poor fellow was utterly bewildered. I could see he had no idea what this was all about, could not understand this strange city behavior of the hooligans. The women in the audience continued to climb over him. He rose suddenly and looking down at me angrily, yelling at the top of his voice, "You there—what agitates the females so? Did you bring a live mouse with you?"

I invited him to the bar for a wee one.

The following evening, my birthday, we were seated with the McNallys in a little private dining room at the Gresham.

Bertie said, "A few friends would be dropping in for the little party."

"Will they?"

Then, led by Maureen O'Hara herself, in strode the Irish Pipers, in full marching regalia, playing the music that has sent the people to death, battle, liberty and freedom. There were tears, Jameson's Irish whisky, toasts across the sea, hands across the table, and more Jameson's.

The next day we went to Galway, in the western part of Ireland to watch the sun go to glorious fire down on the Bay. The McNallys presented us both with the rings of Cladaugh.

Bertie explained, "It's the traditional ring of Galway, often used as wedding rings."

"It's pretty."

"The ring itself was originally designed by one of the early kings and a beautiful design it is—two clasped hands beneath a heart with the crown above."

I said, "So I see. And thank you."

We spent one night at Ashford Castle and then stayed two nights with Bertie's brother-in-law, who lived in a tiny place called Kiltiemaugh, and it was just all the corny shamrock-filled pictures of old Ireland, land of saints and scholars, we no longer believed in.

I came around to thinking the old Irish themes were really all there.

We drove back to Dublin the following day and had a wonderful visit with Eamon DeValera, President of Ireland, even if born in Brooklyn—an old hawk of a man, nearly blind, but still with a fire in the face of a dedicated fanatic. During the rest of our stay, we lived with the McNallys right outside of Dublin. We met the late President Kennedy's sister, Kathleen. She was to meet a tragic death, in a plane accident in England.

We visited Killarney which Thomas Moore referred to as "Heaven's reflection . . . where angels fold their wings and rest." And of course, we visited Blarney Castle, and after being lowered to an uncomfortable position, I kissed the Blarney Stone with all the enthusiasm of a man who wanted the whole works on this trip.

When we again visited in Ireland, we met Robert Briscoe, the first man of Jewish faith to become Lord Mayor of Dublin.

Eloise said, "There is even hope for a Protestant some day."

I was impressed by Briscoe. He spoke three languages fluently, Gaelic, Hebrew (so I heard) and English. His English has a lilt that was definitely lyrical. He was endowed with a sense of humor and appeared a most erudite citizen.

Mrs. Briscoe said to Eloise, "I love your husband when he plays the priest in the films."

I looked up from the gefilte fish. "I've played so many priests in pictures and television that at every meal our entire family discusses everything in Latin."

The mayor grinned. "O'Brien, since I have been elected Lord Mayor of Dublin, I've attended so many masses that on Friday, fish comes to me automatically."

The Briscoes were of the Jewish Orthodox faith; they had a daughter who entered a convent. Eloise asked Mayor Briscoe how he felt about his daughter becoming a nun.

"I'll tell you, Mrs. O'Brien, all my life I've been preaching tolerance and now I'm going to have to practice it."

I wallowed in all of Ireland—Galway, Cork, Killarney—the so green hills of Eire, that green no artist could ever transfer to any canvas. I even loved the outrageous description someone gave of the rain in Ireland: "Sure, it's not rain, at all, 'tis only the harp-strings coming down from Heaven, and 'tis holy water on the windshield."

John Ford, during a flight to Ireland, on his first glimpse of the Emerald Isle said, "What a glorious green." Then he added, "But what are those black spots I see there?"

"If they move," replied the stewardess, "they're cows. If they don't they're County Council workers."

The quality of the Irish is ever evident: their gentleness, their kindly thoughtfulness and graciousness at all times, and their natural wit.

We regretted bidding farewell to the McNallys and Bertie's bowler.

Cardinal Spellman had arranged for us an audience with His Holiness, Pope Pius XII in Rome. We flew back to London on one of the Irish planes, and the name of the plane was *Brigid*, like our daughter's. All of the Irish planes have proper names.

From London we flew to Switzerland and from there we were to fly on to Rome over a Europe all clouds and ancient hillsides and ruins of history and recent wars. An old sad landscape, but full of the grandeur of age missing in America. When we arrived at Geneva we found the planes grounded because of a strike and were told we couldn't get to Rome. Eloise and I drew on our faith. We found it was possible to engage a car, but were warned against the hazards of the trip. The road to Rome lay over mountains. We took the train to the border. There we were told we would drive at our own risk because of bands of brigands known to be infesting the mountain passes. Our attention was further directed to a downpour with the assurance that driving in such rain on the mountain sides meant our roads would be blocked by landslides. But nothing would weaken our determination and faith.

After two hours' sleep in the tiny Italian village, we squeezed ourselves into the tiny car. It seemed no bigger than a watch fob. In the front seat were two Italians who spoke no English. It was four o'clock in the morning, dismal, forbidding, foggy. Eloise and I held hands tightly. We were too busy with our prayers to talk at all. All that rain-drenched day we drove, and all that night and through the next day. At midnight we arrived in Rome.

Those who know the terrain look unbelievingly at us when we tell of how we drove across the Italian frontier. Sometimes I wonder if it wouldn't be more truthful to say: "Our faith transported us to Rome."

Our audience was set for 11:10 the following morning. I had been told, "They mean eleven-ten. Believe me, Mr. O'Brien, they deal in exactitudes in the Vatican."

The McNallys had made reservations for us at the Grand Hotel. We were two tired-looking gypsies in the ornate old-world lobby of the hotel. The clerk half closed his eyes.

"O'Brien? Your suite is held for a Grecian Princess. We did not think you were going to get here."

"But we did arrive!"

"The hour had grown so late. Sorry, signore."

The clerk spoke English fairly well, I saw. "My friend, you had better tell the Princess to stay put in Athens, because the O'Briens have arrived. We have the reservations."

"But signore, a Princess."

"We're moving in *right* now!"

Wild gesticulations and vocal explosives. At the dramatic moment when I was climbing over the counter, a gentleman who had been sitting just off from the lobby, watching the fun, rose and came over to the desk.

He asked me: "Could I be of any assistance?"

I climbed down and told him who we were and what had happened.

"Ah yes. I am one of the Vatican secretaries. I have been awaiting your arrival all evening."

He quickly straightened the whole situation out.

"Ah, now you have the rooms."

Eloise said, "The poor Princess—what about her?"

The Vatican secretary smiled. "A heretic, but charming. I've seen her pictures."

Now that we had someone who knew all about the procedure at the Vatican, we eagerly plied our new friend with question after question. In the course of our talk, I explained to the Vatican secretary that I was all prepared, sartorially, for the audience, as I had brought the full dress suit in which I had been presented to Queen Elizabeth with me. Carefully he explained that it was no longer customary to present gentlemen in full dress suits except on very formal state occasions. The procedure now is for the gentleman to wear a business suit, preferably dark, with a dark tie. I was a bit dismayed at this announcement, not only because it deprived me of another opportunity to wear my splendid full dress suit, but more importantly because I did not have a dark tie with me and didn't know how I could secure one before the audience the next morning.

Noting my concern, our new friend asked me what was the trouble. I explained my dilemma to him.

He smiled radiantly and whipped his own dark tie from around his neck, presented it to me and said, "Now you have a dark tie."

I thanked him profusely and our last crisis of the evening had been resolved.

27

Our Great Moment

Rome is a beautiful stone city, a holy city of sacred purpose. It is also a living city, alive to time and faith.

In Rome, Eloise and myself, after passing a sleepless night, eagerly awaited instruction for our forthcoming visit with His Holiness.

We tried to dress simply, yet with a feeling of respect worthy of the event. Eloise wore a black lace mantilla. I had my shoes shined and wore my borrowed black tie. At ten o'clock, our new friend, the Vatican secretary, arrived to escort us to the Papal chambers. I gripped Eloise's hand and I gripped it hard. After all, this was to be one of the great adventures of our lives.

At last, after passing under sunny cloud-flecked Italian skies, we were walking down that long corridor in the Vatican, with various representatives of the many nations. We saw the Swiss Guards in their bumblebee uniforms by Michelangelo; they were kind enough to allow us to be photographed with them. We arrived at a small gold and marble waiting room outside the Pontiff's official chambers. It was exactly 11:05. A little old Italian monsignor, who looked copyrighted by Walt Disney, spoke English quite well.

"Now, as you say in your beloved country, now, you are on your own."

"Thank you." He motioned us forward.

The door closed behind us. We stood quietly as though hypnotized. At the end of the not too ornate room sat a slender man robed in white. There was a gentle smile on his face. He beckoned us with a delicate hand gesture to approach. Gripped by awe, I don't mind confessing, we advanced.

"Be seated."

I said, "Thank you, Your Holiness."

The audience, private, had been arranged by Cardinal Spellman of New York, who had been a classmate of His Holiness during their pre-ordination days in Rome. A private audience: Pope Pius XII, Eloise and myself; that was all. His Holiness possessed penetrating eyes I felt, and in a wild comparison, I thought he resembled a kindly district attorney. He seemed aware of our apprehension. He asked in most articulate English, "And how is your beautiful Santa Barbara?"

"You know the place, Your Holiness?"

"I am the only Pope to ever visit the United States, as Cardinal Pacelli."

"Of course."

"Your California missions have a serenity and beauty. The Santa Barbara mission in particular."

Eloise said, "It's our favorite too."

He spoke of politics, questioned us about America in general, and then glancing down at the introductory note on his desk from His Eminence, Cardinal Spellman. I looked at Eloise. We were good enough actors to appear very calm. Maybe she was. The most frightening thing about the audience was its normality. Here was a human being, not a symbol.

"Ah, O'Brien—Irish—yes, the Irish have made great contributions to the world."

"Not great perhaps, but valid, Your Holiness."

"You have a family?"

I leaped to my feet as if on cue and spread the pictures of our four children before him on the richly carved desk.

"That we have," and in a voice not too shaded with humble awe, I recited their names and where they went to school.

Eloise plucked nervously at my sleeve, trying to quell my vocal enthusiasm, before—she said later—we were apprehended by the Swiss Guards. But the Pope only smiled. He didn't seem to have any desire to end the audience. My mind said we were coming near the half-hour. It was asking me, "How do you know when to leave?" At the command performance in London, there was a definite protocol as to your arrival, presentation and departure. Everything was done on precise very British timing. When we visited DeValera in Dublin, his secretary unhesitatingly told us when our visit was terminated. "It's all the time and strength himself has for you now." Visiting with our ambassadors, it was much the same. Someone always made it obvious that our visit was at an end, often when the martini jar was empty.

But now we were sitting with the Supreme Head of the Catholic Church, and he seemed to have all day. No bell was rung, no lackey approached to say our time had gone. There was no indication that our audience had been completed. Nearly in a flop sweat, I got a message, a sign, a feeling that must have been heaven sent. Suddenly we arose under our own almost coordinated power, and slowly backed away from the man behind the desk, his hand raised in benediction as we made our backward departure. The last impression I have was of the most delicate sign of the cross from a fragile hand that might have belonged to a surgeon.

As he made the gesture, he kept repeating softly, "My blessings upon you and your family and your friends and your friends, friends, friends, friends." It was an echo from the mystery and center of things earthly and celestial.

Outside in the sudden white Roman sun, in the sound of hysterical Italian traffic, Eloise and I just looked at each other and grinned. It had been a wonderful stage exit.

As we were driven back to the Grand Hotel, we still could not speak—just sat happy and close *and* wept in the streets of Rome. We were definitely in a state of pietic hypnosis, so powerful was the impression of the audience. It cannot, by me, be fully expressed on paper. In a show business term: "You had to be there."

I remembered what Cardinal Spellman had told me in New York before I left. "Pat, you and Eloise are going to experience something in your young lives no words can describe to you now—a certain atmosphere and magnitude of what will occur in the presence of His Holiness. When you come back, come to tell me if I am prophetic."

After our audience, we spent two days in Rome, visiting the Coliseum, the Catacombs, the usual splendid, often ruined sights that tourists enjoy. Italians are a cheerful people, living on ruins doesn't frighten them. The men are publicly amorous—pinchers, as Eloise found out.

"Call a policeman!"

"Now honey, it's the custom here. Besides, the cops look like they know the game."

From Rome we took off for Paris by train. Maurice Chevalier, still bouncing, was most kind to us during our Parisian visit. He took us to a dubbing studio where they were at work making a French sound track for *Angels with Dirty Faces*. You have not lived until you have heard Bogart, Cagney and O'Brien converse in sharp hep underworld French in an American gangster atmosphere.

Eloise said, "If we could have lifted a clip of this, we could have sold it for a featurette and made a fortune!"

But we were longing for home—the sights and smells, the faces, the places we knew best. So we went there.

We stopped over in New York for a week. I was being honored by the College of St. Francis, in Loretto, Pennsylvania. I was to receive a degree of Doctor of Literature along with Cardinal

Spellman, and Doctor of Law degrees were to be bestowed on George Buck (brother of Gene), Governor Duff of Pennsylvania, Frank McKinney and General Fleming of Washington. Not a list of Nobel prize winners, great novelists or poets, but at least it was free of scientists preparing to blow up the world. The back of my hand to them. Father Walter Plimmer, who at one time in his career had been a very talented actor and had in the end chosen the cloth, was responsible for my receiving the honor degree. To make the occasion practical, the Cardinal and I broke ground for the Shrine of St. Genesius, patron saint of actors.

Back in Hollywood, we kissed the kids and read the mail. A première of *Fighting Father Dunne* was to be held in Atlanta, Georgia; Atlanta, where I had been a very young actor twenty-five years before. Memories fairly lunged out of yesterday. Young dreams, magnolia blossoms, hunger, fun, laughs, southern fried chicken, corn pone, the Georgian Terrace Hotel, hasty, amorous, quick exits. Fuzzy Woodruff, the theatric sage of the South, the Erlanger Theater and the daffy night the football team marched down the aisle onto the stage when we were appearing in *Broadway*.

Jane Wyatt accompanied Eloise and myself on the trip. One of the scheduled events was a music festival at the Atlanta Stadium, the night before the première. The civic leaders and various sports celebrities and local bigwigs were to be present. As our car drove in, accompanied by a motorcycle escort of ten, with Eloise and Jane seated in the back of the sports job, I sat in front with the driver, taking cheers and waving like a goon, through the gates, and there was a fantastic burst of applause. Our car passed slowly before the stands, I stood up and bowed and bowed again. I said proudly to Eloise and Jane, "They sure love me in Atlanta."

Eloise yanked my coat tail. "Sit down, you idiot! They've just finished playing the state song."

The following afternoon, there was an interview with the editor of the paper, the Atlanta *Constitution*. The editor spoke with great pride of his prize possession. "The desk belonged to Jefferson Davis; given to me some years ago."

"It's a good bit of wood."

"A great man, a great cause. We were never beaten, sir."

"History never gets all the facts."

"Jeff Davis' own desk. Yes, sir."

I opened my big Irish mouth. "Eloise and I too have a very prize possession—the desk of Abraham Lincoln."

The silence was suddenly on us—the social barometer rapidly dropped. The interview was over.

On the way back to the hotel, Eloise said, "Well, Paddy boy, you did it again."

I said, "What did I do? We were just talking furniture."

"*This* is Georgia, not Illinois. We're Damned Yankees here and Sherman is *still* marching through, as far as they are concerned."

"Our desk is nicer than his."

"Better get North before you make a speech about the surrender of Lee to Grant."

"I'll play it safe, honey, and wear my gray suit at the première."

Back to Hollywood, and I began to readjust my career. All seemed well. I had two years more to go on my RKO contract which would terminate nine years of a wonderful association. When I left the studio, the new head man was the *same* one who had brought me to Hollywood twenty years before—the strange dark worker, Howard Hughes. One of the workmen on the lot said to me it had been announced Hughes had bought the studio. "He'll never get it off the ground." About this time, Mr. Hughes, on the taxpayers' fifty million dollars, was building a gargantuan plane at Long Beach, that flew only once, and was retitled the Ruptured Duck.

Shortly before the conclusion of my studio contract, I dropped by the tropical *Typhoon* set. A very torrid love scene between John Wayne and Laraine Day was in progress. I was warned that Dick Wallace, the director, had just seen Leo Durocher, the very new and ardent bridegroom of Laraine Day, enter the set and sit down quietly behind the cameras. The director tipped the two stars off, and told them, "Really turn it on and make the scene a scorcher."

They did as I saw, and went into an embrace that out-Garboed Garbo and John Gilbert and made Taylor and Burton look like members of the P.T.A. I took a look at the new bridegroom. Durocher was in a sweat and the scene went on and on as though it would never end. A stand-by painter I knew, winked at me as Durocher started to squirm. The painter said, "Pipe the kisser on Durocher. You'd think somebody just stole third base!" After that, Leo the Lip didn't appear on the set much.

My last picture at the studio was with George Raft: *Bail Bond Story*, a real dog. "Everyone," my agent said, "connected with it should have been locked up without benefit of bail before it ever went into production."

No one knows where it ever played, probably the shelf in the cutting room. But it was not the cause of what now happened to me, something odd and sinister.

I was confronted with a strange situation I did not think could ever happen to me. I suddenly couldn't get my foot inside a studio gate. I could not figure out what had happened. Whatever it was, I was now unable to get a job in pictures.

I was not a political figure, either right or left. I wasn't a sex maniac, dope user, dog molester, nudist, enemy agent, flag or barn burner, epileptic, leper or vampire. But I was out. I also had responsibilities: Four kids, three homes to maintain (Mother's, Eloise's parents and our own place). I couldn't afford to sit around and try to brood on it.

I decided to hit the saloon and night-club circuit. When I broached the subject to the William Morris office, their shortest agent (they are bred for size) said, "Pat, what could *you* do in a night club?"

"Just book me as the Irish Myron Cohen."

I was booked into the Desert Inn in Las Vegas, followed by the Mapes in Reno and the Broadmoor in Colorado Springs. It was remunerative, but sometimes a little disconcerting, learning to battle the sound of knives and forks and glasses, slaps and digestive sounds, and all the drunks who wanted to rewrite my act. However, I enjoyed the work. The audience was alive, and the inebriates never bothered me much.

But in the dark sleepless hours, I still wondered what had happened to me in Hollywood. A man's world can change so suddenly that the pain, as from a bad wound, is delayed; the pain comes later and the throb of it continues for a long time, in the emotional scar tissue. That no major studio would use me seeped in slowly and stained my few remaining illusions as to the show business man and his habits, the loyalty (none) of corporations, and the helpful existence of new friends (they dissolve at a crisis like a sunflake).

It was the late forties in Hollywood. Politics during the war had run like a mad cloudburst through the studios. I have spoken of the far Left and the claims of blacklisting of the Unfriendly Hollywood Ten and their friends. Some, it would later seem, very unfairly. Now somehow I had gotten onto another kind of blacklist, made up of people of the center and the right. For the left remained powerful in the studios, and actors like the late Adolphe Menjou lost out on a couple of dozen film parts because of his vocal voicing of his far Right opinions. I never felt heated up enough to call for a birchwood soapbox. With Shakespeare I agreed: "A plague on both your houses." I was against Communists, I was against the methods and the procedures by which they and fellow travelers had, it was reported, infiltrated the studios. But I hadn't made a full-time crusade of it. Yet here I was with a score of my films playing all over the world, and soon to flood over into television, an unemployable actor to the motion picture studios. Why? Who?

The dreadful part was not knowing why, not being tried, faced, accused. Only the great numb silence and the tepid voice of the agent. "I can't get you a thing going, Paddy baby."

It was for me living in Kafka's novel, The Trial. The accused man never knowing why and how it had all come about, what his crime was. Some of us broke, some died by their own hand. I was lucky. I had strong walls: my family, my home, my loyal friends, my faith. I couldn't go as far in prayer at first so as to say "Forgive them, Father, for they know not what they do." They knew damn well what they were doing. But I didn't bear any great hatreds. Hate is a rust that eats inwardly, and destroys the hater much quicker than the object hated. I was once tempted to try some voodoo dolls *and* long pins. But there my belief failed me.

So I played the clubs—and the only problems, besides laundry, bad checks and cold water, was when one of the audience who wanted to hear the act took care of a drunken heckler.

Then irony took a hand. A group of movie actors were sent to the Uruguayan Film Festival to represent Hollywood, of all places. Eloise and I were among those in the delegation.

"How come, Pat, they picked you?"

"Honey, all the other actors are busy working. I'm not."

"We'll fool them and take the free trip."

Our headquarters were in Montevideo. It was a fascinating, widening experience. Stars from all over the world were present to represent their various countries. The highlight of the trip was Eloise and I celebrating our twenty-fourth wedding anniversary. Mercedes McCambridge had arranged for an anniversary Mass for us at a tiny chapel at Punte del Este on the sea. The Bishop of Uruguay conducted the service and we received Holy Communion. A young English couple, Dickie Attenborough and his wife, Sheila Sims, had their tenth anniversary the same as ours, January 21. I smiled. "They have only ten years to our twenty-four."

I hoped the trip would clear the tracks for me with the studios. It seemed as foolish as to ask the condemned man if he wanted to be measured for a beach suit. Upon our return, the film gates were still locked tight. I did the lecture and banquet circuit again. This paid well, but it meant being on the road too. The children were growing up. Sean was in the Air Force, stationed at Dreux,

France; Terry at Loyola, Los Angeles, and the two girls at Mary-mount.

I wanted more than fancy saloons to play in. I shall always be grateful to Tony di Santis in Chicago. Tony had a great love for the theater, and when I first met him, he was operating a tent show in Evergreen Park, Illinois. Today his fame is nation-wide.

He said, "Pat, we would love to have you appear in *Front Page* in my tent."

"Can they hear in there?"

I knew he was not prepared to pay the money I had been making.

"So what do you say to being Hildy Johnson again?"

We shook hands. "You pay me whatever you can afford."

"I'm ashamed to say it."

"Say it Tony."

He did, and I said, "It's a deal anyway."

I wanted a real stage, real people who loved plays.

Tony over the years made tremendous progress, and his theater, the Drury Lane in Chicago, is one of the good things in America.

For years I played, and still do at least once every year for Tony. Eloise and I have broken a couple of box office records for him.

I had made the full circle. I was back where I had started so many years before; on stage. I was still ham enough to enjoy it. A hard life after Hollywood ease, but I was happy.

Shortly after my break in Chicago, Mel Ferrer approached me with a play called *Strike a Match*. "I would like Eva Gabor, Richard Egan and you to star in it. Plan to open in La Jolla."

"Sure."

It played fine and we went on to San Francisco and on through to Texas. A successful tour. But frankly, none of us felt the play was ready to go into New York. Eva was a darling girl. Dick and I would drag her to Mass every Sunday. She went under duress, flinging Hungarian limbs in all directions: "Dose two c-r-r-r-azy Irishmen, darling, dey *make* me go to Mass e-ver-r-y Sunday!"

On one of my trips to New York, I entertained an important

311

Hollywood guest at the Lambs Club. He enjoyed it so much I had a two-week guest card issued to him.

"Pat, this is the greatest."

One night at the club, he was in a real swinging mood. I don't mean belligerent, but he was making a good study of the whisky situation in the human system. It caught up with him and he wrecked the Grill Room. I knew nothing about this. I was opening some mail at home and there was a letter from the Lambs telling me I was "suspended for ninety days. Your guest has made a perfect ass of himself and because you are responsible for getting him a guest card, etc., etc." I was chagrined and tore up the letter so Eloise would not see the kind of people I was getting into the Lambs. Loss of club rights to me was like having a leg chopped off. I cheered myself in the flame of an old saying around the club. "You are not a real Lamb until you have had a suspension."

I wouldn't have minded it so much if I had been expelled for fighting, like the famous Louis Calhern–Walter Catlett bout, but for some lout misbehaving, *that* burned me up.

I returned to New York for a television commitment, the ninety-day suspension still in effect. I used to pass the club (on the other side of the street) and look longingly at the warm, lit window of my friends.

I must have acted like Oliver Twist asking for a refill, or the bum starving with his nose against the eating-house plate glass window. A lot of the fold interceded for me in my misery. I received a wire at the hotel: COME HOME ALL IS FORGIVEN. I was living at the Astor Hotel, just a block from the club and when I received the notice, I raced to the Lambs. There is no truth in the rumor I was barefooted. I made a novel entrance through the door, to the Grill, and then into the bar, at high noon, *crawling* on my hands and knees. The gesture had its effect and got its laughs. But it was more far-reaching than I expected.

Some weeks later, back home having dinner, Eloise looked up: "Why didn't you tell me about your suspension?"

"How did you know about it?"

She handed me a clipping from Winchell's column: "The greatest gesture of abject humility was displayed by Pat O'Brien recently, when, after his ninety day suspension had been lifted at the Lambs, he made his entrance as a meek supplicant, crawling on his hands and knees all the way from the front door to the bar."

"Honey, I guess I was too embarrassed."

"How did it go?"

"I got a great laugh."

"That's my boy. Did you count the house?"

I was soon to put on my traveling shoes again. The Cerebral Palsy Association, in Johannesburg, South Africa, to raise money for their cause, hit upon the idea of getting a group of American entertainers to come over and do a week's variety show to raise a substantial amount of money. Tex Ritter, the singing cowboy, and his wife organized a group of performers, among them Zsa Zsa Gabor, Don DeFore, Felix Knight, Martha Tilton and Robert Hopkins, and our spouses, to make the trip. It was the first time in theatrical history that a troupe went halfway around the world to raise money for sufferers of a dread disease. I had no idea at the time South Africa was the Alabama of Africa.

Twenty-five years before at Warner Brothers in a picture called *The Great O'Malley*, I had met a little seven-year-old girl called Sybil Jason. At the completion of the picture, she returned to her home in Johannesburg, South Africa. When we arrived in South Africa, I finally got Sybil's last known number. It was a place some miles from Johannesburg. Her aunt answered the phone, and I went into a full explanation: "I know this is a surprise, after all these years, but I sure would love to see Sybil."

Her aunt laughed: "I'm afraid that would be a little difficult, Mr. O'Brien. Sybil lives in Hollywood!" (After we returned home, we looked her up and found she was married, and had a child.)

South Africa, for all its color, prosperity, hurry and modern look, is a sad place. Everyone is waiting for the dam to burst. And it must.

Back in Hollywood, Tay Garnett, the director, contacted me. "Get out the priestly robes once more. I have a part for you in a picture with Mickey Rooney: *Fireball*. It's a chance for you to pick up a few fast bucks."

"You think they'll let me work?"

"A guaranteed flat of twenty-five grand, or ten thousand dollars with fifty thousand dollars deferred till after the release."

"No deferred Tay. The ten thousand dollars."

And that was all I *ever* got.

But it provided a major breakthrough back into films. Not with the big studios. There I was still unkosher.

For Ben Bogeaus, I went into a Damon Runyon story, *Johnny One-Eye*. It was a success. So I was indebted to Ben, because he not only assigned me a role, but gave me my asking price. Ben broke into films by owning a camera crane for high shots. He would rent the crane to studios at a daily rate. One day the crane not working, he decided to shoot a picture of his own.

But now that I had a toe back in the studio doors—the studios were in trouble—the little picture tube was king.

One day I was approached to work in a television pilot in which Fay Wray was to star. The role I was to play in the venture was just a panelist and was to be for the one show only, to enable Fay to get the show sold. Fay Wray is best remembered as the girl King Kong carried up the side of the Empire State Building. Johnny Mack Brown was the other panelist. I thought the idea was a good one. Every week there would be two guest stars who had been active in athletics in their college days. She would question them on physical fitness and education. I worked very hard on the script they gave me. Fay made her entrance on camera, and really looked gorgeous, even without King Kong. She introduced her two panelists.

I felt at ease, a cigar in my mouth. Then a voice over the loud speaker interrupted the show: "This is 'This Is Your Life.'"

I thought we were cross-wired. The voice came over again: "One of these three people will be the subject tonight of 'This Is Your Life.'"

I felt very happy. I was sure it was to be Fay Wray, she looked so beautiful, and was part of Hollywood's great past. The voice of Ralph Edwards said, "Fay Wray? No, it isn't."

And then: "It *might* be Johnny Mack Brown—but it isn't! Pat O Brien, 'This Is Your Life!'"

I made like a goldfish; all eyes and open mouth. I was lifted from my seat, whisked out of that place and into the studio where Ralph Edwards was smirking in person. I came down the aisle, still in a daze. I suddenly realized all the bunk about Fay's pilot was a complete farce. So I stood and waited while my life passed. The first to make his entrance was Dae Shawl, my boyhood friend and shipmate in the Navy; followed by Allen Jenkins, and Wally Ford from *Broadway*; Jimmy Gleason, who had given me my first part on the stage; Mary Brian, my first leading lady in films. I could only smile, bow and try a few bits of small talk. Then in trooped Eloise and our four children. Suddenly I heard a lovely, musical voice over the loud speaker (piped in from far away, or so it seemed). The voice grew louder: "And when Billy was a little boy"—I was known as Billy O'Brien as a child—"when Billy was a little boy and his mother brought him to school that first day, he cried and cried, as all little boys do."

I said to Ralph Edwards, "That *couldn't* be Sister Mary Norbert, my first-grade teacher!"

Ralph answered, "It not only could, but it is."

And on she walked. My delight really left me speechless. My first instinct was to throw my arms around her in loving embrace.

"This Is Your Life" had set up a TV set for my mother, who was confined to a hospital bed, and I kept saying, "How about that, Mom! I can't believe it, Mom."

Sister Mary Norbert could not attend the party that was given at the conclusion of the program. She did come out with another nun to the house for lunch the next day. Her companion was very austere in mien and bearing.

"Sister Mary Norbert, I didn't dare kiss you in front of thirty million people. But—now—*here*—"

"You wouldn't dare, Billy!"

315

I picked her up and waltzed her around the room and gave her a big kiss.

Sister was of the B.V.M. (Blessed Virgin Mary) Order.

"All around the country, Billy, the B.V.M. nuns were alerted and permitted to watch the show."

"That's only right."

Sister reached into her habit and brought out a telegram. "See what I received this morning. It's from the Mother General in Dubuque. It reads: 'DEAR SISTER. COME HOME SOON. DON'T SIGN UP.'"

"Don't let the agents see you."

In 1958, I prevailed upon Eloise to come out of retirement and get on stage with me. "The theatrical world can always use talent."

"Too old for Pollyanna—too young for Lady Macbeth."

One of the kids suggested *Charley's Aunt* in reverse.

Eloise couldn't make up her mind, but the day I caught her raiding my make-up kit for grease paint, I knew she was back.

It was great for me. She alleviated all the loneliness on the road, and we played opposite each other, and so enhanced our joy. Then, too, I must have mentioned, we broke a couple of box office records. And I've become used to her by my side.

We were doing *Dear Ruth* at the Drury Lane in Chicago at Tony's annual nuns-only matinee for a benefit. I had Sister Mary Norbert planted in the first row. I introduced her to the assembly at curtain time: "I want you to know that Sister taught me over fifty years ago. Many of you probably saw her on 'This Is Your Life,' a born scene stealer."

Sister acknowledged the introduction graciously. She would have bowed all afternoon if we had let her.

If I went back to the stage because it was the only way I could earn a living, I soon had the satisfaction of knowing I was playing better than ever, getting a variety of roles that would never have come to me in Hollywood. And the stage, I began to see, is the true place for the actor. I can say that now, since I've done a few independent pictures from time to time since; had my own television series, "Harrigan and Son," and appear in other acting mediums.

The stage is more than the lifeblood of acting, it's also the marrow, the muscles, the true brain center.

An actor needs all his courage to survive. I saw my friend William Gargan show the greatest courage when illness, serious and deadly, hit him. He was told he had cancer of the throat that they would have to remove his voice box, if there was any hope for him. An actor without a voice. What was the use? But he went through the operation and came out mute but alive. Painfully, months of teaching himself to talk again with a new system of air pressure in the throat brought back a new voice. He has devoted himself to teaching and lecturing among the thousands like him that had been left voiceless. He gives them hope, and a method by which they would again be able to talk with the world. Bill's work is so little known in this field I had to put it down here. He'll phone me, I know, and *tell* me I shouldn't have done it.

Perhaps if I had saved my voice in *Miss Lonelyhearts* I would not have been in a thud the play made on Broadway in the late fifties. But it was a good play, and out of town it looked a hit. In New York the critics felt its message of gloom was too heavy. For me it was Broadway again, and being on the stage there was almost worth the ache and the sadness a play creates when its hopes fade and the closing notices go up. Ironically, the Lambs were giving me a party on my "return to Broadway" the night the playhouse went dark. No one took down the signs with my name on them for months, and I would suddenly, for days, find myself suddenly staring up at: PAT O'BRIEN in *Miss Lonelyhearts*.

28

Great Loss, Some Gain

A man putting down his life should include a sample of everything. The happy, the unhappy events, the eternal and the transitory.

My mother had been taken ill in the late forties. She remained alive and alert, but bedridden until 1956, when she died at the age of ninety-two. Among other heritages, she left me hope for a long life, if I could afford it. During those years I could not secure employment in any of the studios while I had to find thousands of dollars for her care. I did not of course resent this —only thanked the dear Lord for the privilege of being able to take care of Mom those last years of her life. I never missed a day seeing her right up until the fearful parting hour of her death. She had had a full and wonderful life.

From 1950 to 1964, fourteen years, I made only three pictures for the major studios. There was little relenting against my mysterious punishment. At MGM, because my old friend Spencer Tracy insisted I be assigned an important role in his production, *The People vs. O'Hara*. Dore Schary, the perpetual wonder boy, was the man in charge at MGM. Spence had to put on a wild, desperate fight to secure the role for me, even threatening to walk out unless I was signed. Then, John Ford, pal since *Airmail*, asked for me in *The Last Hurrah*. Billy Wilder also phoned. "I got a part for you in *Some Like It Hot*."

Billy is a demonic ironic genius and a bit of a practical joker.

I also did an independent picture, *Ring of Fear*, for which I am indebted to John Wayne and Bob Fellows. Nothing else broke the condemned man's sentence to unemployment in films. I continued to be mystified. There seemed to be no answer.

We continued playing the theater circuit. Eloise and I have played all over the country. As to money, it has been rewarding, but naturally we disliked being away from home and family, especially during the kids' formative years.

In 1956 I went to England and did an independent picture there. I was the only American in the production *Kill Me Tomorrow*. The weather almost killed me every day.

But I had work. I thought of the hundreds of talented men and women in Hollywood who just rust away, waiting, waiting for a call that never comes. They stand in front of Schwab's, testing free toothpicks; sit at home in some shabby room, looking at their youth on television's ancient movies. Some end life suddenly; some exist, but no longer live.

All through these hard years, I kept playing night clubs, lecturing, toastmastering and every year, a six-week engagement for Tony, in Chicago. I survived and worked—and survival and work to an actor is all.

I never put on a poor-mouth or solicited anyone's aid (nor shall I). I was a happy guy, with a wonderful family. And counting my blessings, I would say (corny as it sounds) they were these: memories of a happy childhood, strength to work, good true friends, a happy marriage, the great merciful privilege of receiving

319

the sacraments of my church. There is a quotation from Oscar
Wilde which I recalled many times: "Misfortunes, one can endure,
they come from outside, but to suffer for one's own faults, ah,
there is the sting of Life." But I have had no soul-shattering suffering, only the sting of the meanness of certain people in absolute
power.

After we built our new home, we tried to unload our Spanish
home next door, in which we had lived during the constructing
of Tara. One day, my attorney phoned me.

"We have a chance, Pat, to sell the house—and for cash."

"Who is it?"

"Don't know—he's some guy that plays the piano or something
—seems like a nice Joe and I think we can cop the deal."

We did.

After purchasing our former home, the piano player, (it turned
out to be Artur Rubenstein) converted what had been my library
into his music room. Every Sunday, I would tilt my chair against
the wall facing his place just a few feet away, and listen en-
raptured, while he hit the keys for hours. The only thing that
took me away from my own private Sunday concerts was twelve-
o'clock Mass.

Meeting me over the garden wall, Artur Rubenstein asked: "Pat,
do I annoy you these Sunday mornings when I practice?"

I said dead-pan: "Yes, Artur, I do have a definite beef."

He looked at me querously. He was a small handsome man,
the sire of a couple of generations of children, and looked like
a king pixy, proud, yet artistic.

"Beef? What is this beef?"

"A complaint—where the hell is Heifitz on Sundays?"

He laughed. "Maybe it can be arranged."

At the Rubenstein official housewarming, some weeks later, we
were present, and he summoned all the guests into the music
room.

"Myself and my fellow concert artist, Jascha Heifitz, are about to do a command performance because one of my guests, Pat O'Brien, had a beef."

It was a darling party.

The Rubensteins were our neighbors all too short a time. With the expansion of the virile old man's family, they sought larger quarters. They sold the place to Alida Valli, the Italian motion picture star known briefly to fame only as Valli. It was not too long before she returned to her native Italy. She sold the house to Lady Sylvia Ashley.

Eloise said, "Our former house has sure turned into a League of Nations."

"United Nations, honey, is the better term."

"Your birthday parties are great for the United Nations; the one Maureen O'Hara gave in Ireland, and the one General Randall gave in China."

"It might be a great topper, Mommy, if Jessel game me a birthday party in Israel."

By 1960, I wondered if I'd ever be coming out of limbo. My manager, Bill Shiffrin, called: "Cy Howard has a great idea for a television series."

"Not a Western?"

"No."

"Or a head-feeler? doctor? sick-people series?"

"No."

"What *else* is there on TV?"

"Come and listen."

The name of the series was *Harrigan and Son*; a lawyer and his son—human, amusing, yet earnest. Everyone was enthusiastic about it. I loved the series and everyone associated with it. But after thirty-six weeks of what we thought was a most successful project, the Ivy League-suited gods of Madison Avenue thought otherwise. It was replaced with a chimpanzee show, half ape, half human. I have never ascertained whether those chimps passed the legal bar to practice. We were a happy group of people in *Harrigan and Son* till it went ape. One of the finer actors, Jerry Mohr's wife, Mai, was our script girl. Shortly after the demise of our series, they did a TV pilot for their own series in Acapulco, Mexico, and contacted Eloise and myself to play in the first segment. We have great hopes that it will sell some day. It has a good adventurous theme and gets around to two or three continents.

But there are *no* parts for chimps in it.

Our boy Terry, who was enrolled in Georgetown University in Washington, won a scholarship at the University of Madrid and spent a year in Spain. He was (and is) a great boy, and while no father can be trusted to estimate his offsprings, Terry I thought of as a doer. Shortly after his return to Georgetown from Spain, I was in New York City. He was singing with the Georgetown Glee Club, and phoned me at the St. Regis from school. "Dad, it's a special event—be a good guy and give the glee club a little party at the hotel."

"Little or big—come on."

They were due from Washington for a singing engagement in New York. I felt that was the least I could do for a kid who had brought such joy to his parents. I arranged it big; champagne punch and a parade of hot and cold hors d'oeuvres. Terry arrived from Washington around five, looking great.

"Son, it's all set. Class A all the way—for your party tonight."

He looked at me unhappily. "Dad, I forgot to notify you in the rush of everything, it's changed to tomorrow night."

I did a long stare in Jack Benny's best style.

"That's just great, Terry. The whole champagne and fish-eggs bit is set for six o'clock. There's no way I can cancel now. The caterer and his staff will be here in half an hour."

"Maybe we'll be *very* hungry, Dad. We can try to use it all."

"No—you're too young, I'm too old."

"So—?"

"Call the valets and all the bellhops, Terry, and maids and anyone else you roust out in the domestic coterie of the hotel. Invite them all. Cocktails and free chow at six."

"You're a sport, Dad."

"A chump."

322

I wish I had had a camera record of the binge that evening. It was a big night for the common man and his girl. I had to repeat it all the following evening for the glee club. All involved at both parties had a wonderful time. Young people make me happy. Even young actors.

I am frequently asked by embryo actors, "What is the secret of acting? I mean is there a secret, Mr. O'Brien?"

"After having spent forty-four years in show business, kid, my answer, while not original, is always the same. It is based on a philosophy I have used all those years."

"What is it?"

"Only a quotation from Edwin Booth, who, when asked the same question by you guys, always answered, 'Don't act!' "

"Oh."

"A young actor can't go wrong by following the advice of William Shakespeare in Hamlet's address to the players: 'Speak the speech—etc. etc.' "

"Oh, that one."

"Also that old stuff: Hard work and sacrifice that become an integral part of life for an eager thespian, plus—if you care—a reliance on prayer."

(Speaking of prayer, some years ago in New York City, a rabbi and his friend, a young priest, and myself were attending the fights at Madison Square Garden. As one of the bruisers left his corner, he made the sign of the cross. The rabbi turned to the priest: "Will that help him?"

The priest winked at me. "Only if he can fight.")

"So in acting, prayer can be good for you, and can't hurt you a bit, but you also must have some born ability on a stage, and must apply yourself zealously and conscientiously all along the way. I wish there was an easier way—but there isn't."

Most people think "Method" acting is a short cut, and consists of scratching and nose picking. It certainly is talked about a lot.

My ideas on "Method" acting, I can't discuss because I have never known what "Method" is. John Barrymore once said:

323

"Method acting, to be perfect, should throw out the Method and leave just the actor on stage." I buy *that*.

I have always held and always shall that acting is more than just a vocation. It can be a great art. Some may have something given them at birth that moves them along the way a little faster. But at its best, true acting requires study and a concentrated effort and a belief in one's self, and a hell of a strong stomach. Personally, I have learned more by human contact, watching my contemporaries, trying to absorb some of the artistry that has been the trade mark of the great performers. I shall continue to do this as long as I am here because I have no intention of retiring until the Great Producer upstairs nudges me: "There's your cue."

I sometimes get the idea that in Europe actors are viewed as artists. But here in the U.S.A. we are looked upon as artisans and glamor-pusses. In the old days of the stock companies, I put in rigorous work with every role I played (a juvenile, old men, middle-aged characters, buffoons). I kept *learning* all the time and I find even today I *keep* learning all the time. Even unlearning a bit; that's harder—unlearning.

Is it all worth it—the moment's glory at curtain call, a hard, often frustrating life? Yes. Acting at its best, is a long, hard pull, often to nowhere. Try not to become embittered along the way. The cynic sees only the horse dust, never the pony. When the studios barred their gates to me, I could have gone sour, had I not been strong in my knowledge that those years of apprenticeship where I had worked and studied so religiously could never be lost. I'd find a place for them. Even if I had to work in a drugstore window. The thing about Picasso I admire (not his politics) is his remark: "If I were a prisoner chained, hands behind me, I'd still paint by spitting on the walls."

Whatever else gets lost in an actor's head-over-heels life, the magic of the stage hardly ever all seeps away. I still get a young man's pounding in the chest when I enter an old theater, smell its layers of historic dust. I know the lives of all who have used the ratty dressing room washed and made up at the leaky faucets, stared into the dimmed mirror. A new play script is an adventure, like hope for finding a lost continent, discovering some scientific fact for the first time. Each new play I read may be the greatest part of my life, a new character may make me immortal in the theater. That it doesn't come off doesn't mean anything. There is always the next one, the one after that one, and after that, maybe not even written yet. I can wait, an actor learns patience, and hope. Like Hemingway's bullfighters, he too must have the courage of "grace under pressure."

I reject nothing. The new theater, the *avant-garde* stage of the absurd, the kook drama, the surrealist comedy, the baffling special pleading of despair-crazy philosophers, the half stage, the moving, open or in the round. As long as they use actors, I can get interested. It doesn't mean I have to accept any of it. A lot of it seems nonsense, most of it is windy talk often by life-defeated people. But I don't reject out of hand. I listen. I watch. I try it on.

There are no sure answers for most things. On the Crosses, I know one thief was saved—and I also know one was condemned.

For an actor to live in the past of the theater's glory is a kind of death. For a performer to say, "Those were the good old days. They were greater than today's, better, more heart and feeling," is to kill the present. And we live in the present. I, too, at times look back with a glow, but I walk like a wary hunter in the present, and I even have hopes for the future.

The ideas that go into good plays are amusing, sad, sometimes seem revolting, but are not really new. They began with Adam, who must have hammed it a bit when things got dull in the Garden of Eden, while the apples ripened. But what *is* always new is the ferment in the human mind, spirit, soul, always attacking the problems and enigmas of life. Trying to see it with new facets, to say something about it that no one has said in just that way before. It is this; wanting it fresh, or repolished, or reworded that makes new plays and great parts. And puts actors on stage to try it on for fit.

Eloise and I were approached to tour Australia. It meant starting in Brisbane and continuing on for several months, but we wanted a two-weeks sabbatical in June, when Brigid graduated from Marymount in California. The following Monday, Terry graduated from Georgetown in Washington.

I had told the producer, "We can always go to Australia, but we can only see our kids graduate once."

"Listen, I know. I've six myself. Two weeks free in June is part of the deal."

For those keeping score, here are figures for the records. Today, as of *this* writing, the parents of four children are also the grandparents of six. And here at Tara we are ensconced in the surrounding of family joy, that abounds in fun, love of God and love of life.

Brigid, our youngest, did at various times have six to eight of her Marymount classmates as house guests for a day or two. Eloise and I played charades with them often till three o'clock in the morning. (You've heard of that fast Hollywood life.) Sean brought home a French bride, named Monique. Our oldest, Mavourneen, married David Garton, a Scandinavian. Sometimes I dream Terry, after his graduation from the Diplomatic School of Georgetown University, will be appointed ambassador to Ireland.

Over the big trellis at Tara hangs an inscription partly translated from the Gaelic:

"Come in the evening; come in the morning,
  Come when we expect you and come without warning.
  Cead mile failte you'll find here before you,
  And the oftener you come, the more we'll adore you."

The translation of the Gaelic phrase "*cead mile failte*" is "one hundred thousand welcomes." The Irish believe in quantity as well as quality.

Tara is close to the hearts of us O'Briens. It is our home. Home is all the wonderful days a family has known together. The day a child was born. The day of the christening. The bittersweet memories, too—like the night I spent on my knees when they said my daughter was dying. And the morning they said she was well. It's the memory of your daughter coming down that stairway on her wedding day.

Ours is a kind of mad, merry household, a family of friends. Like all parents, Eloise and I wonder if we've done a good job of preparing our kids for the tough world we're handing them. Like it or not, parents teach by example. Parents can't fail to go to church and expect their kids to. They have to go it together—in all ways. It's a big assignment, this parent business, but don't kid yourself that you aren't living a better life because you are one.

There isn't much to write—I stand or fall by what I am. I don't like labels. Do I have some?

I have heard the word "liberal" overdone, abused, condemned, praised through the tall years of my career. The word that fits the O'Briens best, I hope; human. Bea, our housekeeper has been with us for over twenty-seven years. Bea is colored and a Baptist, as is Ella Mae, who is also part of the O'Brien household. Our gardener, Ascensión, is a Mexican. Our family doctor for thirty-two years, Stanley Immerman, is a Jew, as is my manager, Bill Shiffrin. My lawyer is a Congregationalist, my secretary a Presbyterian, my wife Eloise a convert, and with four Catholic kids and six Catholic grandchildren, and me who came close to embracing the priesthood, I'm sure that the real meaning of the word "liberal" fits all our lives, or should. If I can add a few atheist readers as friends, I will have it made.

I remember Ring Lardner saying: "Don't think an atheist hasn't got a rigid religion—he has. His religion is *not* having a religion."

I have heard that when one of the great Dukes of Alba, in Spain, was dying, his deathbed confessor, before giving him the last rites, said, "You must forgive all your enemies."

The Duke said simply, "I have no enemies, I have hanged them all."

Unlike the Duke, if I have enemies, may they be few, and as I write this, I forgive them all. This is no noble gesture. I see

327

myself for what I am, with neither rank nor honors. Except for my acting I am an ordinary man who has lived according to the values of his society and his creed. I have the normal amount of children, one wife, a settled home life. I have done no great deeds to carve on stone, only on birthday cakes. But also no great evil. I have been tempted at times, I suppose, to human weaknesses, but I have tried not to do any unkindness. All in all this record is not of one who was a conqueror, nation builder, inventor or trail blazer. And alas for certain readers, not a great sinner or criminal. Perhaps it is the lack of those things that are enduring fame or notoriety that has made for my personal happiness. I am not cut off from the everyday world, don't inhabit an ivory or nylon tower, not lost in a world above and beyond the accepted and the tried.

I have had my Walter Mitty moments. I have had strange dreams and thought of impossible events. But in the end I came back to reality, by a whispered word from the head on the next pillow, the cry of a child, the smell of a certain dish, the shape of a cloud over my garden, the delivery of a quotable line, the group laughter after a good story. All these things, among many others, have kept me not earthbound, but a citizen of some free will, at ease (nearly) in his universe.

My world may not be as wide as Einstein's, as deep sunk in secret darkness as Freud's, as wild and cruel as Marx's, as dismal as Dr. Teller's or as shattered in shape as James Joyce's. But my world is inhabited by the great shadows of Moses and Abraham, the teachings of Isaiah and Jeremiah. And the eternal words and the divinity of Jesus. Of St. Peter and the popes, of Thomas Kempis and Pascal. I run with the yea-sayers, the believers in the Life Force, and the theater of Shakespeare, the feisty Restoration dramas, the declaiming hams beginning with David Garrick and Kean, to all the Booths (except one), Joe Jefferson and the Barrymores. And a bond with old friends: Spencer Tracy and Wally Ford and James Cagney and others, whom I helped set up a make-believe world of pleasure and entertainment that had encircled the world a thousand times and still goes on. Until the last foot of film is shredded away, I shall exist here on earth. It was Samuel Butler who said it best. "No man is gone from among us while one living person remembers him."

In telling my life story here, I have remained onstage—often I confess playing a part—in full view, picking scenes, remembering lines, trying to see what I was, attempting to untangle some of what has puzzled me, and some of what still does.

Writing it down has helped me see the pattern of myself and my times. By looking back I know I have come the full turn.

Is it proper in the life of an ordinary man, a public performer, for him to write of his faith? That which sustains him? I think so. Anyway I shall try.

When anyone asks me what my faith means to me, the only answer I can give them is, "My faith is my life." The prayer of faith I learned at my mother's knee set the standard for living and of living ever since. And I would not surrender it for all the rewards of the world.

Faith, the way I see it, is believing in God no matter how you reverently express your belief—no matter what church or temple you attend. Faith is part of a man's heart, and all of his soul.

Every spiritually minded man has a feeling of love for his religious faith and heritage and I feel the same about mine, for the Catholic Church has meant a great deal to me. Others who have worked for us for years are Baptists. They, too, are extremely religious; they, too, have a true faith. They always have been proud of their strict adherence to their beliefs. So our entire household is blessed with the gifts of faith, each in his own way. You can feel its presence.

My wife, Eloise, has this faith, too, and for us it has borne the fruit of true happiness in our four children. Ours is a home of love and mutual understanding. Truly one of the most powerful blessings and a great stimulus for my unswerving faith—is my marriage to Eloise.

To share a faith, to be dedicated to the same sacred security, has made us one in "sickness and in health—for richer or poorer."

There isn't any doubt about the O'Briens' happiness because we ask for and unfailingly get guidance.

To those who claim that faith is purely subjective, I say with sympathy: You've never given it a chance to act and live for you . . . Ask the soldier who found faith on the battlefield—ask anyone who has come square up against it and found the vital, dependable, saving power of God. Miracles, some call them. The man of faith knows that guidance and help are always available when sought.

When my oldest daughter, Mavourneen, was still a child, she was stricken with a severe illness. Eloise, with the agile loving hands of a mother, worked furiously at her bedside. Suddenly, as if touched by the hand of God, the child became well.

Eloise went all over the house looking for me. She found me praying.

"There was nothing else I could do," I told her.

"Nothing else was needed," Eloise said softly, and threw her arms about me in relief.

A miracle, many people say. But I know it's just the practical and absolutely expected answer made possible by faith.

I've related how, during the war, I traveled by air with an entertainment unit. We flew about sixty-eight thousand air miles to the battles of the Pacific, China, Burma, and India. I grew in stature and maturity talking with those boys, trying to make them laugh, watching them pray—praying with them.

When we were ordered to break it up during our performance at Luchow, I was plenty scared. With Jap infantry, some hundred thousand strong, approximately twenty-five miles away and not standing still, we scrambled into jeeps, raced for the airfields.

I was praying harder than I thought possible. The prayer was part of my heartbeat. But my prayer was only part of a great salvo of faith that night. You could feel it—those guys had it, to a man. Scared, but full of prayer, men of all creeds. You felt that they knew God had His arms around them. I couldn't really tell you how we were evacuated so rapidly, but we were. Technically, General Claire Chennault was the instrument of His care—his planes, his superb precision flew us safely into Chungking.

Faith never fails. Like an illimitable reserve fund, it is always waiting to give protection, inspiration, forgiveness, courage and spiritual joy. I am firmly convinced that anything I am today and everything I have today I owe to my faith. It is a debt that can be repaid only by passing it on to others. I can ask no greater thrill in life than sitting in church on Sunday, my beloved life-partner, Eloise, and my four youngsters, all understanding and trying hard to serve God—all living practical faith. I wish every man and woman in the country could say with the conviction I do: "My faith is my life, my standard for living."

On the stage I began my career, and with good grace, help and hope, I will end it there, facing people I have entertained for more decades that I want to count up here. I know I have given pleasure in my roles; I hope I have brought a little thought and some awe and wonder in those few parts that were bigger than the actor.

And now, after forty-four wonderful years, four beautiful children, six glorious grandchildren, the sons' and daughters' education completed—Mission Accomplished! And now, back to the road again, back to the theater, my first love, and with me, the love of my life, Eloise; so be it. Once again, "half-hour"—"fifteen minutes"—overture, Mr. O'Brien"—then, "Hey Mommy—curtain going up! We're on!"